The Journal of Sedona Schnebly

Lisa Schnebly Heidinger

First edition, 2017
Written by Lisa Schnebly Heidinger
Edited by Nathan Shelton
Cover design by RenSu Yang
ISBN: 9780930831097
Cider Press
© 2017 Lisa Schnebly Heidinger
ISBN: 0930831098

Dedication

This book is dedicated to my daughter, Sedona Lee, who embodies the best traits of Sedona Schnebly, and to my son, Rye Schnebly, who embodies the best traits of Theodore Carlton Schnebly. Also to their father—my husband, Tom, who by saying, "You have a job; you're a writer," made it so

Foreword

I have planned to tell the story of my great-grandmother, Sedona Schnebly, for as long as I can remember.

When I was small, a painting of her hung in my grandfather's study, and I would try to imitate her large-eyed gaze and serene expression. I knew the town here in Arizona we visited every summer bore her name, and that my great-grandfather, Theodore Carlton (T.C.) Schnebly, had named it after her. My grandfather was their oldest son.

A journal-keeper myself since grade school, I always yearned to be told someone had found her diaries, but no one ever did.

I wanted to tell her story. So in my early 20s I flew to Denver to ask my great-aunt Clara, Sedona's fifth child, everything I could think of. Years later I visited her youngest child, Margaret, and learned even more.

And finally I got to sit down with her dear friend Ruth Jordan (by this time her dear Helen Jordan had passed), who told me the story that pretty much closes this book.

My great-grandparents were part of my own story. My now-husband proposed on Schnebly Hill Road, and we were married on the land T.C. and Sedona had owned on the banks of Oak Creek. We named our children Sedona Lee and Rye Schnebly. My father, Larry, likes to say he's the only person in the history of the world who is Sedona's grandson, and Sedona's grandfather.

But until recently, the time to actually put down the words hadn't come.

I knew Sedona had been restrained, quiet, reserved...and since I'm a bit of an extrovert, closer to T.C.'s model of wanting to meet everyone, I wasn't sure I could describe a woman so different from myself.

Then our daughter Sedona grew up.

She not only has a great many of the earlier Sedona's physical characteristics (lustrous wavy hair, petite build, huge brown eyes, sweet voice), but I realized that while she is decorous and quiet like my great-grandma, her inner life is a maelstrom. Also like her foremother, she loves beauty and music, and hates too much attention. (The mother in me is compelled to add that Rye received not only T.C.'s unusual thumbs, but also his ease with and interest in all people, his endless physical endurance, his ability to see humor even in crisis, and a bone-deep love of Northern Arizona.)

By watching them as adults, and having been married 25 years, I was finally ready to write. And write I have. I was delighted to find out from Larry that Sedona had taken an hour a day after lunch to write, because my own children grew up with that same hour of quiet time. So then I wondered: what if she had kept a journal, sealing it to keep loved ones from having any hurt feelings for, say, 65 years after her death? And it had gone with the other family papers into the Schnebly Collection at Northern Arizona University's Special Collections & Archives in the Cline Library? And one day, a box came in the mail, with a letter from Peter Runge, head of said Special Collections, explaining that since it appeared to be family papers, I should be the one to open it?

This is what I would have wanted to find.

Lisa Schnebly Heidinger

Table of Contents

I. The Beginning

New Year's Day, 1950

The first time I saw the place that now shares my name, all I wanted to do was be somewhere else.

It wasn't that there was anything wrong with Oak Creek Canyon, when we pulled around a curve in the road and saw it arrayed in front of us. The fault lay in me: I was so tired the newness and strangeness frightened me. It was completely unlike anything I'd ever seen.

That trip from the wooden train platform in Jerome stays with me...the wagon filled to bursting with precariously piled belongings (God forbid Carl take five trips if something could be done in four). Everything we owned had been left at Jerome, and true to the trainmaster's word, no one had bothered it under the tarp during the two weeks since Carl had arrived before us. He'd made multiple trips already, and this was the last. So now besides the final household goods, plus grocery staples, Carl had Tad, Pearl, and me. Of course the children didn't take up the most actual space, but they seemed to occupy the better part of that wagon. After days of being shushed and still on the train, they were impossible to subdue, and so excited to be with their beloved "Dad" that they were like puppies, wriggling in my arms, making noise, moving around to look in every direction at once. And it felt like every bit of that energy came out of my body.

Struggling to keep them contained, and listen to Carl talk about the wonders of where we were heading, I confess I just wanted to sit on something that wasn't moving. It was hours (although it felt like days) before we arrived. And once we got to our new home, the dwelling was as lacking as the surroundings were admittedly stunning. But surroundings don't protect and nourish a person. For that we had just a tent house, wood-floored and wood-sided up about waist-high, with canvas above it. That's all. A few humble outbuildings, but no welcoming presence bustling out, no smoke rising from a warming fire. All our lovely things had to go here? Bedsteads to be set up, dishes unloaded. Carl had done all he could by himself. But the prospect of having to

wrestle and wrench things off the wagon and in the door before anyone
could eat, let alone rest, gave me as faint a heart as I'd ever had.

More daunting than the humble shelter was the vast swath of wilderness all around it. This was not a place people lived. I'd been to St.
Louis, so I knew what a city was like. I'd never been anywhere so empty
of human influence. Never mind streetlights, or even streets; no houses
for windows, let alone lights shining in them...the only light was fad-
ing around us. The endlessness of all this nature, looming and rustling,
made our tent seem like a fairy-sized dwelling. We were alone out here,
with no protection save Carl and his rifle. Animals, including preda-
tors, outnumbered us by dozens or even hundreds.

But even then, weary and weathered and forlorn, I didn't for a second wish myself back. As primitive as this setting was, it was preferable
to what we'd left behind. Gorin, Missouri, was no place for any of us
anymore.

Getting Here

I remember when I was about five Papa taking us to Franklin for some reason. I could tell he was excited to show us big wagons, surrounded by noise and confusion. We saw a loose ragged line of them, humming with activity and people moving around as purposefully as ants. He explained they were getting ready to head out west. The trip would take a long time, days and days. There were children already looking out of the backs of some wagons through keyholes of canvas drawn tight, dogs running and barking, men talking, women busy with piles of possessions and provisions. At the time I both envied and feared for them.

So when we had train tickets to come west ourselves, some people would say, "It's a good thing you don't have to go in a wagon any more." And I, smug in my ignorance, agreed.

After our trip I was less sure. In a wagon train, the children could have run about and used up some energy. In a wagon there would have been privacy, more space between us and the snoring and sneezing and Heaven knows what-all going on among people. With a wagon we could have reached our possessions, more than one set of clothes. There would have been flat hot rocks on which to lay washed diapers. I know it would have taken longer. But during our train ride, I would have far, far preferred a wagon to a locomotive car.

We'd all looked so nice setting out: Tad with comb tracks in his neatly parted hair, suspenders straight, shoes shiny; Pearl adorable in the dark green dress (I'd felt so smart avoiding light colors that could get ash on them!) and me in the serviceable brown-and-black stripe I had thought impervious to any stain or smudge that travel could inflict.

But four very long days later, I marveled that any of us had ever been clean. Little Tad was downright grimy. He looked like he'd been cleaning chimneys in London, although he'd gamely attempted to maintain good manners when people fell against him going down the aisle. Pearl was a fretful heap of soiled linens; the dark green was milky, scummy and spotted. I was crumpled, wrinkled, frizzy and formless—and tired down to the bone.

Not that it hadn't had its moments. Maybe many things aren't defined by being "good" or "bad," but more by being "intense" versus "forgettable." This had been anything but forgettable.

Since our things had gone out already in the railroad car Carl hired when he'd left in the previous month, I had felt delightfully unencumbered with only a few necessities for the children and myself in our big carpetbag. But that proved to be more than enough to keep track of, and the constant unpacking and packing had made it a mare's nest of diapers in various stages of dampness and cleanliness, handkerchiefs that were two parts soot and one part food stains, small toys the children had tired of far too quickly, and the coin purse I'd kept reaching into as every performed service compelled yet another gratuity.

People had mostly been lovely: a woman plucked Pearl right out of my arms that morning in Gallup when I was trying to maneuver down to get Tad's shoe off the track where it fell as he stepped off. (From then on I checked his laces as the train slowed for each stop.) Kind strangers had talked to Tad when he manfully tried to leave me alone so I could help Pearl eat, and he had shown such good manners my heart swelled with pride.

But people had also been occasionally terrible, cutting in front of us at the Harvey House—even I, amateur traveller that I was, knew the train would not leave until each of us had been fed. Others coughed and cussed as if no one was around. My yearning for privacy had reached a level I'd not known existed.

Technically, we were private at night; the sleeper bunk had a curtain that closed us off from sight. But every whistling snore, bodily emission and other sounds I devoutly wished I'd not heard were sometimes inches away. I was glad the children slept soundly. Each time either one moved, I woke and waited. I'd daren't nod off during the day because they were active, and very restless. So nights became careful calculations of sleep: two hours, then an hour and a half, and if I can just drop off again and get another two…that's a sure recipe for exhaustion if ever there was one.

Because of all this, by the time we were in the wagon, moving toward what we would learn to call home, I was rueful about the wonders of modern travel. Maybe a pilgrimage made by all four of us together, crawling across the prairie, would have had some merit. Campfires and music at night, with Carl's comforting presence. However, I knew almost nothing about Indians, and even that was too much. Everyone said attacks had died down and then ended, but the image of vast open space and our vulnerable covered wagon would have made me wonder, staring into darkness, every night. And what about running out of water—you heard horrible things about how dry the west was.

But after the first hour in the wagon from Jerome to Oak Creek Canyon, I concluded that if I still had a tooth in my head that wasn't loose from the pitch and rattle and jounce of this journey, I would count it a miracle.

Morning

I remember so well opening my eyes that first day, on the mattress on the floor, Pearl wedged against me puffing faint baby exhales. Tad was on my other side, deeply asleep. What struck me was the scent in my first conscious breath; sweet and yet peppery, rich and loamy and....well, even after decades I've never quite found the words to describe what the scents of the creek do inside the nose. My spirits began to rise like fish to the surface of water, looking for good things, even expecting good things. I raised my head and shoulders as gently as I could, and saw that on Pearl's other side, Carl was gone. Easing up, I slid off the foot of the ticking and crept outside.

Then stopped, entranced by the beauty before me. As still as any empty cathedral, it also brimmed with life and energy. I could hear the creek rushing and journeying while the birds practiced their morning songs. The scent was even stronger out here. In all directions were indeterminate shapes of greenness, grasses and vines and trees I couldn't have separated and identified; just a glory of growth. Sunrise made the sky pale, but didn't diminish at all the color of the rock faces. It was Nature at her most abundant and I knew myself to be among the most fortunate of persons to have seen this place.

Carl's brother Ellsworth had urged us with such enthusiasm to move here, saying over and over he'd never even imagined such a spot on earth. He was right. First, the rock was surreal. Mountains and hills and fortresses and then stone spires on top of those other things, all in deep rust-colored richness, some with bands of lighter color as straight as if made by a master craftsman (which I guess they were).

They seemed more three-dimensional than things back home. Then everywhere that wasn't taken up by those endless variations of stone was filled, festooned, decorated by green growing things, and laid over all was the music of the water. Whatever fatigue remained was replaced by energy. I felt healed of some miasma I hadn't known I had. I was galvanized, grateful and ready to begin.

Carl

Carl had been absent when I rose and I still didn't know where he'd gone. But I knew wherever he was, he was working for our comfort and good. I felt so indebted to him; without him I'd still be in Gorin, not even aware there were options. He had opened that door. He had shown me that life could be other than what it was. Even with everything this move cost me, it was already supremely worth it.

There's a poem by Leigh Hunt that has always reminded me of Carl, even though it's written about a girl.

"Jenny kiss'd me when we met,
jumping from the chair she sat in.
Time, you thief, who love to get
sweets into your list, put that in.
Say I'm weary, say I'm sad,
say that health and wealth have miss'd me;
say I'm growing old, but add:
Jenny kiss'd me."

Certainly Carl didn't jump from the chair he sat in and kiss me when we met (there wouldn't have been a second meeting if he had), but that verse has come back to me often over time. Whatever has occurred, whatever I or anyone else might say about my life, Carl kiss'd me. And probably, more than anything, that has made all the difference.

II. Oak Creek Canyon
1901-1905

Moving West

Well, we're off! The first leg of our journey has officially begun. Tad, Pearl and I are on the train, having pulled out of the station within the past hour. It is so exciting. Probably when I'm tired later I will be melancholy for my sisters, but right now I feel like a dog after a snowfall—frisky, excited, wanting to share the adventure with everyone. And we'll see Carl. It seems forever instead of a fortnight. But we are making our way to him.

Before we see him, we will see new country the likes of which I cannot imagine. Double newness: new to us, and new to the very nation itself. We will pass through Indian Territory. Tad, even at three, is fascinated with that. He keeps asking, "When is Indian Territory, Mother?"

Pearl is so proud of her new travelling dress that she's being a perfect angel, sitting with her little boots stuck straight out in front of her on the seat. It's as if she knows she's an absolute picture, with her bright big eyes and soft hair. Everyone who comes through the car whispers and smiles, pointing her out to whomever they are with. I know God grew her, and I was just the vessel, but it makes me proud even so.

The only hard part is that we've already finished the lunch I packed, and we are just an hour out. While I brought some comestibles, I suspect I will end up buying meals at the stop houses, whatever they are called. Carl left me a little money; all he could spare. But then over the past few days, each friend who visited one last time would press a

handkerchief or envelope into my hand, "Just in case you need it, dear."
(It could almost be profitable to leave one's birthplace.) I felt guilty for
still being glad to go, in the face of those kindnesses. But it does make
one concern about this journey vanish: we are well-funded.

Tad and Pearl in Gorin, MO, 1901

Oct. 9, 1901

Sakes, am I tired of riding. Accurately, I am not tired of the riding itself; how can a three-day journey feel as if it's lasted three weeks already—and we aren't even there yet? I am tired of Tad's and Pearl-girl's being tired of riding. I have walked the length of this train more miles than it's gone down the track, I vow. We have colored on paper, we have made up names for flowers, we have counted everything imaginable. We have asked questions to guess what one of us spies with our little eye. They are actually momentarily entertained playing finger games, giving me a few minutes to reorganize our bag and write a little—a blessed respite that makes me feel I regain an important part of myself. I have struggled to be sedate and comport myself in the manner becoming to a young wife and mother, but at the next stop, a town called Gallop, we are going to do just that: gallop all over as fast as we can, so they come back to our seats good and worn out.

Well, we did indeed gallop. Only the town is either misspelled or intended to be another word: it was "Gallup" on the depot sign. I took Tad's hand firmly in mine and carried Pearl past the tracks and platforms, through the station to the boards that make up the sidewalk. Then I put her down, and we walked. They scurried and stumbled a bit, but then they began to run, and laugh. I strode between people, being amazed at the Indians we saw, but not pausing to gaze upon them.

Tad ran smack dab into a pair of long legs, and the man bent down and picked him up.

"You all right, young cowboy?" he asked genially. Tad looked bashful, then delighted, and valiantly told the truth: "I'm not a cowboy."

The man smiled at me, and put Tad down. "Well, you could have fooled me." He tipped his hat. His was an attractive face, with eyes brown and soft as a deer's and a square chin. The gentleness of his expression seemed in contrast with his frame, as lean and powerful as a racehorse. But somehow his countenance made me think of a pilgrim.

"Begging your pardon, ma'am," he said. "You don't appear to be native to our city. May I help you find your destination?"

I knew half of Gorin would shudder if I did more than politely dismiss him, but we weren't in Gorin anymore, and there were enough people around that he couldn't have abducted us. I no more think he would have kidnapped a young family than Carl himself would.

"Actually, we don't have a destination other than where we began," I said, "We are on the train. Well, not on it now, obviously, because my young ones here are more Indians than cowboys, they're so restless. I planned to walk them tired, then find something to eat, before we have to re-board." I glanced at the watch pinned to my lapel. "We have another forty minutes. Do you know a small café near here?"

I waited for directions, but instead he turned around and offered me his arm. I looked up and down the board sidewalk; there were small shops stretching in both directions down the long thoroughfare, with a scattering of people moving in and out of various doors. A few wagons in the wide dirt road had Indian drivers, or bearded men who looked like hunters, in buckskin or dirty calico. There was only the occasional woman, and I wondered if that's why he was making certain we were going to be accompanied.

"If you'll let me have the honor, I will escort you to my favorite place for breakfast. It's run by a woman; her prices are fair and her food is good." He picked up Tad to carry him while I held Pearl. "By the way, so you won't have to wonder if you should be gallivanting around with a stranger, my name is Atkinson."

Clearly, now, I could tell he was a westerner. A back-home fellow never would have approached and addressed a woman he didn't know; he would have found a mutual acquaintance to introduce us. But I decided he wasn't brash as much as just from a different place.

And part of the point of this coming west is to decide who I want to be. I want to be a welcoming woman…not just welcoming to the "right sort" but welcoming to the world. In whatever form it arrives.

So I told him our names, saw there were plenty of people around who would pay attention if I turned out to be a horrible judge of character and needed to cause a ruckus. We walked with Mr. Atkinson to a little restaurant, where a large woman with eyes like watermelon seeds watched us almost suspiciously as we came in, but when she saw the children, she smiled, and her face reminded me of one of those dried apple dolls.

The room wasn't large, but it was scrubbed and uncluttered: tables with ladder-back chairs, a door to the kitchen, a counter. Cloths were crisp, and the flatware looked clean. We sat down and ordered a prodigious breakfast: eggs and flapjacks and milk for the children, oatmeal and toast for me. I saw it would cost almost a dollar for this but didn't give a fig right then. And it was a fair price: my oatmeal came with brown sugar, currants and real cream, while the children were transported with delight by the fluffy butter and maple syrup that came in little containers on separate saucers for each child. Mr. Atkinson just wanted coffee. That was fine; I would have been happy to purchase him a princely repast in exchange for his protection, but coffee gave him less to disagree about.

What an amazing man our companion turned out to be. Mr. Atkinson is what's called an Indian Trader. At first, my face may have betrayed I was wondering if there was a slave market out here I hadn't heard of, but he quickly explained he travelled among the tribes in the New Mexico and Arizona Territories, buying the silver jewelry and woven rugs and blankets they made. Then they had money to buy tobacco, or tools, or coffee at the trading post. He said more people are coming west just to tour the land, and that they want to take home souvenirs to remind them of their travels.

I didn't say it, but I thought he was a shrewd man to be able to figure out what people were willing to pay for. I don't know what he will do when everyone who wants to see the west has visited, but he seems so bright he will surely find a different career once all the sightseers have come and gone.

Mrs. Koenig, for that was the name by which he greeted the proprietress of the café, seemed charmed by Mr. Atkinson. Indeed, he seemed to treat everyone, women and children alike, as if it was oneself he had been anticipating meeting all day. Tad ended up on his knee, poking flapjacks into his mouth whenever Mr. Atkinson let him, and Pearl giggled and looked at him through downcast lashes. He laughed, and asked me at what age I had begun giving her coquette lessons. I swore she had never observed me carrying on so; that it must be something in the female psyche that emerges unbidden.

He told me an amusing story of coming in once and finding a set of false teeth in a syrup pitcher! It seems Mrs. Koenig no longer has her own teeth, and put them in a pitcher to soak, and in the morning the kitchen help filled pitchers without removing them. But it was a spotless establishment as far as I could see, and I could imagine Mrs. Koenig's chagrin. Mr. Atkinson says he admires her because she supports a family this way, without a husband. He said as a businessman, he has a great deal of respect for anyone who makes a way in the world, and especially a woman. We talked about whether women should be given more opportunities, and he said women are more capable of making good decisions than many men he's met.

It was a delightful and unexpected conversation; one doesn't strike up such a discussion with strangers in Gorin. That might be because there aren't any. It occurred to me once back on the train that had I actually ever bothered to walk down to the station in Gorin I might have met people just as interesting. (Although there would certainly not be Indians in wagons on the street.) I guess part of the difference is in me. At home, I walked my same circle like a donkey in a yoke. Here, every footstep takes one somewhere new. It's so easy to feel lively and happy when there is no routine.

And it worked: Tad and Pearl are both snoozing next to me.

Arrived

So we're here. I feel I should write, "We are home," or some such, but this feels too strange and unsettled. We are…nestled, for lack of a better word, among these giant chiseled rock upthrusts and towers, with turrets and shelves, each shadow changing as the sun rises. And the colors! Rust, auburn, port, caramel; it looks not unlike the shelf of a magical alchemist's shop, with all the liquids and essences side by side. There are more varieties of "red" and "brown" here than I knew existed.

Between us and the rocks spread layers of vegetation: grasses, trees, low plants whose names I will learn later. And I hear the creek. Carl says our home will be six strides to the left of where this tent is. An irrigation ditch the man named Owenby dug before Carl got the property is next to the home site.

Eighty acres. Carl has as much land as Gorin occupies, I swear. From the creek bank to my right, all the way to a ridge a distance away on my left, and in front of me to a slight rise, then however far back 80 acres goes. Carl's brother Ellsworth, who described this place in letters urging us to move. told us the creek floods often, but that our homesite is far beyond the perilous area. Behind me? I don't even know. I hope I don't lose the children in their new world.

Carl's already got plans for most of it: corrals here, orchards over there (he's already begun planting the seedlings he brought), garden, outbuildings. I will feel like landed gentry.

I am delighted that Carl is so optimistic, so full of plans; almost giddy as a boy, and I feel bad for my hesitation. Part of me wants to stand square in front of him, look him in the eye and say, "Do you realize how much work all this will take?" I don't think he has any idea. Or maybe he does, and it bothers him no whit.

Oak Creek Canyon. I wonder if it's inspecting me as I am inspecting it. Sizing one another up; while I think, "So this is where I'll make a home..." the land thinks, "So she thinks she's going to impact these plants and places..."

The scent of wet foliage by the creek wafting up is heavenly, and there's a beautiful brisk breeze just starting to stir and ruffle the leaves. It got cool last night, but not uncomfortably cold. Carl says the breeze goes upcanyon at night, and comes downcanyon in the morning. The trees haven't lost leaves yet, so I know we have some time before frost sets in.

I'm overwhelmed by all there is to do. Unpack, learn the lay of things, meet the men Carl has working here. And yet, I feel strangely like a child out of school—free, and unfettered, as if work in this place might not feel like actual labor, because it's all so new. Nature is encompassing; it seems one would feel the presence of outdoors even when indoors. I wonder if we can make it feel civilized here; seem anything but wild. It's an exciting feeling, and yet there are moments one wants a cozy feeling instead.

Carl says we will go to Jerome or Flagstaff for things like mail, but he's already planning on getting a grocery business: selling the products from his orchards and gardens in those cities, then bringing canned goods back for the other families here. I'm worried about how long we will last on what we have before we can earn money selling our fruits and vegetables. Carl laughs when I ask him; I don't know if that means we are ridiculously rich from his hardware store share (which I rather doubt) or that he knows life is always an uncertain venture, and we may as well meet it with optimism.

I hope the women like me. Meeting new people scares me. I don't think I'm snobbish, or terribly shy, but they already have lives that function perfectly well, and throwing a new neighbor into the mix might not be to their liking. On the other hand, it's not like we'll be cheek-by-jowl with anyone. You would have to plan pretty carefully to happen into someone around here. I see no sign of anyone, from where I sit.

Ellsworth has told us there are five families spread across the region, but that's a relative thing to figure. Oak Creek is miles long. No one appears to live within two miles of us in any direction. He reckons the Dumas, Chavez, Schuerman and Armijo families are all within about five miles, and Indian Gardens upcanyon has several families.

This is a very different desk from any I have ever used. It is a rock. A fairly large rock, with enough room for my book, and a flat spot on the ground for the tin cup of tea I brewed (a new occasional habit; I get so exhausted sometimes). Carl was so grateful when I brought him tea. He hasn't been making any during his bachelor days here. It felt good. For a moment, handing him his cup, I felt as much at home as I ever have.

Oct. 27, 1901

Step by step, we are creating home. Even before we came to the half-wood tent, Carl had a plan already outlined on the ground for our actual house. Every day, he and other men he pays from the hardware store money are bringing it into being—almost like they sketch and paint a new element on a blank canvas of ground. In the meantime, I distribute our belongings in the tent house in as homey a way as possible, although with the wild surroundings it feels like pouring a cup of tea in the path of a forest fire. The featherbeds got partially wet, so half the down was replaced with pine needles, which scent our dreams but prick our backs. Everywhere is roughness: splinters come up each time I sweep, no shelf can be dusted or hold a figurine steadily. So all the breakables wait in crates.

Despite all the rawness and newness, I feel a stirring sense of ableness. Rather than being in a string of baby ducklings following the mother, I set the course. I figure out, I improvise: the first time Carl hadn't had time to hunt or fish a main dish for supper, I toasted bread and sliced it into hot milk. Tad said it looked like dog ears. Pearl laughed so delightedly that it has become their new favorite dinner. We got chickens almost as soon as we arrived, so there are always eggs, and later we will have chicken for dinners. Gradually, seeping in around the edges of my bewildered confusion, there is confidence. I think I will write to Lillie that while in Gorin I encountered shoals and breakers of inadequacy, in Oak Creek I find mastery. While Carl supervises the building of our house, I am learning what it means to build a life.

And somehow, while conditions are far more harrowing to child-drearing than the streets of Gorin were, I still find it easier. Even with having to watch them every second by the creek, and last week killing a rattlesnake all by myself with a rake and having to sit down afterwards because my knees wouldn't support me, even with rudimentary sanitation and everything else so raw and wild, I seem to be more the kind of mother I want to be. I take time to answer Tad's gruff little excited summons by going over to where they are playing instead of calling, "What is it?" And it is something new each time: a turtle on a branch sunning itself with a smaller one on its back; the slap of a beaver tail on the slowly moving water, a new berry or bloom about which to ask "what is that, Mother?" (Pearl calls me Mama, but our boy has always said Mother.)

I've never said, "We will find out, won't we?" so much. And at evening meal we all bring our questions to Carl. If he doesn't know, Ellsworth does. Ellsworth is Carl's aide de camp in most things, although he teaches during school hours. But he often takes meals with us, and shares the second tent-house with the lean and laconic Ned, who has worked silently alongside Carl since the day after he got here.

I have decided while observing him that the west must be a welcoming place for men like that, with no great prospects back home. Men with weak chins or stutters, men with a fondness for cards or drink or worse, men who may have felt lesser around the rich and powerful members of society back east, out here can be something more. They can be trusted, turned to, counted on. (Although Carl is no fool, and which boards under our bed hide the strongbox will never pass his lips.) "Good work!" can follow these men rather than derision. And where they walk and scatter seed, or in our case plant the seedlings Carl bought, comes life: trees grow so fast we can almost watch the progress, root vegetables spring eager and firm out of the loamy soil Carl is endlessly creating by turning wet decaying leaves into the red clay that made it a warm nest for young shoots.

Home

W̶e are at home! Our house is done. I was starting to worry about getting a real roof over our heads before snow flies, but no more. This is not a palace by Gorin standards, but compared to the tent house, it's grandeur. A big rectangular box, with windows on all sides and a wonderful porch all across the front. We have five rooms downstairs: kitchen, parlor, guest room, a big gathering room with the

Schnebly house in Oak Creek, 1901

dining table at one end (which can hold Sunday services until there's a church) and a combination washroom-storeroom.

There is even a full basement below, which will be wonderful for drying laundry when there's no sun, with plenty of shelves for preserved food. Upstairs are six bedrooms. Carl, ever resourceful, said we should build extra and fill them with paying guests until we fill them with children. Which means right now we could accommodate five rooms' worth of guests including the downstairs room, which would do wonders for our finances. He's talked to people in Flagstaff, who tell him lots of travellers want to lodge in Oak Creek, although some prefer a more rugged experience, like camping. The tent house can keep the rain off and still qualify as a highly rustic lodging.

I feel the chatelaine, queen of the kingdom, keeper of the keys. Carl has been lavish, ordering glass windows and a heavy front door with carving. It wouldn't raise eyebrows back home, but I have seen families larger than ours living in one-room soddies, like so many prairie dogs. This wide-boarded porch, the open rooms with sunlight pouring through all that glass, the spacious upstairs—it's heaven. And Carl does nothing by halves. His doorframes, chair rails, and window frames are simple, but carefully crafted.

The shed (which some kind souls refer to as "the ranch house") has been home for stored possessions, and will double as sleep space or perhaps a playhouse for the children. We face the creek. I want to be able to open the door and hear its song. The front bedroom on the upper floor facing that direction is ours. The whole place smells of fresh-cut pine and sawdust. Already the floors have a fine coating of red clay dust, also, but that's what brooms are for. I can't even imagine being bothered by having to sweep those smooth planks.

The first thing I want to do is hang pictures. Before I put together bedsteads, before I unpack the rest of the kitchen, I want to put up a few photographs. What I've missed the most being in the tent is not being able to see those images. They say, "This is where we live" to me.

Our home has been here, even before its existence. We walked the outline together; we planned which way it would face. We placed the stones forming the fireplaces, front and back, until I could reach no higher and the workers took over from their scaffolds. Here our family will flourish and grow. The bedrooms will fill, the table will be laden for holiday meals. Holidays seemed like a burden at Mutter's house; she was tense from cooking and things had to be impressive. At this house, holidays will be festive! Strangers and friends will be welcome. If there aren't sugared almonds or the roast is late, it won't ruin the day. We will have fun here.

Dear Lord: I feel awe and responsibility, walking these rooms. Help me share Your bounty. Bless this home, and those who will dwell within these walls. Give me humor and compassion, to be a woman who deserves this fine place. Let our children be olive branches around the table, and give us joy all our days here. Thank You, Lord, for the gift of this new home, this blank page of life, waiting for us to write upon it. Amen.

Billy Wallace

Carl came home yesterday and told me he'd met the man who lives up a ways by the creek.

Of course he did—Carl meets everyone. I'm so fortunate that one of the things I dread most, introducing myself to a stranger, is one of Carl's most favored activities. We have noticed and wondered about the occasional campfire smoke we see from that direction, and I've glimpsed a man walking about, with a gun on his shoulder or a fishing rod in his hand. But we knew nothing of him.

Carl paid him a call, and found out he answers to Billy Wallace. He was—and this is so exciting, like touching history with a fingertip—a Rough Rider.

"He lived in Flagstaff, and answered the call to join up with that unit when it came," Carl said, relishing retelling the story as much as he enjoyed hearing it himself the first time. "He said they trained just like any sharpshooting cavalry unit, even though they were actual cowboys and Indians and some rich college boys, with a few retired officers. The government recruited in Arizona, New Mexico, Texas and Oklahoma to get men who knew a thing or two about heat. Teddy Roosevelt himself came out to see them." I reminded Carl that he'd read me of the Spanish American War out of the newspapers for days when Tad was a newborn baby.

"That's so. Anyway, this Billy Wallace fought in all the battles. Hearing his story about going over to Cuba on the boat was like reading a novel."

Billy survived, but didn't escape scot-free.

"He was wounded; he says it's listed in the records as a neck wound, but it was his head. He got cracks in his skull and it was swelling underneath, and they took the bone pieces out. But then they couldn't put it all back together. So," said Carl with great relish, like a chef unveiling a grand dessert at the end of a meal, "they put a metal plate in his skull instead."

Tad was close enough to key in on the fascinating part. At almost four, his little ears are tuned to hear things like this.

"What, Dad? A plate in his skull? Like a tin plate you eat off of?"

Carl smiled and picked him up. Tad, all shiny of face and neatly combed of hair, was ready for bed and obviously looking to distract his father from that fact. Carl shot me a glance over his head, acknowledging the ruse and hoping I would let him hold his boy for a minute. I smiled back the parental understanding. He hugged Tad, who looked up to watch his dad's face while considering this remarkable thing.

"It would have been a piece of metal, probably round, and curved a little like your head, so there wouldn't be any sharp corners to push through his skin," Carl said, curving his hand around Tad's head. "I bet they used something strong, but not too thick. Then they sewed his scalp back over it, and here he is."

Tad's eyes were wide.

"Can I meet him sometime?"

"You can meet him tomorrow. He's coming to supper." He set Tad down. "Scoot up to bed and Mother will come and tuck you in."

I did, and returned.

"So he's coming to supper?"

Carl nodded. "He is. He relishes home cooking. The reason he's here is that when he went home to Flagstaff (he has a wife and children there), the cold made that metal plate burn something fierce. He knew the climate is milder here. With children in school, and them having a fine house, he goes up when the weather's good. But he has a great little outfit down here. A tent house, with hooks and beams across for hanging things; it's snug and tight and he keeps it shipshape. He has planks outside where he can skin what he hunts, and gut fish...." Carl told me all about the finer points of Billy Wallace's living quarters.

So this evening, Billy Wallace did indeed appear for supper, clean and genial. (In Gorin, we had breakfast, lunch and dinner. But here the men work so hard that we have a big breakfast, dinner at noon, and supper in the evening.) Billy Wallace wore a hat, and I noticed Tad staring intently when he took it off. You can see, if you look, that his hair is combed long over part of his head, but there's no shining silver to indicate the amazing surgery. He's clearly a father, because when he answered Carl's questions about the Battle of San Juan Hill, his answers were nuanced. He didn't use "bloody" or "massacre" and such words. Carl had read me a great deal about the battle at the time, and getting a first-hand account made us feel closer to a momentous event.

Billy Wallace greatly admired Teddy Roosevelt and Buckey O'Neill. He still mourns the loss of Captain O'Neill. He told us that his captain had led Troop A, which was the Arizona Unit, and was a fine man. Then he bowed his head, and quoted Lt. Col. Roosevelt's report about O'Neill's death: "As he turned on his heel a bullet struck him in the mouth and came out at the back of his head; so that even before he fell, his wild and gallant soul had gone out into the darkness."

Tad and Pearl were quiet. Then Billy smiled at them.

"You know who else was in our unit? Two Buffalo Soldiers."

Tad looked puzzled. He has seen pictures of the great shaggy beasts, but was probably wondering if animals could be soldiers.

Billy kept talking.

"They were brave men who have very dark skin, and joined the Army right here in Arizona Territory. They didn't fight buffalo, or even ride buffalo. But their hair is thick and tight, and reminds some folk of buffalo. So that's where they got that name. I tell you, they were smart and strong, and I think they trained twice as hard to make sure everyone knew they would pull their weight. I have a lot of respect for those men. I haven't ever had to live as a stranger in a white man's world, but I've seen how mean and small white men can be. Those Buffalo Soldiers had a hard road to hoe."

Carl was fascinated: Buckey O'Neill, Roosevelt, and Buffalo Soldiers? Billy Wallace is an entire repository of stories; a one-man acting troupe. He talked the lamp down pretty low. I had put the children to bed, and finally the men tore themselves away from the good talk and table. I believe we will see a great deal more of Billy Wallace, and I look forward to that.

First Christmas

Dec. 24, 1901

We have a small tree. We decorated it here in the main room after Tad and Pearl fell asleep. It's humble by any standard, but we were able to string cranberries Carl brought from Flagstaff. (It was a long trip; he has to go back through Jerome and up a place called the Verde Valley, so he was gone eight days, which I won't even write about because I was so shamefully skittish and scared.) He also brought popcorn, which I popped this afternoon; the children helped me string about six inches, eating and breaking most of it. We finished tonight.

I did bring one small box of ornaments from Gorin, and those share space on our three-foot tree. As long as it's as tall as Tad, it's tall enough. Carl also brought back the gift I had asked him to find: a sling-shot for Tad, who may as well begin to learn humble marksmanship if he's going to be a western man. I cut up pieces from the ragbag to make dresses for Pearl's doll Windy, who gets dragged everywhere and needs regular washings.

Normally Christmas is all feasting and leisure after church. Since there is no church here, we will sing some carols and say some prayers together in the morning. We will perhaps work a little less, not beginning any new projects around the property.

Most of all, we will wake up together in our home, in our place, in our new life. My heart is full.

Judgments

People back home have no way of knowing how different things are out here, because they haven't ever seen another way. You don't even know that your way is a way. As if everyone in Gorin walked backwards wherever they went...and people would think it the only way to walk, so it wouldn't seem like an aspect of life. You wouldn't mention it, describing Gorin: wrapping up with, "and everyone walks backwards."

I didn't realize growing up there was a class system there. (Now, of course, I realize that it's easier not to be aware of it when you are near the top.) I guess I observed the results—who paid calls to whom—but I thought it was simply part of the world, like leaves turning in the fall. I didn't know it was elective.

One thing I've recalled from the WCTU convention in St. Louis had nothing to do with abstinence. (Well, in a way it did, just abstaining of a different sort.) One of the older women, delightfully lively and candid, was originally from the Deep South—New Orleans, I think. She described to the group at our table her brother's amorous arrangement when he was a young man. A successful planter, he had a mistress. (It makes me smile to recall how we all sat circumspectly, wearing careful expressions of only mild interest, while our figurative tongues were hanging out.) She explained the men of that city engaged in the practice of setting up a mistress, only they called them placeés there. This happened, she said, because most marriages were for business advantage or plantation land acquisition. And what made it even more scandalous to us was that the mistresses were women of color. Octoroon, quadroon, or mulatto. (She added that those were one eighth, one fourth, or one half Negro blood.)

The most surreal aspect involved the grand balls. On the same evenings that polite society held a gala event, right next door, divided by a curtain, there was a quadroon ball. So the men slipped back and forth between the two, dancing with their wives, dancing with their mistresses. The wives pretended their husbands had just ducked out for a cigar, even though everyone knew. And the mistresses didn't pretend anything. Anyway, the point of this recollection is that the storyteller said that while it sounded shocking to outsiders, in New Orleans people merely shrugged and said, "the custom of the country." That's just how it was.

So I didn't realize while I was growing up that in Gorin that everyone was judged primarily on advantages beyond their control. We always knew Papa was "the second-richest man in Gorin." Like his name, this simply was fact, unquestioned. How did we know that? I never saw any numbers; I doubt anyone did. But it was the custom of the country. So our elocution lessons, our four spoken languages, our dancing and singing skills were settled upon us; we didn't earn them. They were still our social currency.

Here in the west, many people came to get away from somewhere. So no one ever says, "Who are your people?" because that isn't the important thing. One's bloodline, or the money that came down from forebears, doesn't figure into the scale upon which your value is weighed.

How hard will you work to save a neighbor's crop? (And are you strong enough to finish the job?) Can you be counted on to bring food and sit vigil after a death? Are you kind to strangers? Those are what matter.

I love that about Oak Creek.

Building

Carl is going to get to build his road.

He went up to Flagstaff yesterday to meet again with the head of the Board of Supervisors there, a Mr. Babbitt. He'd gone before to explain the foolishness of having to go south to get north. Jerome, Clarkdale and Cottonwood are a long day's trip, but getting to Flagstaff takes four, and that's the best produce market: the cold there makes growing peaches, cherries, apples, and most other produce impossible. Ours will be in keen demand.

The route Carl wants to use probably began as an animal trail, and then the Munds family used it. Making it a good wagon road would get produce to Flagstaff in less than half the time it takes now. Last time he went, Carl showed Mr. Babbitt the map he and Ellsworth had been studying every night, puzzling over, tracing each section like small boys with a secret treasure map. Maybe in some ways it is. Getting to sell so much more of our bounty so easily would bring welcome relief to our budget. Between Carl's constant improvements around the house and orchards, setting a good table, and keeping a family almost constantly outdoors in clean, serviceable clothes, I hate seeing our cache of bills under the floorboard dwindle.

Anyway, Carl has been telling the men around here his vision, and they thought it made sense.

So he told George Babbitt he has $500 to get started right away, and asked if the county could match that. At this meeting—I'm guessing the board approved the proposal—Mr. Babbitt said yes. I know Carl already had commitments from the Armijos, Chavezes, and Owenbys, because it would make all of our lives so much easier. Carl could bring mail more often, and all the other supplies he fetches back for everyone (coffee, sugar, flour and salt). They are such constant requests he now buys in bulk and stores them in our basement, selling them like an occasional storekeeper to anyone who comes by when he's home. Of course when he's gone, I am Mrs. Storekeeper. It's hard for me to ask for money; I let everyone put things on account and figure Carl will deal with it later. Which he does most often by throwing away my carefully noted transactions. He knows who can afford things and who cannot pay as much.

Anyway, the road. All of us down here have picks and shovels, and Carl bought a big scraper from Mr. Babbitt's store—I guess there are things like that out in back of the store, in addition to things on shelves. It's a sheet of curved metal wider than a wagon, with handles that men use to guide it while walking behind horses that pull it. He told me the county can lend them another such scraper to get the job done more quickly. Out of the $1,000 between himself and the county, he will pay anyone who wants to work on a road crew $1 a day. Except you know he won't pay himself. "We will be the ones who get the most use out of the road, Dona; that's all the payment I need." He has already said so.

Oh…and we celebrated my birthday with a small cake; I never dreamed growing up I would turn 25 in a setting such as this! The weeks fly past and I hardly touch my journal; my precious hour of writing time after midday meal is spent sending letters: to Lillie, to friends, occasionally even to Papa and Mutter, knowing they won't answer since I am no longer their daughter. But I suspect one or both may read them secretly before tossing them onto the parlor grate.

When the road builders were first getting started, I could take Carl his lunch. With Pearl on the saddle in front of me, and Tad on his pony feeling like a real cowboy, we would ride up this new road to see Dad, instead of him coming home midday. (Pearl has a pony named Pet, but both pony and child are a little too young for her to ride that distance). Most of the road crew workers live farther away, scattered through the Canyon, so Carl stays with them at midday. It's always a different group, because who can make it away from field, farm and family changes daily.

They use what they call the Mormon scrapers with picks and shovels. And—Tad's favorite part—on occasion they use dynamite. We don't go on those days, because Carl tells me that morning, but Tad hears the explosions and shivers in delight. I thought it would take a year to get through, but these men work industriously with only Sundays off. In only a few weeks they pushed so far we couldn't make the noontime trip.

Life is so different here! In Gorin, I never even wondered who built a road; roads seemed as much a part of the world as the trees, or clouds in the sky; they simply were. But now I see every convenience we had there was begun by someone, nameless but contributing to the good of all. I guess now Carl is one of those people: a founder.

There are so few families here, and those who are so scattered across a good distance. The Chavezes seem to get about easily, or maybe just love other people and count it worth the effort of bundling everyone into the wagon, hitching the team and making the trip over rough roads, animal trails and half-visible paths between most of our places. Tommy Chavez has become Tad's favorite playmate. We've also been to see the Dumas family several times. Tad loves Grandma Dumas as much as if she were related by blood. He can be shy with strangers, but something about her gets past his natural reserve. He runs to her, vigorous with his hug, chattering away and holding her hand as they go in to see what surprises await in the cookie jar. I find myself wondering sometimes if children and dogs can see in a way the rest of us cannot, based on how they respond to people. They seem to instinctively sense gentleness and kindness—or some ill intent. For reasons not visible to our eyes, they gravitate to, or from, someone new. When I do happen to see a neighbor, the talk these days is all about the new road. It's a good thing Carl is doing.

April 3, 1902

Carl is never done. Now he said he's applying to be the first postmaster here, and perhaps even get a telegraph machine. In order to apply to be a postmaster, he needs a name, which could possibly end up being a town name if more people move to the area (and already we are not the newest residents, less than a year after arriving). We have Indian Gardens upcanyon, Red Rock Crossing and Grasshopper Flat out west, Big Park to the south. But he wants something new. Lengthy conversation after dinner while Ellsworth was here has narrowed it down to Oak Creek Crossing or Schnebly Station. It will be interesting to see if they take his first or second choice.

Montezuma Castle

May 2, 1902

Tad is fortunate to have two parents.

If it had been up to me, I never would have let Ellsworth carry him all the way up the tall ladder at Montezuma Castle to see inside.

I'd heard of it and Montezuma Well, but not thought to go. They are an Indian ruin and a huge round lake over in the Verde Valley.

We made a day of it, going over in the wagon at first light, Pearl wrapped in a quilt on my lap, sleepy but interested. On the way through Big Park, Carl and Ellsworth pointed out Bell Rock. Many of those remarkable formations do not yet have names. The way they are shaped, sometimes sloped, then sometimes so straight of side, in terraces, is how sandstone apparently reacts to rain and wind. And they are red because they quite literally rust. It's iron in the rocks. Who ever heard of rocks rusting? At home stones are quite inert and inactive. They just lie on the ground. Anyway, the color is arresting. I wish I could paint; I would try to recreate some of them to send home. I can barely draw.

The ride to Verde Valley was long but pleasant. Verde is Spanish for green. And it's greener than the surrounding area, although not as green as Oak Creek. The Verde River is their watercourse.

Montezuma Castle may or may not have been built by the Aztecs—Ellsworth says he thinks some huckster thought of the most exciting Indian name he could—but it's a grand spectacle. You have to be fairly close to even see it. I was wondering as we approached how on earth there could be a castle anywhere nearby; there's so little level land, and nothing showing. Then Ellsworth pointed up at the cliff near us. At first I was just looking at a cliff. Then, gradually, my eyes made out a building tucked inside there, also of rock. How anyone, Aztec or otherwise, was able to get handholds and footholds up to that hollow cave in the sheer wall and build all the rooms with windows and doors is beyond my ability to imagine. But they did it, and Tad was mad with excitement when Ellsworth said he always climbs up to look in.

So I watched my four-year-old boy get smaller and smaller, like a knapsack on Ellsworth's back, as he climbed what seemed increasingly spindly ladders up the face of the ruin. Once when Tad let go of Ellsworth's neck to point at something, I clenched Pearl so tightly in my own arms she gave a surprised squeal and started to fuss. (As if holding onto her would keep him from falling up there.) But after a while, they came back down, both panting and flushed even though Ellsworth did all the work. Tad described some pots and fire circles inside.

It's a majestic place, in a very different way than the French courts we read about in school. Did they not know of these wonders in Gorin? They certainly never told us about them. I know I didn't realize that Indians were apparently every bit as ingenious, and industrious, as our own forebears were. To engineer and construct this place takes talent far beyond what most builders in Gorin were capable of creating.

We took our lunch back behind Montezuma Well, which is just a short wagon ride away; surely the water supply for the people who looked out of those windows up in the cliff. The well is an oval pool of water that looks like someone built it. But it's a natural limestone sink fed by a spring. Ellsworth says no one knows how deep the well is— they've not been able to dive to the bottom yet. After we looked a bit, we went back behind to a shaded area. We had to lift the children over things and scramble, but the result was worth the effort. There were very large sycamores by water that runs deep and cool, flowing out of the well through an ancient canal to a natural river. Tad was clutching a piece of a pot he had found, cinnamon with black zigzags, like lightning. He was very proud of it. I wondered aloud if a mother had made it for her boy a long time ago, and he beamed, putting it carefully in his pocket.

The drive back never seems to take as long, and I sang to the children; they are learning some hymns that way. Being in the sun that long made us all yawn on the return trip.

We will sleep well tonight.

Named

Carl came back from Flagstaff last night. Ellsworth was here because it's Friday and he generally has supper with us on weekends—there's no rush to grade any homework for the next day. When he taught in Verde Valley he couldn't see us during the week, but would often walk here on weekends. I don't know how many miles it is, but it takes hours. That man purely loves to walk. "Claiming miles is like a game," he says. "And it's time to think." Now he's closer in, teaching families west of us.

He was drinking water and visiting with me in the kitchen when the children heard the horse nickering and neighing, calls of being home, and hungry. The children ran out to meet Dad's wagon with Ellsworth following more slowly; he helped unload while I got supper on.

When Carl and Ellsworth came in, they were grinning like boys with a secret. I figured they'd tell me when they were ready, so I dished out the chicken and dumplings, passed the beans and biscuits and tomato relish, and waited.

Finally, after some catching up about the day, Carl pulled out a letter from the U.S. Postmaster General in Washington D.C. It was the application he'd sent, returned to him with "too long" written in the margin by his town names. It struck me as a little terse, a little rude. Like correcting a composition. But then, I have no idea how many applications they have to deal with. Maybe politeness would slow things down to an unacceptable pace.

The idea of Schnebly Station being too long launched indignant conversation about how they make fort names fit on cancellation stamps, and then every two-name post office any of us could think of. But at the end of it, the Postmaster General is sitting in his office, where we are not. His is the power to grant or refuse.

And that's when Carl came to why they'd been so tickled when they walked in.

"So Ellsworth said, 'why not name it after Dona?' And I think that's a fine idea." Carl waited, watching for my reaction.

I didn't know what to do, or think. A post office with my name? Maybe a town with my name? At first I was proud that they'd think of it. Then I was embarrassed; it was like saying I was important. Queen Me. But it does have a pretty sound, Sedona. And no one would know where it came from anyway.

It's an honor, a tribute from these two men whom I both love and respect.

I said thank you.

Travois

When you meet someone, you have no way of knowing if it
will be a one-time conversation, a casual acquaintance or
something more. I'm thinking this might be more.

June has been hot. So hot that I was working in the garden in a
dress I'd all but cut the sleeves off of, and hemmed up to my shins. My
hair wouldn't stay up with pins – they kept sliding out and driving me
to distraction. I stomped into the kitchen and flung the pins on the
table, then braided my hair firmly into one long plait. Get out of that,
I thought with grim triumph.

I did all this quickly, because Tad and Pearl were allowed to play in
the irrigation ditch; it was that hot. Since I was weeding near them, I
felt safe, but didn't want to be inside more than a moment.

As I came off the porch I heard, "Hallo, the house!" and saw a man
coming out of the glare. I turned (my sunbonnet keeps me from seeing
anything except right in front of me) and saw him—a little on the tall
side, burnt dark and not hatted, which is unusual, and also foolish in
this climate. He was shabby looking, but strong, and strode rather than
walked. Tad looked up and checked my face to see if I seemed alarmed,
but I felt perfectly safe even though Carl was working up on the road.

Feeling at a slight disadvantage in my informal attire, I nevertheless
smiled and walked forward, taking my bonnet down once I was out of
the sun. I introduced myself and said he looked as if he could use a cool
drink.

He made kind of a shy wistful face and said, "and a bite of something if you can spare it, Mrs. Schnebly. I can pay." (He knew my name, so he'd obviously been in the area; word travels fast in a remote place when anyone new settles.)

I shook my head at the offer of pay—Carl and I both feel that if we have enough, we won't take money—and invited him to sit on the front porch. Tad came up and looked at him, Pearl following with her fingers in her mouth. I pulled her over and wiped her hands on my apron.

The man smiled at them.

"Thank you for sharing your shade with me. What's your name, young man?"

"I'm Tad, and that's my sister Pearl. Who are you?"

I was listening, because he'd not offered his name.

"Well...they call me Travois."

"Truh-voy?" Tad repeated.

"Right. Do you know what that means?" Tad shook his head. "It's what Indians use to carry heavy loads. They drag poles with something between them that can hold things, behind horses usually. And an Indian friend of mine gave me that name, because he said I always look like I'm carrying a heavy load, even if my hands are empty."

That was pretty poetic, I thought—and could even be true. Plenty of men out west don't use their given names, I suspect, for all kinds of reasons. Hiding from a family back home, or the law, or just bored with a previous dull existence and wanting to be someone more interesting out here where no one can question it. But Travois seems a cut above most: he fits the part. He's one of those men who seem painted in deeper tones than most of us. I guess it could be called charm...but also something slightly secretive. Not clear and open like Carl. If it weren't for Loring, I would have thought Travois a dashing figure. But charm doesn't go very far with me anymore. While he talked to Tad, I went inside to get lunch together. Carl had taken his with him that morning, so there were four of us to feed.

We ate on the porch, trying to soak up any stray breeze. There was Sunday's ham, some stewed peaches, good bread and cool water with ginger and lemon. Travois appeared to savor it all. Tad and Pearl ran back to the ditch as soon as they were finished, and I picked up our plates, planning to just scrape and soak them so I could get back to the weeding before it got even hotter, as it does until late afternoon. Then after a few still hours, the breeze starts to stir, and you know sundown is on the way.

I explained I needed to get on with the work, and he nodded.

"I'm handy," he said. "Give me a digging stick." Digging stick. He must either be half-breed or maybe just feels an affinity for Indians. Either way, I wouldn't turn down help. I had an extra screwdriver in case Tad had felt inclined to help, so I handed it to him.

He worked quickly and lightly, moving easily. Sort of graceful, I thought.

As far as his bloodline is concerned, he was enigmatic. Not anything about his people. Nor much of anything else, except that he's had adventures, talks very well, and seems inclined to melancholy.

He asked a few questions, saying he'd heard our name the last time he came through Oak Creek. I told him a bit about Gorin, and asked where else he goes. He talked some: he's been as far north as the Rocky Mountains in Colorado, and spent the winter trapping. "And doing some looking around for the folks back in Washington," he said. I added this piece to the puzzle I was fitting together to share with Carl when he got home. Travois spoke like a cultured man. I asked where he was staying, and he said he would camp not far away. I thought about mentioning our tent house for use if it rained, but decided Carl should meet him first; he's good at taking the measure of a man, so this was his decision to make. I asked Travois where he was from.

"Originally, back east. Now, I'm from wherever I just left." He shook his head. "I've never been one who could stay in one place. But when I saw you in the garden with your hair swinging and the children playing, it made me wonder if I might not be missing more than I realized."

He was looking at me when I glanced up, his eyes dark and earnest. I didn't move, but I felt something inside me back up. Not because he was dangerous; it was just a little bold, too familiar. He must have seen my expression, because he shook his head.

"I forget what it is to be around ladies. I'm sorry if I overstepped. Talking to just myself most of the time, my manners have gotten rusty." Perhaps, I thought. Or perhaps that's something he says to women everywhere he goes, and depending on how they react he either apologizes, or is encouraged and continues sweet-talking. He sounded very rueful and sincere. I am just not the right person for it.

Sedona

June 30, 1902

I realized today I've not written because I'm embarrassed, but I should record that we now have a Post Office with my name.

Carl and Ellsworth were overjoyed when the official designation came, and got silly egging one another on about all the endless jokes that could be made.

"So, if your sister wrote you here in Arizona Territory, she could write, 'Sedona, at Sedona, AT!'" Ellsworth crowed at one point. Carl had to beat that: "She could write Sedona AT with a 2, like squared: Sedona AT Sedona AT!" They were off again.

I'm certainly honored, but also a little ruffled and unsettled. I have no idea how the subject of a post office name should act. Will this be a nuisance? As Carl pointed out, it's not like he's making me preside over a ribbon-cutting. I think he thought I should just relax a little about it.

I'll try. Easy for him to say. We should have named it Carl.

The Kings

W e're getting the most interesting people about. No one in
this group needs to sleep out. When folks come down to
Oak Creek with Carl and the supplies, Carl unloads their bags, intro-
duces them to me, and says a word or two (or several paragraphs) about
each guest.

The lung patients sleep in the old ranch house, or the tent cabins.
Since tuberculosis is highly contagious, it wouldn't be safe for our family or other guests to let them sleep inside. The rest board in the house.
At first I worried that the ones consigned to other lodging might feel
rejected, on top of already being sick. I had Carl get extra bedding, of
very good quality, so no one would ever be cold. But rather than feeling
hurt, the people recuperating seem to love their quarters. Hearing the
creek so close at night, breathing the fresh air, being in such a setting
are wonderful, they assure me when I take trays down for breakfast.
Supper and dinner are in the house, but no one should have to wait for
the first meal of the day. I'd even learned to make good coffee, or so I'm
told. I have actually learned to enjoy the scent of it, but I haven't tried
to like the taste.

Anyway, yesterday Carl brought down a couple from back east
who will board with us awhile. When the woman came up the steps
of the porch I felt a little shy, as I used to when Temperance meetings
included speakers from big cities. She was tall and slender and beautifully dressed, in a fawn-colored suit of what appeared to be faille. (But

not at all fussy; no jewelry or furbelows, just a perfectly lovely hat of rough straw with a wide brown velvet ribbon circling the crown finished in a large bow.) She did look hot and tired when I welcomed them in. They are the Kings of Boston, Massachusetts: Dorothea and Jacob.

He's been ill, she told me, when she came downstairs after freshening up. I gave them the back upstairs bedroom I like best, with the quilt all pieced in yellows, and the big rug. (Thank Heaven that while Lillie embroidered table runners and tea towels, I enjoyed creating quilts out of the rag bags; it was like being an artist to find all the scraps, patterned and flowered and plain, with the same set of colors.) Dorothea had changed into a simple dress. Her hair is almost the same color as mine: not black, but too dark to call brown; sable, perhaps. She's fairer of skin than I am, with beautiful hands. I tend to notice women's hands because mine used to be nice, and now are rough, red, cracked and cut more often than not. Loading firewood into the stove means splinters and small gouges; dragging washtubs to the creek, harnessing horses—it seems everything we do out here includes small hurts. But Carl always says to whichever child holds up a fresh oozing injury with a stricken face, "Count the day lost you don't draw blood." I say it myself now.

Back to Dorothea King. Far from being Boston snobbish, she's a delight! She said sincerely she thinks our house is lovely. Part of me hesitated to believe her, because they clearly come from money: Jacob is in banking, she said, which is the kind of thing wealthy people say. (I've learned a lot from our boarders: poorer folk eagerly tell you exactly what their work is while the wealthier ones are more vague.) Anyway, she couldn't be more fun. It was as if we had been sisters and not seen each other for too long. I remember the Gorin house, and how much grander it is than this, but fussy and full of knick-knackery, stuffy and crowded and cluttered. She said she loves how clean and bright and open this house is, with the children's things about, and for some reason I believe her. Life isn't all about money, and this woman clearly holds her own values.

I asked questions about Boston, so much a part of our history. She described the Old North Church, the road to Concord, the harbor where the Boston Tea Party took place. She talked of Faneuil Market, where all manner of merchants have been selling goods and food since the 1700s. She speaks rapidly, and is very intelligent. But she seemed truly interested in what it's like to do the laundry at the creek, and pick the fruits for canning; she loved the idea of being able to sit outside listening to water and birds, instead of the clop of passing horses with buggies, and myriad unintelligible voices from streets.

We talked nonstop through dinner preparation; she says she can't cook at all, but that even she can chop something and set the table. And she is lovely with the children, cutting up apples for them and asking them questions about their playhouse. She doesn't have children yet; she said she's only recently married, although I believe her to be a bit older than I.

If I'd met her in Gorin, we probably wouldn't have talked in the first place. She would be staying with some very wealthy cousins, and I didn't move comfortably in those circles, even though we qualified to. But being in the west is a leveler. People meet with fewer preconceptions, and judge one another more on real values than possessions. I'm so blessed we moved here.

Dorothea says she's going to have me help her make a few dresses like mine that she can wear while they tour the west. She says she plans to take them home and start a new rage in Boston. She has so much spirit, she just might.

Flagstaff

What an adventure! Dorothea, Tad, Pearl, and I went with Carl to Flagstaff this week. I'd never gotten to go: we often have boarders, and even if we don't, I don't know how we would take the children. Carl can sleep under the wagon if the weather's bad, but they couldn't. Dorothea wanted to go back to Flagstaff to see the town. Carl had collected them right off the train, so they came straight to Oak Creek and she wants to see more of the sights there. Mr. King—she calls him Jacob, but I am too shy—thought it would be great for us to go, since the weather's mild. (I found out he picked up some sort of lung fever in Egypt or somewhere he was travelling, which is what brought them here.) Anyway, she asked us to come with her since Mr. King wanted to stay in Oak Creek to fish and walk all day, and she insisted we should stay in a hotel! She said spending the money on a hotel room for us wouldn't deprive her of a thing, but being there without me to explore with would be a deprivation to her.

Travois is our only visitor right now, and he doesn't have to rely on me for meals. He said he'd be happy to water the stock, keep the trees irrigated, and eat pickup with Carl for two nights, adding, "It will be good for you." It makes me feel funny to have a man who isn't my husband talk about me as if I'm a person. That isn't said well, but it's an odd thing that I don't have any experience putting into words. He cares about how I feel, even though he isn't responsible for me at all. It matters—I matter —to him. Which, rather than offending Carl, makes him glad when Travois is there. "There's no one better to look out for you and the children," he says.

In any case, Carl knows Travois will do fine bringing the cattle in at night and turning them back out after milking, and could handle any minor emergency like a coyote getting after the chickens. So we all went. Pearl and Tad couldn't believe they didn't have to wave good-bye to Dad, but got to clamber up into the wagon instead. (Which I now realize will create a hue and cry next time he leaves without them, when they will confidently expect to be able to go.) We all sat in the back of the wagon, while Carl managed the team on his new road. It's primitive to anyone who expects a road to be paved, but the fact that he could look at the rough canyon and see where it should go amazes me. It's wide enough for a wagon, but over much of it if two met, one would have to back up.

Of course nothing thrills Carl more than getting to show the area to someone new, and he told about the time Mantle Rock calved off after the big storm.

"I only wish I'd been there to see it actually fall! What a crack-and-shot sound that must have made, when the inner panel just split out and slid down the slope. You can still see the scree where it tore up all the plants and the ground on its way down. That's why I call it Mantle Rock, because now it looks like a fireplace, where before it was just a flat front."

Dorothea has a natural touch with children; she had them looking out for bear and deer, which Tad and Pearl found as exciting as actually seeing them, and watching ravens soar on updrafts as we climbed the canyon. Their caws of ownership of the air followed us most of the way. One even flipped upside down, and turned right back up like an aerialist at a circus! It must have been just for fun.

About halfway up, Carl turned two horses back for home, since the road levels out and he no longer needs four. His drive back home is all downhill; he's said he could pull the wagon himself. When I'm home, it's always a good feeling to see those first two horses return; it means

Carl met with no accident that far up. They seem like ambassadors bringing his greetings.

Now I know where he unhitches them: it's about the point where the pinyon and juniper trees give way to tall Ponderosa pines, and the growth gets thicker. It must snow more here in winter,; the breeze cooled noticably. Then we pulled up onto the higher ground, out of the canyon, and it was a flatter drive into Flagstaff.

You can smell fresh-cut timber before the town is even in view. I guess all these trees make that a natural enterprise. Carl learned somewhere that Mill Town was what it was called before someone cut the branches off a pine tree and fastened a flag to it, celebrating the Fourth of July in 1876. That's when it changed to Flagstaff. This is a rough town by Gorin standards; the streets aren't paved, and the houses look raw. Most of the people on the streets are men.

We went to Babbitt's store to meet the people Carl always sees. The clerk told me whenever someone comes in who is either tubercular and needs fresh air, or just wants to see the west, they are told at the railroad depot to come to the store and wait for Mr. Schnebly. They won't be disappointed.

Anyway, Dorothea and I got to explore the town with the children. It's very cool, very green. The pines smell heavenly, even in town; a rather sun-baked, breeze-borne spicy scent. And from the mill, issues the sound of saws, and the more roasted smell of lumber being cut. Tad couldn't believe all the wagons, and Pearl loved seeing children. Poor thing—it hadn't occurred to me how rare a little girl playmate is in her world. So we walked to the grand new school on a slope just out of the main village. It's a pretty building with a stretch of actual grass and some pines, and a few children were running around there.

They had such a time! Ours joined them in shrieking and rolling down this gentle hill in front of the building. The school is very impressive; blocks of quarried russet sandstone three stories high, with turrets and lightning rods. It looks like something back home, except odd, sitting by itself. A woman watching her own brood play told us it was first supposed to be a reform school, and then an asylum, but now it's a normal school for teachers.

Tonight we will eat in the restaurant at the Hotel Weatherford. It's reminiscent of the St. Louis hotel where we stayed for the WCTU conference, with red brocade carpet and a staircase with carved spindles and an elaborate banister. The children have already been promised they can walk up and down as many times as they want after the evening meal. I am so excited. I feel as if I'm on vacation abroad. I will sit down like a lady to a meal I had no hand in preparing. I can't think the last time I did that. Well, I guess it was on the train trip out here, but that seemed so frantic: the children were younger, and I didn't even really know where we were. Now, we are guests of a very generous woman, in a town where Carl is known and respected. I will not put on an apron. I will have dessert.

Interlude

July 20, 1902

F̲ew things are as pleasant as peeling peaches on the porch in late afternoon; poorly alliterative, but I'm too content to care. Obviously, I'm taking a brief respite from the fruit work to gaze at, and bask in, this tableau. Tad and Pearl have been so happily engaged this past hour I haven't bothered them. They've constructed a village of some sort, using twigs and leaf canopies with various pits and peels from my basket; from the sound of it, one resident is named Erlie and

Tad & Pearl outside Oak Creek house

one is Poppa Pie. As long as they remain even remotely clean, and are safe, I am content.

Oak Creek summers are different than back in Gorin; there's a lissomeness here that I don't recall from growing up. All of Oak Creek is a more sensual climate. Maybe because the outside is still so untamed, and we spend so much more of our time in it. The view is always fascinating, with light constantly changing the look of the abrupt upthrusts and crags of the deep rust rock. I feel much more a part of…I was debating between writing "nature" and "weather" and realized it's more than either of the two.

There's something about this place that magnifies, intensifies any emotion. If I am pleased, I am more than content; I am soaringly grateful, filled with felicity. If Carl is away and I wake up in the night, it isn't with nervousness; it's with a startling terror that makes my heart hammer and breath come fast. Thoughts seem to go deeper here; love comes stronger. It's as if the potion, the alchemy of what goes into a life is distilled here. It's boiled down, some of the liquid steamed away, so you imbibe the intoxicating core instead of essence diluted by filler.

July 23, 1902

What an interesting conversation with Dorothea today.

I knew she had no children; she said that early in our talks. But she is always so natural with mine that it seems a shame she has none of her own. She speaks with Tad and Pearl as if they are equals, and they are as comfortable having her wipe their hands as they are with me.

I've always rather wondered whether her husband didn't want children, or what was involved, but today she told me she can't have them. She had a fever when she was younger, and something happened; she can never be a mother.

She was helping me make blackberry jam; she actually seems to enjoy kitchen-y things more than I do. She says it's because she never gets to do them at home—the staff shoos her out. And of course to me, they are survival, not option. In any case, it's so much more fun when we talk while we work. Today it was about the exciting life she leads, travelling all over the world, seeing things I will probably only read about.

"I would choose what you have in an instant," Dorothea said. That's when she told me about not getting to have children. She said at first, she was very bitter, and she cried, and "had a funeral of feelings for myself."

Then she said what I've thought of ever since.

"Happiness is like a muscle," she said. "And if you want it strong, you have to exercise it. I know a lot of wonderful things have happened in my life, and if I don't enjoy them—if I'm preoccupied with what I don't have—I won't be happy. I just don't have any patience with that. Maybe someday things won't go so well; I could be tested. If I've worked the happiness muscle to be really strong, I'll get through anything."

She added with a flash of smile, "And if I'm never tested, just think how much happier I will have been from all the practice."

She's so right.

Since then, I've been aware of times when I merely go through the motions of my day, mentally running on a schedule like a late train: on to this, on to that, then to here. When I stop, and realize that I have a choice between barreling through a day enduring, or actually enjoying, I see my life differently.

Right now, for instance. The children are in bed; Carl is washing up. My home is in order (to a degree I can live with). We are safe, and abundantly cared for, with a surplus of food and energy and love.

I could have missed this surfeited feeling of blessings if Dorothea hadn't said that.

I am fortunate to have her in my life.

Storm

Travois was here today. I was weeding when he came up; he's the quietest walker I've ever known. He had some fat fish for us. He isn't officially boarding with us; he generally sleeps down by the creek in a rudimentary branch shelter closer to the sound of water than any of our buildings. But frequently he comes for a meal, usually bringing some contribution. I always enjoy seeing him, because I know he will leave me thinking about something. He and I can quote poetry or plays back and forth almost like a contest.

After I thanked him for the bounty, he sank down beside me and started helping with the weeding. (The rain we've had makes them grow like—weeds?) By and by he said he'd been thinking about me. That's a powerful thing to tell a woman, especially a mother. I don't think of anyone but Carl thinking about me. They may call me, or need me, or depend on me, or expect me. But thinking about me implies something different. It's a considering of me not with a demand, but as if I'm interesting and worthy of pondering. It made me feel like an entity unto myself.

I'm uncomfortable writing this. Sometimes, when I'm around Travois, I feel...what? A little different than around any other man. I know how much I love Carl, and I adore our children. I wouldn't have my life different for an instant. Even so, being in Travois' company carries a little extra sense of being a woman, and worth talking to.

I'm not foolish enough to think the mirror doesn't reflect both ways. There could be some dry goods clerk at Babbitt's in Flagstaff with auburn curls who makes Carl feel a little confused and frisky. It doesn't mean he's supposed to marry her, and I expect there's no real harm in it.

But it feels disloyal, to even write about Travois. And yet it flustered me when he said, "I wonder if I'd met you sooner, if I would have needed to travel all those years." So I need to write to sort it out and make sense of it.

"You have a travelling bone," I said. "You would be restless with anyone."

"But you take me places without having to stir a step," he said, and then he laughed, with kind of a rakish look.

I just laughed at him.

It's always interesting to watch Travois talk to any woman who might be around. He has all the elements of a dime-novel hero: he wears furs in winter, buckskin in summer, and seems to fit the exact definition of a wayfaring stranger. He is definitely good-looking. And yet part of me always pulls back a little bit, like if I don't watch out, I'll believe something he says. Thank goodness for Loring. After him, to me only Carl exists in three dimensions: strong, kind, and true. Others might possess any number of qualities, but only in two dimensions, not three. Carl is always glad to see Travois, because they are both talkers. He makes Carl laugh, and that makes me glad. I feel better if it's the three of us sitting around after dinner. I don't linger if Carl is away; I get right to the dishes.

But there was a day I haven't written about, a few weeks ago. I'd been stringing beans on the porch, aware of a storm blowing up; the brisk little dust devils in the side yard, the scent of extra dampness. There's a general quickening when a summer rain is coming over Wilson Mountain. Travois came past from the creek, where he'd apparently gotten a good bath. His hair was damp; he'd shaved and was wearing clean clothes. He settled on the porch step about a person's distance away, and we were talking, mostly about the Indians around here and what he thinks we should all be learning from them.

The breeze picked up and started rattling branches, then lightning seared across the sky. We agreed we love the wildest types of weather. Then we fell quiet as the storm descended with a huge Old Testament vigor. The drops splatted large and heavy, and we could hear the wind tossing the cottonwood branches. There was a heaviness all around, and I was so aware of Travois next to me.

It was a sense of being a part of something as rough and all-consuming as the rainstorm; as if he and I were just as much a part of nature as this thundering deluge.

Before the storm ended, Travois abruptly stood up and walked off. I didn't see him for a few days, and neither of us has mentioned it. But I know it isn't because either of us forgot. It's because we both remember.

I tried to tell Carl about it a few days later; I didn't like feeling as if something were unsaid between us. But he stopped me one sentence in, with, "Do you love me?" "Of course!" I said. "Then that's all there is," he said.

I don't understand men. But I am so impressed with Carl's strength, and his clarity for what matters most. As long as the children and I are protected, he will gladly bear any foolish feelings on my part without complaint.

Indian

Now I don't know what to do.

I've been letting Tad and Pearl pretty much run free. At the age of four, he is well able to keep an eye on her, and wouldn't get them into anything dangerous. Foolish, sometimes, like building such a village out of clay near the creek so that they came home looking like red mummies. But not dangerous.

Then this morning, I look out and they are sitting on the corral fence, which isn't so high it scares me. But they are having a conversation...with an Indian!

Where did he come from? Who is he? Why was he here? I started outside and realized he was walking calmly away, and the children were waving at his back.

"Tad," I said, brightly, "Who was that?"

"Well, I don't exactly know his name, Mother," he said. "But he's our new friend."

"Where did you meet him?"

"Right here. We were just sitting here and he came to see us."

"Did he speak English?"

(By now my heart was slowing down, and it was becoming interesting rather than terrifying. It amused me that Tad actually stopped and thought a moment.)

"I guess he probably didn't."

"How did you talk?"

"Umm...I guess we pointed. And...I don't know how we did, but we did. He was hungry, so I showed him where the chickens were and the fruit in the orchard."

(More mixed feelings. I would have fed him, quickly and abundantly. Are we now going to have hordes of his friends descending on our stores?)

"That was kind of you. We always share, don't we?"

"Yes, Mother. He was funny! He sang a little song."

Tad tried to imitate it—low and a bit guttural, but with a definite cadence. It made Pearl laugh and she joined in. The two of them were so entertained I smiled and walked back in.

He must have been Apache, since Carl says any natives remaining here are of that tribe. He seemed healthy enough, and content. I don't think he intended any harm, although it was probably easier than he expected to pick the plumpest hen in the flock. But he waited until the children invited him to.

I guess since they were actually within eyesight, I won't do anything differently. If a whole horde of marauders set upon us, I would have bigger problems than the children being outside. One woman, albeit a very protective one, wouldn't last long against flaming arrows and tomahawks (or rifles and knives from white men!) even if the children were behind my skirts. Carl swears any Indians still here are respectful souls, who still go once in a while to Indian Gardens to harvest some of what they quite likely planted themselves before they were sent to live elsewhere.

Oh, that's interesting. I was about to write, "Not by us, thank goodness." But surely some lived here before we did. Why is it all right for me to be sovereign of what was probably their land, as long as I was not the one who specifically drove them out? You, Sedona, have a bit of hypocrisy in you.

I'm glad I've apparently been able to keep my fear of "red savages" from the children. I very much wanted to. That's not how it is here. But I grew up in a different world, back east, where stories came in whispers about settlers in wagon trains being desecrated and witnessing unspeakable things done by Indians.

I guess there's a difference between the groups we think of, and then the people we meet.

Pantheist

Sept. 2, 1902

Interesting conversation with Travois today.

He brought by a brace of jackrabbits, which I will stew with pleasure (and some sage, pepper, and rosemary, which grows abundantly here). Not only tasty, but a dinner of vengeance, since those pesky creatures don't leave my garden alone unless I'm standing in the middle of it waving my hoe. I invited him into the kitchen; he frequently accepts a cup of coffee, which I keep on the back of the stove. I never have developed a taste for it, but I do love the scent, and most folks seem to feel any time of day is appropriate for a cup. I was latticing piecrusts, so he was welcome company. Tad and Pearl like him, although after they asked to see the bear tooth he wears on a thong around his neck, they didn't stay around long. Travois has nothing on the leftover scraps of pastry with which to decorate their mud pies. "We know! We won't eat any," Tad called as they ran back to the playhouse.

I mentioned to Travois that there was a circuit preacher coming through this weekend, and how nice it was to be getting some kind of regular worship. I asked how long it's been since he's been to church. (Most people I would never question as I do him; Travois is as familiar to me as a relative, somehow. I just feel I've always known him, and that anything I say is acceptable. In fact, I'm more constrained with Carl. I guess things are more important with Carl—how he feels about me, or his reaction to something, has a greater affect on my life. Travois is once removed.)

Anyway, "Depends on what you mean by church," he said. "If you mean a little closed-in building where a man stands up front and gets paid too much to lecture and scold me about being a greedy sinner, I am happy to say it's been longer than I can remember.

"But if you mean being in a holy place, where I feel full of the spirit of life, grateful for all my blessings and willing to be part of the greater good, I guess I go about every day. I am almost always in the cathedral of nature."

Well, he never does give a boring answer.

"That's fine as far as it goes," I said. "Let me narrow this down. Would you consider yourself a Christian?"

I was curious to see what he'd say. I don't know much about how Travois was raised: he came from family in Indiana, and speaks of his mother with regard. I've learned that when he wants me to know something about the life he's had up to now, he'll tell me. And never a word more.

"Would you consider me a Christian?" he parried.

"Travois. I can't judge from out here. What do you consider yourself?"

His dark eyes crinkled; he looked like a happy bear holding a coffee cup.

"A pantheist," he said.

"A what?" I'd not hear that word.

"It's an atheist…who plays a flute. With goat legs." He laughed.

Then he explained: a pantheist (Travois says) is someone who sees God in everything in the universe; who believes that all things are a manifestation of Him.

"Even evil?" I asked. I agree with him that there are times I can feel God's presence more clearly while I'm scrubbing diapers in the creek than I do trying to keep both children quiet during a service; God does seem more present here than back home. But I didn't want to blindly accept some pagan definition at face value.

He cocked an eyebrow at me. "God didn't make everything?" He asked. "The Garden of Eden didn't happen?"

"Oh, a scripture war!" I said. "I'll win. I always do."

Travois held up his hands.

"Sedona, I would never fight you. Although depending on what kind of combat, I might relish the loss. Do you ravage your prisoners?"

Now, I don't know why I don't take a rolling pin to that man, or show him the door. When I write that down it sounds shockingly unacceptable. But Travois speaks with such good nature, it just seems a part of who he is.

That's exactly the kind of exchange one would never have in Gorin. If a man spoke to a woman like that and she put it on the Harpy Telegraph, he would be shunned. But here, people are judged more for themselves. There are too few of us to be snobbish; you need a bigger group to have room for a clique. I love that about Arizona Territory. I doubt Travois would make such a comment if Carl were sitting at the table, and that makes me feel a bit odd, but I also know I would never do wrong by Carl. Travois' conversations make me feel interesting. Carl can tell. How he can be so generous is beyond me. "See if Travois can stop by while I'm gone," he says sometimes.

I think that's a courtesy married couples can give one another. I can't be all things to him, and he recognized long before I did that he couldn't be all things to me. So he urges me to fill in those other spaces myself. He is my lover, and nothing changes that. So he is secure enough, wise enough, to give me wide pasture.

And I must do the same. I think there's indeed a shopgirl at Babbitt's that holds an allure for him; sometimes he'll mention Candy a bit fondly. At first I felt tight and nasty, hearing her name. But as Carl pointed out the time I let myself act waspish, he always comes back. If Candy gives him a few moments where he feels like the biggest rooster in the henhouse, what of it?

Travois and I talked about when we like to be out of doors. He prefers nighttime; I prefer earliest light. When I'm up around dawn, preferably alone, the day feels like a secret few people share. I love the hush, the anticipation, the peace before sunrise.

Travois got up to leave as we were talking about that.

"Well," he said, setting his cup on the sideboard, "I'm sure I'd like dawn better if I were with you."

He flashed a big white smile at me, and ducked as I threw an apple core after his head before he closed the door.

That man.

Now that I read what I just wrote again, I wonder why it's even remotely acceptable, but then I know the answer. He's as fond of Carl as he is of me—perhaps more. He respects Carl, mentions his strength, his drive, his endurance. I believe even if I went crazy and asked him to take me away, he would never really do it. He just likes the talk. His loyalty to Carl is a deep vein. There. Now it's all right.

The sun doesn't just set here; it stages a finale. I could imagine if dusk were such an event in St. Louis: carriages would halt, everyone would face west, watching together. Back there the sky pretty much just gradually darkens. Here, the whole horizon fills with colors, from vivid thistle and coral, to gradually paler shades of lemon and whisper pink. Meanwhile, below, the rocks are burnished in shades of taupe, amber, rust and ochre, gradually but inexorably, until the color fades and vanishes, leaving the observer in sepia-stained silence. There is never an encore, no curtain call. But another show always begins at sunrise.

Telegraph

Since he's now postmaster of the new Sedona, Carl wants us to also be able to send and receive telegraph messages. A man with an eye to success, he bought a Morse code manual in Flagstaff and brought it home before he asked if I would want to learn it—he knew I'd fuss at the waste of money if it didn't get used. He praised my ability at the piano, and assured me this would be very much the same thing. Since I do enjoy the way my fingers seem to remember which piano keys to touch without me having to think of them each in their turn, I let his flattery work and said I would attempt to master Morse code.

"There's no need to worry," he promised. "At first you can look up each letter if you need to, before you do any dots and dashes."

He knows me well enough to know I'm not able to do anything gradually. I studied that manual every free moment, spelling things out in my head as I said them: "Dinner!" in dots and dashes, "-.. .. -. -. . .-.;" "Pearl, pick that up," " .--. . .- .-. .-../ .--. .. -.-. -.- / - .... .- - / ..- .--." Soon it was easy.

Today Carl asked if I would stop peeling potatoes to send a telegram. One of the Armijos had news to get out. (I would never write down what anyone said in a message. One of the first tenets of being a telegraph operator is confidentiality.) Carl watched proudly while I read it over and made sure I had it in my head before tapping out the message. He relishes seeing me play a role in modern communication. I confess it is fun. Now if I can't fall asleep, I turn the children's names, or nursery rhymes, or even "rutabaga" or "umbrella" into Morse code just to make sure I don't lose it.

So we are the center for all communication with the larger world, telegraph station and post office alike. Carl still brings mail from Flagstaff. He shows me my name—Sedona, the town's name—written on envelopes with real relish. It's odd, as if I'm getting mail with somebody else. But of course there's never my last name. Just "Arizona Territory" or "A.T." I don't know if all post offices stay in business forever, or close up when a postmaster moves on. But for now, Sedona is a place name. I wonder if Carl had fallen in love with my sister Minnie, would that be its name instead?

Pauline O'Neill

March 3, 1903

While I think anything difficult for us is also good for us, and I love seeing Carl return home, when I see more than his silhouette in the wagon, I have to take a deep breath and make myself smile as I come out to greet him and a visitor.

Which is most times. It doesn't take people long once they meet Carl to discover he's never met a stranger—only friends that haven't been introduced yet. When people get off the train in Flagstaff and ask at the station how to get down to Oak Creek Canyon, they are told to walk over to the Babbitt store and enquire when Mr. Schnebly will be coming back. Then they can ride down with him (I presume if it's a matter of days, they seek lodging; sad to be propped on a chair near the hard candy, yawning in perpetuity). When Carl arrives there, he conducts his business and brings them back to Oak Creek in the wagon.... no matter what. It might be consumption that brings them west. They may be shady or surly; traits and disposition wash over him like the color of someone's hair; it simply is. He is genial and welcoming to all.

So we've hosted the proverbial beggars and kings; while those who Carl quietly assesses as being comfortable of purse pay a dollar a day, visitors just as often look like their last coin has already disappeared. With them, his vague, "Well, we'll settle up before you go," is usually the end of financial discussion. Then they are handed off to me upon arrival, and shown to one of the bedrooms. Or two, or three, depending on their number.

Now a woman who can afford the most is turning out to be my favorite, even though I tend to feel shy around gentry, and sometimes defensive about my everyday dress. I forget fashion marches onward back east, despite Lillie's descriptions of her new wardrobe every season. So when I saw Pauline O'Neill, I felt my chin duck down. Both she and the pleasant-looking boy almost grown, whom I found out was her son, were impeccably arrayed, and the satchel Carl handed down from the wagon was a fine tan hand-tooled leather. I've never seen anything like it.

But she gave me such a likable smile—with a handshake as firm as a man's—that I smiled back. And so have come to know a remarkable woman.

Pauline didn't go upstairs to wash the trip off; she followed me into the kitchen and asked to wash her hands so she could help get dinner started. Seeing her son, introduced as Maurice, lingering uncertainly in the doorway, I told him my son Tad was a good bit younger than he, but out somewhere between the house and creek, down that way. He caught his mother's eye and shot out the door, probably glad to be tearing about freely, and no longer responsible for keeping her company.

Over the next few days, I have learned more about her life, and we have much in common: we both taught school before we married, joined Women's Christian Temperance Union, and came to Arizona as adults. She was elected president of the Arizona Territorial Women's Suffrage Association. We have talked about politics and the movement with the delight of young girls finding a friend. It was several days before I guess she felt comfortable enough to tell me how she happened to be travelling with her son with no apparent purpose save her curiosity to see new places.

Pauline said she lost her husband in the Spanish American War— and then I remembered him. She was Mrs. Buckey O'Neill! Buckey O'Neill lived all around Arizona Territory and had adventures that sounded like some less-than-scrupulous newspaper man might have made him up: he'd been part of a posse in a shootout in Canyon Diablo.

He'd met Wyatt Earp, who got in the famous gunfight down over to Tombstone. Buckey also worked a mine up by Grand Canyon. He was a sheriff and a mayor in Yavapai County.

Like most of us, his strength held the seeds of his weakness, and the adventure of fighting Spaniards in Cuba beguiled him. Pauline said she wasn't sure if he really thought he was liberating innocents, or suspected it was a actually a war about sugar prices; he had to go regardless. And there with the Rough Riders, who were hoping to get Arizona enough good attention that we could become a state, he died before San Juan Hill was captured.

I told her about Billy Wallace, who was one of her husband's men. At first, she smiled like an eager young girl, and then her eyes filled with tears. She shook her head and took my hand.

"I can't tell you how this feels. Buckey's gone, but thinking of being able to meet and talk with one of his men…" Few people alive could tell her firsthand recollections about him. We had all read about the Rough Riders, and their bravery and stalwart service; while only about 100 died in the battle, one of them was the Arizona captain, Pauline's husband.

I took her down to Billy's camp the next day, after we got breakfast cleared. I came back to get things done around here, and he escorted her home just as I was setting out plates for supper. She didn't talk much about seeing him, but she looked like she'd been through something. I surmised the conversation brought up a lot of memories; while a blessing to have her husband in some ways brought alive by talking with this man who had been with him at the end, it also meant mourning him all over again. The next day, we talked more about it.

It's a puzzling thing, how a hero happens: partly brave deeds, certainly, but also a lot of story. Someone captures our imagination in a way someone else, probably equally brave or courageous, does not. Reading about the Rough Riders back in Missouri, they seemed almost the stuff of myth. But then coming here, where that Arizona unit trained and lived, it's a completely different feeling. Perhaps like actually seeing a court where King Arthur could have walked, or the Holy Land. People you only read about become real when you see where they lived.

Pauline told me that she'd not been surprised Buckey became famous. She said he'd have been famous somehow, no matter what.

"Maybe it started with his nickname," she said. "He got that by 'bucking the tiger,' betting against high odds, playing faro. 'Buckey' stuck because everything he did was against odds. Becoming a newspaper writer when he was 20, then militia captain of the Prescott Grays at 25, and after that setting up a very successful mining operation at the Grand Canyon before he was 30. You can't do all that if people don't believe in you. He made everyone a partner in the adventure that was his life as soon as he met them. Buckey had this elemental mix of authority and dash. If a group of people were sitting in a room talking about how they didn't like him, he would walk in as if to say, 'I'm going to make you glad you were born.' Then he'd do it. By the time he left, they'd forget what they'd been saying about him."

Mercy. He'd done so much in a short time, it was as if he crammed four people's lives into his one. His mines made him rich, but he still worked for the love of being involved in things, and the call to fight was too stirring to ignore. Pauline said he had hated leaving her and their son. She had told me they had adopted Maurice after their tiny son, with the given name Buckey after his father, died at two weeks. As if that wasn't enough loss, it was the next year her husband died.

Then, she'd married his brother.

"And I still don't know if that was a good idea or not," she said rather whimsically, while we were peeling apples on the porch mid-afternoon.

Fortunately for our visiting time, even though Maurice was a young man compared to Tad, boys out in the Territory welcome any company, and Maurice knew wonderful games that made Tad his adoring acolyte from breakfast to dinner. I am grateful to Maurice, who two days in a row asked for their lunch in a pail so they didn't have to come back midday.

She may have seen me start to ask where her current husband was and realize it wasn't seemly, because she smiled again.

"Brady seems to feel better when he's somewhere I'm not," she said. "Maybe I was hasty—Buckey'd left me more money than I could count, between life insurance and the mine. I certainly didn't need a husband. But Brady was so kind, and I guess we just rather...fell into it. Maybe we both missed Buckey so much we were actually each loving him with someone else who missed him, and thinking we were loving each other.

"So I travel, and get to do my work on women's rights. And he is in Phoenix, or sometimes Los Angeles, meeting important men about important things. I've wondered if being Buckey's brother would be its own particular hell no matter what; always being the one who didn't live that large, grand life. And now, to wonder if I'm comparing..."

Her voice trailed off and our eyes met. We both knew what she meant.

"Anyway, here we are," said Pauline. "And I've learned that getting older is just adding to the list of things that don't kill you. I had thought watching our baby boy leave us was the worst thing that could ever happen, 'til I got word Buckey wasn't coming home. When we lost our baby, we grieved together. But after Buckey died, I woke up alone in that bed, hearing Maurice in his crib saying over and over, "Papa? Papa? Papa?" I was heartbroken for us both, but more alone, having to be cheerful for Maurice. I'd have a hard time getting up in the morning. I'd bring Maurice in with me, and then just lie there, picturing Buckey's body under some cruel sun on a hillside. I felt empty, and so very sad. But the worst was doing my very best being two parents for Maurice, all the time just being so tired. I was dragging around like tail feathers on an old rooster. In fact, one day I decided it wasn't worth it. I decided I'd rather join Buckey. I took Maurice to our neighbor, then came back and just laid there for maybe an hour, I don't know. And then I got up and washed and got Maurice again. You can't simply decide to die and get your wish. That wish is one you'd have to work at, harder than just lying in bed, to make come true. Granting yourself that wish would involve violence and cruelty and a curse on your children and family.

"People said, 'You're a wonder; you're so strong. I don't know how you do it.' And I'd think, 'Well, it's easier to do it, than to figure out how to actually stop doing it.'"

Cook

I am getting accustomed to having a cook. When Carl returned from Flagstaff last time, he came in looking a little mischievous and also slightly nervous.

"Dona," he said, "Someone is here, and I hope you're going to let him stay. His name is Charles Rutledge, and I think he will be a wonderful cook for us. With all the guests we've been having it's too much for you. He won't live in the house," he said hastily, as I opened my mouth. "He said he'd love the old ranch house, and we can still have guests out in the tents."

Because he seemed hesitant, I said, "There's something you're not saying, isn't there?"

He nodded. Watching my face carefully, he said, "He's from China. He came here to do railroad work, but he's always loved to cook, and speaks fair English. When I went to Babbitt's store, they told me he'd asked to be recommended for any position at a restaurant, but nothing has come open, so they thought we might want a cook. He won't ask much in the way of wages, since he'll have room and board."

I thought for a minute. While sharing my kitchen wasn't appealing, sharing the workload very much was. There's always so much to do.

"Let me meet him," I said, realizing that it would be extremely difficult to deny him the position once that had happened. I wanted it to work.

Carl came in with a slightly built man who appeared extremely interested in everything. He bowed to me.

"Charles Rutledge," he said.

"Dona," I said.

We smiled at one another.

I figured everything else would work itself out.

It's been fascinating getting to know Charles Rutledge, who always refers to himself by both names, making it difficult for me to think of him as one or the other. Because his English is limited and my Chinese non-existent, we don't communicate a great deal beyond the basics. But Carl, who loves to plunge into conversation with anyone, probes a great deal more, and told me that after coming from China, perhaps in Jerome where he lived before going to Flagstaff, Charles Rutledge had met a kind man of that name, and after they parted company he adopted it as his own.

The only time I was alarmed was when Tad came in to see me, gravely concerned because Charles Rutledge had seen one of the barn cats and offered to catch it to put in the soup.

I reported that to Carl that evening, who seemed to enjoy finding out that in China meat is very scarce, so any animal is looked at as a candidate for a meal. But since game and stock are so abundant here, the cats are in no danger.

The other thing in short supply in China is wood. Charles Rutledge can't believe how much kindling I put into the stove without even being aware of it.

"In China, that wood make fire for a year," he says. I'm glad he's happy with how things are here. He won't eat with us; I'd wondered how that would work. He is delighted that he can have anything in our larder to make his own meals, and I see him walking to the old house, carrying a bowl of vegetables and meat, leaving only a pleasant aroma in the immaculate kitchen. I haven't yet asked where he learned to cook, but he keeps a spotless work area, and he seems equally at ease with baking and plain cooking.

Our seedlings are bearing so much fruit! So now besides plain cakes and cookies, we can now do pies, tarts, cobblers. All from this rich, wonderful red earth.

Carl, Sedona and Tad peeling apples outside

Rain

July 11, 1903

Yon it comes: a summer storm. Having been here this long, I recognize how heavenly they are.

I thought I'd seen big rainstorms before coming west. I was wrong. The thunderstorms that blow in on summer afternoons seize Oak Creek in a maelstrom of wind pushing anything loose in its path, then jagged spikes of lightning followed almost immediately by crashing thunder. They demand total attention. And, spellbound, we give them their due, standing on the porch unless we're driven inside by hail, or called inside by piteous cries from alarmed children.

It's sticky in the morning, like waking up in an oven where pans of hot water have been steaming. Sometimes there's a bit of a breeze upcanyon, but it doesn't last past sunup. We puff and sweat just getting dressed. I confess to wearing less than I'd have ever dreamed I would. But just a dress and drawers with a full apron are so much cooler than all the layers and accoutrements. Mutter would have a conniption...but Mutter's not here.

Around lunchtime, you can look west to see the clouds building. Huge piles of them; from brazen white on the sunny tops, to a quiet cream underneath. They billow higher and higher, and about mid-afternoon a breeze kicks up. The trees toss and rustle, and the scent, the promise of rain, comes next. It's unlike anything else—a piercing pureness, a light lemony note over damp green, with a hint of sweetness. Then, you hear the first ominous rumble of thunder, but to me it's music. Soon all the clouds are a deep grey, almost menacingly dark. Sometimes it isn't five minutes before the sky is filled with a chorus of surly booms. And because the canyon throws off so many echoes, each thunderclap generates several encores of itself. It's a celestial symphony of timpani—God's own kettledrums, rumbling and rolling, like a call and response duet. It's a German opera, sturm und drang, quite literally the "storm and stress" I remember from late 1700s opera we were taught about back in finishing school.

Sometimes lightning strikes a tree, and we get a short fire nearby before the rain quenches it. So far we've been lucky; nothing on our land has fallen or burned too close to the house. I worry just a little about that, because the rain often doesn't last long; it might not extinguish a blaze if one did start. But if it's close enough to see the lightning strike, there's also a piercing—well, not a smell. More like something astringent you can feel in your nose. It's almost too clean. Carl says that's the ozone from lightning.

For the most part, I hang on the porch railing, watching the flashes of light against the deepest charcoal-colored sky you can imagine, breathing in the heavy air, feeling the quickly cooled winds around the corners of the house. Sometimes it turns into a steady gentler rain, lasting an hour. They call that a grass rain. But often it's fierce, and subsides too soon. The drops change from hammering to falling, then lessen, as if leaving reluctantly. You start hearing the drips off the house. Birds come back out, water runs off the clay so fast that you can walk anywhere by suppertime, if you avoid the few standing puddles. The children venture from the house to beyond my sight (but within calling range), each assuring me they only stayed inside because the other one was scared. Tad, of course, said it first; Pearl was able to understand then, that is what kind and brave children would do.

Pregnancy

Respite...naptime. With two months to go before there are three of them, the hours when both children are resting are precious indeed. Tad doesn't sleep; he's allowed to do anything he wants if he's quiet on his bed. He loves the few books we have that he can read parts of, and he can look at pictures in a few more. I don't remember getting as tired when Pearl was coming. But I was living like gentry last time, in a town down the street from a store that would deliver many things that I now have to make from scratch. Kind and calm Dr. Asin was nearby, humorous and interested but never alarmed. In addition, any mother or grandmother you encountered offered advice that varied with the stage of pregnancy. Chores were mostly indoors, with much less hauling and dragging and wrestling large heavy sheets.

I feel weak and worn out, and fear if I weren't a harsh taskmistress, I would simply stop doing it all. I must keep myself in line; withhold flattery, for fear of turning uppity and lazy.

But if another woman rose at dawn, got the fire going, started the oatmeal, brought in water and washed up, cut bread for toast and turned it in time, spent a moment holding each child as he and she wandered into the kitchen, blinking and warm and sweet, opened windows, shook bedding, retrieved shoes and clothes and brushes for the day to bring downstairs, fed the dogs, dished up breakfast and measured molasses, supervised the blessing, brought Carl a hot cup, and only then sat down for a moment, I would think her day well begun.

And from there, it doesn't change: always in the service of family. Pack Carl a meal, whether he's heading out to the orchards or up the hill to Flagstaff. Pack him a bedroll (yes, he could—he's a grown man, but he doesn't...just sleeps in the same clothes and comes back extra tired from not having good blankets and it's a small service I can perform to make him feel loved at the end of a long day), help around the edges of his loading crops and baskets, hold ropes while he ties down the load, then console the children, who hold me to blame that Papa leaves. "Not because I want him to," I want to say. But instead I say softly and brightly, "I know how much you will miss him...but he always comes back, doesn't he?"

Then, the animals to feed. Chickens would take less than half the time if the children didn't either insist on helping, or just hang on the fence wire begging to be let into the yard. Bread to get started rising, laundry to bring down (even if I don't do the wash that day, it must be collected). If I heat water for washing clothes, wash the children as well. We never bathed so often back in Gorin, but we weren't running wild all day in red dirt and creek clay.

There's always clothing that needs mending, so bring that down in case there's a minute while something comes to a boil. Sweep out the kitchen, pick up the front rooms. If there are boarders, of course, we have a full breakfast and conversation time, although I can begin clearing up some of the utensils and skillets while they finish. The children want lunch when it seems like I only just put away the last plate from breakfast. Wipe the two of them off, fix them something; maybe they can eat outside on the front step and avoid yet another sweeping. This would all be so much easier if I weren't also the source of all answers for the crew. Does Carl want the trees thinned out now, or after harvest? "Didn't he tell you?" "Yes, but Hugh swears he said to wait, and I heard plain as day to do it now." The fire goes out; someday I'll learn to keep a better eye on it. A dog throws up on the porch; the children are horrified and riveted at the same time. Bring a bucket of suds, clean it off.

And on the hours go. Now the sun's overhead. We need to work in the garden a bit; weed, pinch buds. But a traveller stops; has questions, needs a drink. How far to Jerome? Does he want to go there? (What kind of question is that, anyway? Do I want you to? Yes! Right now. Get out of my squash.)

It's the total surrender of self, of will. What would I like to do? What do I want to concentrate on? It doesn't matter. It doesn't matter if I'm hungry or tired—someone else must be fed or tucked in to rest. It doesn't matter if I'm so discouraged I could weep—someone else must be soothed. It's the constant suppression of one's own desires that makes motherhood so daunting.

And I feel guilty for even writing that down: I would want no other calling in the world. I cherish these small people who I am given to help and watch; I love Carl and I am glad he gets to be out on the road; he would be diminished in his own eyes if he had to stay put. What is it in me that can't glory in being of service to these people?

Sometimes I think about being in a hotel, alone. Drawing a hot, wonderful bath, then soaking, with a book to read more than a page at a sitting. Not speaking at all. Not constantly reacting to someone else: the luxury of an independent thought. But that's not to be, for now.

Dear God, I am sorry to be so mulish about the life You've given me. I don't mean to be unappreciative. I fall into bed so tired every night, Lord, and I worry about being able to start over with a brand new baby on top of all this. Sometimes I think I'm not strong enough for this. But You understand my reluctant spirit, and you love me anyway, even as you loved David in spite of his dark thoughts and actions. Thank You for this moment of quiet. Thank you for the baby, moving more because I sat down. Help it be a good quick delivery. Oh, and Lord, please let Carl be here! I don't know what I will do if he's not.

Iron With A Dog

I just wanted to get this down before I forgot.

This afternoon Alice Johns, Bea Hazeltine and I were talking round while I snapped peas. They're both down here with their husbands, who are fighting tuberculosis by sleeping out in the tent houses. The children were off helping Carl pick peaches; by the laughter, I know less is getting done in the orchard than in the gardens of their hearts. Anyway, Alice and Bea and I have gotten to know one another a bit since they arrived last weekend, and the conversation came to husbands.

I realized it's pretty nearly the same conversation I've had with a score of different women since we've become hoteliers down here.

We talk about how the husbands don't ever ask questions as if their fate hinges on our opinions anymore. We talk about how once you've had children, sometimes men just seem like one more pair of larger needing hands. We talk about how they don't praise us for ourselves, and one gets to wondering if they love <u>this</u> woman, or just <u>a</u> woman with whom they happen to share a bedroom. And there's always this guilty, assuring paragraph of talk about how we know what fine Godly men they are, and we would never want another. Which is all true. But there's still this puzzling, this bewilderment, among women…as if each is realizing, "I married a man who seemed to love me exactly the way I yearned to be loved, and now instead, there's a man who looks and talks and smells like him, but seems to love me more in the manner of a good gun or a good horse; something that satisfies a need, so he's loyal to it."

Well, since the guests revolve through this chat, and I am the lynchpin in the middle, hearing it over and over, I think I've figured something out.

You can't iron with a dog.

You really can't.

You could heat the poor thing on the stove till it sizzles, you could hold the legs six ways to Sunday, you could push down till you sweat, but that poor creature is never going to get out as much as a single wrinkle. Not an inch of ironing could get done.

So we are with men. We continue to wish, dream, believe they will retransform into the creatures we perceived them to be when they courted us.

I watch, I listen and I know. These conversations on the porch are the same over and over; only the names change. That courting element is something that God must have put in men so they could marry and procreate. It's like a fuse in them that's ignited by a likely woman—a prospective bearer, a vessel for seed. The fuse burns strong, bringing from a man's lips words like, "How did you get here, Angel? Did you come from Heaven to save me?" and "What do you think about when you write?"

Entranced, we women think we've finally found the man who wants to know not just what's under our dress, but inside our soul. And then, poof! Sometime after the banns are read, and the rice is thrown, this fuse that was needed to set off the rocket has done its job, the firework explodes, and it's gone. It can't be relit any more than a bottle rocket on the Fourth of July can be gathered up as sparks and stuffed back into the paper wrapping.

In fairness, I'm sure that—should they spend time thinking like this, but I don't believe they ever will—men would discover they have a similar set of lonely surprises after they marry.

How willingly at first she melted in his arms every time he turned to her; how tenderly she stroked his hair whenever he was in arm's reach. How she labored over his favorite pie. Then, later, once the shaving brush and hairbrush have shared space for a while, her questions changed from "What can I do to make you happy?" to "What border would look best on the tea towels?"

We all do it, I guess—can't seem to help ourselves. We change, or life changes us. And sometimes, for moments, when children and meals dissolve into the background, we see flashes of those people again. Often, Carl has a little lightness, a teasing, a twist in his voice which recalls the suitor, that I can sometimes for a moment respond to. I remember how proud I was he loved me. I still treasure him, but I confess sadly that I don't celebrate him the way I did. I still bring him his breakfast, and the best moment of the day is when he comes home and puts his arms about me, and while I am resting my head on his shoulder sometimes I'm so overwhelmed by the power and safety of his love my eyes fill with grateful tears. But I'm weary, and there are children and boarders and duties requiring my presence.

I hope I am able to treat him as a king in his castle again—when the harvest is in, when the children are grown...sometime.

In the meantime, I sometimes suggest to women on the porch, oh, so mildly, that you can't iron with a dog. We'd be better served to just save them a good bone, and urge them to be next to us, and talk to other women about those topics deep in our hearts.

But I don't think Alice and Bea would have wanted to hear that today. I think they feel if we talk about it, long for it, resent it enough, some alchemy will occur. And, I think that will happen when the shower of shiny colors in the sky can be sucked back into the bottle rocket.

Goldie Genevieve

W e have another girl.

The labor wasn't long, and Carl brought Grandma Dumas, who promptly rattled off a list of things she needed him to do and sent him away. In a mercifully short time, during which I was mostly trying to be quiet so I didn't frighten Tad and Pearl downstairs, we got our new daughter to come meet us.

Carl edged in then, and his hands looked quite large holding her. His smile was so tender, and then turned to me with a deep gratitude in his eyes. I think they might have been a little damp. (It's already a bit blurry to remember; why does that happen?) We'd talked about names, so we didn't have to puzzle that out. She is Goldie Genevieve after my sister Goldie, so she will be called by her own new name, Genevieve. She's still a bit small in her skin, but that will pass quickly. I need to rest a bit before I brush my hair and see the older children. Odd to think Pearl is older than someone. She's been our baby for so long this may prove difficult for her. On the other hand, she's now got someone to talk to in the superior tone Tad sometimes takes with her. I hope she enjoys being a big sister more than she misses being the only girl.

And now Carl has brought them both in, peeking out from behind him as if maybe I would be very changed from having a baby. They seemed relieved to see me, and I loved gathering them close, telling them that every time a mother has another child, her heart grows bigger, so I love each of them more rather than less. They are back downstairs, laughing while Carl chases them. I don't care when they go to bed tonight. They should remember their sister's birth as a special thing, a good thing.

Charles Rutledge, since I've taught him to make noodles, delights in adding noodles to our meals. Just now Carl brought up a tray with chicken noodle soup, which is delicious, warm and nourishing. I think I will even ask for a second bowl. Lying in this bed, I imagine I know how it would feel to survive a shipwreck: things were terrible, and now they are good. My body will probably hurt more tomorrow, when the gauzy edges around my awareness have receded. But for now, all that matters is that we have another healthy daughter, I am in a clean nightgown on clean sheets, and I can put behind me the chaos I've come through. Tomorrow I will go downstairs again.

Having three children takes some getting used to. I always had enough of a lap for both children, but now if I'm holding Genevieve the others are circling me like cats to get space. Pearl has somehow transformed from looking like a baby to looking like a great big girl to, compared to this very tiny fragile sister who mostly either eats or sleeps.

Until now, Tad rode his pony and I held Pearl on the saddle in front of me when we went to round up the cows; not every day, but if Carl was travelling or involved in a project. It's not hard; the horses keep them in a fairly orderly group coming home. But when we are ready to get back to rounding up, Pearl will be promoted to getting to ride her own pony, Pet, instead of just bringing him carrots and riding slowly while Carl walks next to her. She's a true western girl.

Pearl with Pet

This has her incandescent with joy. Tad's always been on Racer, but she's had to ride with Mama. We let her start on Pet a few weeks ago so she wouldn't feel pushed aside. She doesn't. She seems to like being a big sister.

And both children are the most wondrous creatures in Genevieve's world. She watches her big brother and sister with rapt fascination, and a wide smile comes across her face whenever they appear. They perform for those smiles and are always rewarded, whether they make a face, turn in a circle, clap or talk to her. She's very calm, not at all colicky. I think God knows what we can handle. If she were like Pearl, who was constantly twisting and struggling to get down whenever I held her, I don't know what I would do.

Genevieve. I have wondered what her personality will be. If you can tell at this early age, she will be quiet and easy-going. Or maybe she's still getting her bearings in the world, and will become a formidable force. Right now, she just needs to be fed.

Thanksgiving

Thanksgiving was typical in many ways: the amount of planning and preparing far outweighed the day itself. I still don't have as many good serving dishes as I'd been accustomed to, and had to improvise. Therefore one of the sweetest moments of the meal came when Dr. Ralph Palmer, one of our guests, praised the elegant simplicity of a huge squash I had hollowed out and baked filled with seasoned cabbage (he of course having no idea that desperate times call for creative measures—there wasn't a pot in the kitchen big enough). After the mysterious rediscovery of the disappeared gravy boat (which probably involved 'chocolate' for the children's mud pies, so I scrubbed it thoroughly), everything ended up cooked, served and best of all, enjoyed.

Certainly bounty was ours. Since there were 20 of us, and I had no idea what everyone's preferences would be, we covered the gamut of meats. We were able to serve both turkey and goose, each plump and stuffed; a haunch of venison, and a whole roasted pig (although the apple in its mouth and one of its legs turning on the spit had convinced Pearl it had stolen the apple and was trying to get away, which made for several tearful interludes when she remembered it). Add the side dishes: potatoes both scalloped and mashed, dark and light rolls, green beans and okra, cheese sauce and white sauce, and you understand why the kitchen had only two unused spoons by the time everyone sat down. There was a hail of protests when I began clearing to make room for dessert: blueberry buckle and apple cobbler plus pecan and mincemeat pies, along with nut and candy dishes, coffee, tea, and more milk for all the children.

It really was splendid. Any woman who could figure out how to spare the hostess the backache that results from such a day could surely buy a castle and live by the sea. Carl had provided the deer and hog, dressed the fowl, and was as always a genial and inclusive host. But only a woman notices the child wiping his nose on his sleeve who needs a discreet handkerchief, the one thirsty guest who keeps draining his water goblet and looking expectant, the rapid eater tapping a foot with impatient longing for a sweet while the talker down the table picks at desultory bites of the main course. While it was a slightly damp day, the wet leaves provided a plump decaying carpet of sweet scent all around as people came in, and no one seemed eager to leave. Carl thoughtfully suggested everyone move to a circle of chairs by the fireplace so I could commence to clear. As always, women began helping, for which I was grateful. But the hostess then scrambles to answer questions: Where does this go? Do you save this much? Want me to pack this up? (I haven't figured that out yet; I haven't decided; yes, but now you'll want to know in what it should be packed, and I haven't the faintest idea.)

I could hear Carl happily entertaining the visitors with stories of how Wilson Mountain got its name, and Bear Howard's escapades. Bill Lane, who had closed his saloon in Camp Verde and ridden over for the day, told of not shooting a bear near Stoneman Lake...which doesn't sound like much, but in his dry style, it was quite amusing.

Most of all, the blessings of our own table, our own home; after being tossed on the storms of disapproval in Gorin, we had come west and made our family blossom like the rose. The large warm room and gratefully gathered groceries we shared; we did this. With God's help.

Half the guests remained for a pick-up supper and stayed the night because Carl figured if a little holiday was good, more was better. The men rose early to hunt deer, while the women and children remained with me.

Seeing others' offspring always makes me so quietly proud of my own. Tad, as the oldest of the group of children, shepherded the younger ones all day, devising entertainments that make sense only to the small. Pearl at five has started to slender out, losing that precious baby roundness, but Genevieve is still the size that makes everyone wanted a turn with her on their laps. She eventually drops off when she's being held, and people can stare at a sleeping baby the way we can the flames in the fireplace, or falling snow. I loved knowing she was cosseted while I worked. I feel so very blessed.

Every holiday has made me miss Gorin…in some ways. I never actually want to be back there, feeling trapped in the stuffy parlor after the meal, while most of us tried not to nod off over board games. I wouldn't have wanted to be raising our family there, performing someone else's rituals and traditions instead of being out here creating our own. But I certainly thought of Lillie, and how we'd hilariously skewer poorly-thought-out comments and hairstyles after everyone left. I guess what I miss is that: a sister. Here there isn't even a close women friend; just lots of wonderful women I meet, and some I grow to care for before they depart, becoming correspondents. But that's not the same.

Dogs & Elections

Dec. 17, 1904

We've always had dogs—so many over the years, and like people, each one is different. Sterling had a dignity; he would let you love him and you could tell he was glad enough to be with us, but he also always held himself a bit in check—there was a reserve, almost like a visiting clergyman. April was our most tender-hearted dog, the one who would sit with you when you cried; when we walked in she would search our faces to see if we needed anything from her. It was like she thought we were all her babies, needing her protection. To know any dog is to know love.

But I believe Daisy is the dog of my heart, and after her I don't expect to get close to another one in the same way. She isn't the prettiest, or the smartest, or the most anything except the most mine. She is...vigorous. Intent. Whatever she does, she does with her whole body. I am always entertained by how she sprawls with her awkward legs out behind her, chewing so industriously on something.

She is almost crazed with joy when we return from being away, even it was just to the creek with a pail. And if she actually gets invited to go, when we come back to the house she bounds across the threshold and skids theatrically to a stop, as if concluding a grand adventure. She also sighs so contentedly once the door closes on all of us inside, it makes me smile. But she never bows down; if she wants to do something, she does it, and never seems to feel sorry except for the getting caught. None of that makes her less beloved by me.

She's always alert when I walk in—possibly wondering if I had access to food (although she also eats cloth, rocks and bits from origins unknown). She is the one who has somehow crawled deepest into my heart. When it's my time to go, Daisy will be the first one I see, running out to lead me Home.

It was sheer accident that Daisy came to us. It was the last election, and Carl is, along with so much else that takes place, in charge of voting for Oak Creek.

Smart people figure out Carl never says no, so if anyone wants something done but doesn't want to do it, asking Carl is the solution. And being Carl, he doesn't just do it—he does it better than anyone else would have even thought of doing it. Ever clever, Carl broke regular pencils in two and sharpened both halves so more people can use them at once, before he bundles them up to save for the next election day.

When Voting Day arrives, Carl is ready with the ballots and pencils. Then, when someone comes by the house to vote, he's on the porch before they dismount, offering the ballot and ready to check the name off his master list.

Now, this was funny to me. Men seem to love voting on horseback. It would be simpler just to get down, use the porch rail to support the ballot and mark it. But because Carl is fast, a few were still mounted...and by the next election word must have gotten around, because this time a great many of them rode up, marked their ballots, and rode off again. I've thought men like to feel like heroes, ready for action, maybe as if their lives are more urgent or important than they actually are. And some who come from the east yearn to be western men in a way that those from the Territory take for granted. Any Armijo is off his horse in a heartbeat, and comes into the kitchen for a bite. You don't get more western than an Armijo, since their family was here before this was even part of the United States. But the eastern men sometimes settle their dusters a little self-consciously once they mount; while they are talking they might be taking their hats off and looking at them, putting them back on, as if they are playing a role in a school presentation and like way the costume makes them feel.

Mercy, I digress. In any case, Daisy came trotting up behind a couple of men this past Election Day, and I assumed she belonged to them. But then one of them kept shooing her off, and I heard Carl ask, "That dog giving you trouble?"

"Nothing wrong with her except we're going hunting," the shooing one said. "We don't need the extra noise and bother."

I went out on the porch.

"Want me to see if she'd rather eat some gravy than follow you?" I asked. He bowed from the waist, there on his horse.

"You'll be a daisy if you do."

So she is Daisy.

Carl holding Genevieve, Pearl, Tad, Sedona & Daisy next to Oak Creek house

Worry

Travois came through yesterday. He knows when Carl will be gone, and while he always says a lonely man misses the sweet sound of a woman's voice, I think he comes to keep an eye on us. I always invite him to take supper, because Carl's pleased to find out he's been here. Travois does make me laugh. His stories may well sometimes be exaggerated, like when he was being chased by a bear and fell off the Mogollon Rim, but he also says things that stay with me, as if they're carved like a quotation on a marble tablet, in pretty script.

He's surprisingly comfortable holding Genevieve while I work; I am powerfully curious what babies he's been around, but when I asked he made a joke and clearly does not intend to say more. He sang to her, a little wandering tune with what sounds like some Indian tongue. I certainly wonder if there's a woman somewhere who sang that song to a child of his.

I made baking powder dumplings to go with the venison, in stock I brought to a boil with the lid on tight long enough to cook them all the way through. We all ate a good deal, and there was a dried-peach cobbler with strudel topping for dessert. Any breadcrumbs will do, but sourdough are the best to mix with butter and brown sugar. Travois always has a new riddle for Tad, who loves trying to figure it out. When he can't quite grasp it, Travois will slip a hint into something he says, so Tad gets to solve the riddle after all, feeling proud instead of frustrated.

For a man with no children, Travois has earned Tad's admiration. I think his man-sized respect for a boy-sized person is an admirable trait.

After the dishes were done, Genevieve was drowsing in my lap while Tad and Pearl played shadows in the tent house. Through the window, I could see their silhouettes created by the lantern I'd hung up high on the backside hook out of reach. Travois spoke about a women he had loved and lost. He'd never spoken of a particular one before, and he was cryptic now. Travois may know, with the instincts of a good teller of tales, that when you don't say everything, a mist of mystery drifts around the edges.

Laura was a well-bred eastern girl he loved when he was too young to do so properly, he said. It ended sadly, and I didn't press, but it's quite possible he was the one to end it. I suspect he goes to see her from time to time, even if she isn't aware of it. He may simply observe and fade into the shadows again. But there was something possessive in his voice when he spoke. I'm sure in his mind, part of her is still his.

He said the world is safer when he doesn't fall in love, because he brings pain wherever he walks. I think he's possibly half right on that score, but not because he was born flawed; he just doesn't want to be responsible and put in the time. He's better moving in and out of others' lives. This way many people spread over a great distance can savor his company and remember his stories.

I suppose it's like the land: knowing what should be built where. You wouldn't put your crops on the edge of the creek, because flooding would wash them away. You wouldn't build a dock on a mountain, but put it by water. Travois is best as a sometimes friend, not one who is tethered to one spot and has to walk the same ground every day.

When I mentioned I was worried about Carl, so often alone on the road where he could be hurt, robbed, left for dead, Travois said it reminded him of once when he was travelling with a Navajo man he knew; he called him an elder. Travois was worried about something, and they rode their horses side by side for some time. Finally the elder said, "I know what you are doing."

"So do I, Grandfather," Travois said, explaining to me that was how to address a respected older adult, having nothing to do with blood relation. "I'm riding along here next to you."

The old man ignored that, and went on as if Travois hadn't spoken. "You're praying to the devil."

Despite his slightly unorthodox lifestyle, Travois has a Christian foundation of knowledge, so he took umbrage at that and denied it.

Unperturbed, the elder reiterated that Travois was praying to the devil, and then a third time, said it again. Travois sat in the saddle, angry and confused. So the Hosteen explained.

"You are quiet, and you are sighing. You might call it by another name. You might say you are worrying. But it is praying to the devil. God is now. God is here. When you go places that are not here, and not now, you are asking the devil to come and ride with you. That's praying to the devil. You are not appreciating the gifts God is spreading out in every direction for you in this time."

Travois also said once that men see everything as a win or a loss; every conversation they have, every encounter with a stranger, leaves them with a mental tally of victories and defeats. If they lose too many in a row, he said, they will abandon all good sense and become reckless in their pursuit to win a round. He told me that this had come from another man who lived on an island in the Great North, and had been through a great deal of loss in his life, which made him wise. So if in the company of a man who is becoming reckless out of a desire to win, Travois said, find a way for him to win. Set up a conversation where he can have the last word, or state a mistaken fact he can correct. He said it brings things back to a safer level. And he added, with those deep brown Travois eyes locked on mine, that no one is better at making a man feel like a winner than a woman.

He doesn't flirt...I don't think. He is simply given to want to idolize women. I told him I think he appreciates women the way some people do water; they always want to live in sight of the sea. "Or a lake, or a stream," he said. "A puddle will do. But the best, you know...is a creek." And his deep look again. Which made me smile and swat a hand at him.

I don't believe he means any disrespect. It's like some dogs have to chew, and others to chase. Even if they're chasing their own tail, it makes them feel alive. I'm thinking Travois has to be constantly getting a reaction from someone, in order not to feel alone.

❦

He always beds down out front in the dark; I think to keep a silent watch. We've never had trouble here, but Travois lives on the edge of the civilized world, and has probably witnessed a lot of things people weren't expecting. It makes him more watchful than most, and we're both grateful, Carl and I.

This morning, I rose early, got the fire going and made coffee. Travois was on the porch breathing in deeply and hopefully when I opened the door to bring him a cup, which made me laugh.

Feb. 18, 1905

Tommy Armijo just left after spending the afternoon playing with Tad. I tried to keep Pearl with me, because Tad had asked if just the boys might walk over to Bear Wallow, and I said they could. He is so good to his sister, and I want him not to feel resentful, as he might if he is forced to let her follow him everywhere. I brought out a sheet of paper dolls Carl had brought down from Flagstaff a while back. She intently cut out all their gowns, and since then, they have been changing their clothes for purposes other than those intended by their designer: they put on ball gowns to go to the Verde Valley, then were changed into tea gowns to pick vegetables. Now they are wearing furs and long coats to go fishing.

Tommy sees much better than Tad; I heard Tad asking, "How can you make that out so far away?" about something. We need to get his eyes checked, although where we would get him glasses I hardly know.

Tad is a great reader already, picking out words in the Bible as I have taught him to do. He's eager to learn. I worry about his schoolling: he couldn't walk to Uncle Ellsworth's school with his long-striding, tireless teacher. But I won't be able to give him a complete education beyond the basics. I need to talk to Carl about this.

In the meantime, it's fun to see him run off with his friend. Tommy is dark and Tad is fair, but in their straw hats and overalls you can barely tell them apart. I'm glad he goes to Tommy's house, and comes back asking why we don't have tortillas and beans for lunch. All my friends growing up were of similar heritage and circumstance. Certainly none of their grandmas could have taught me that "thank you" in Spanish is "gracias," and how to sing a Spanish little song about a rooster.

Tommy has joined Tad and Pearl making mud pies a few times. He's always nice to Pearl, having sisters of his own. Today the boys get their own adventure.

Alone

March 11, 1905

Carl is away tonight. I always feel very alert when he's gone. You'd think I'd become accustomed, but I never seem to. However, he had a wonderful load in the wagon, and says he thinks that for the first time he might make $75 from all the sales.

People in Gorin would be appalled at how much folks will pay for fresh produce in Flagstaff. Sweet corn brings 35 cents for a dozen ears, a very small box of berries is 20 cents. Tomatoes, strawberries, peaches, apricots all sell at high prices. (Once he got a dollar for each large sweet apple, which made him feel bad, and he said he wouldn't do that again even if begged to.)

Daisy's restless as well, looking for Carl. She lies near the door and gives me this baleful eye, asking, "Am I the only one who has noticed someone isn't home yet?" I tell her I miss him as well, and we will see him day after tomorrow. He likes her being with the children and myself. She's so smart she could probably even go get help if she had to (I hope not to test that theory).

When Carl's on his way home, he builds a campfire on the road, hoping I can see it from the house. I can't. I want to be able to, and he looked so hopeful telling me he thought I could, that I was temped to lie and assure him it's a wonderful sight. But I can't do that. I think of all the women during the War Between the States who went years without getting letters from their husbands who were off fighting, and then I feel like a pretty dismal piece of person having a hard time when it's only two or three days. But things are just better with him here. And him being gone reminds me of the myriad ways our lives could suddenly be forever changed.

Lawless men could follow him out of Flagstaff and set upon him once he's alone, slashing his throat and taking the money.

Lightning could strike a tree above him on the road and make it fall, crashing across the wagon and pinning him, helpless and thinking of us.

A horse could fall and pull the wagon off the edge of the road at a sheer cliff, hurling produce—and Carl—across the canyon.

Why am I doing this? Not on purpose…it's not as though I have to look for those horrid ideas. They unspool in my mind as if I'm just watching them.

Enough.

I will have a bite of the sourdough loaf with the new butter, say my prayers over again as a penalty for this lack of trust in God, and let Daisy lie on the foot on the bed.

Think about something cheerful first.

Last time Carl came home he had a big book of wallpaper samples the Babbitt store didn't need; I guess a newer one came. I'm going to save it and let the children make valentines, and maybe we'll do some paper dolls with fancy clothes. It's a good feeling, knowing it's here for the next stormy day when they can't play outside.

Shoreline

We've had a group of guests come from back east this week: two men and their wives.

Monty and James talk of nothing but hunting: when might Carl act as their guide to go hunting, what did they hope to shoot while hunting, and with what weapon would they shoot it? They were as enthusiastic as boys with new Christmas slingshots. Generally most of the carpetbags, valises, what-have-you, that Carl unloads from the wagon (always before he unloads our supplies) are met with female cries of, "Oh, that's mine!" But this time even more of it elicited a male "there's the rifle case!" and "oh, good, the hunting gear!" as it was brought forth. Monty and James have rather appropriated the east side of the porch to sort, inspect, try out and exclaim over special sights, fishing gear, hunting knives, various whistles and pipes to lure animals; occasionally a bleat or throaty roar will waft over, followed by laughter or reverent silence.

The wives (Kitty to Monty and Violet to James) are tolerant, while amused. Tomorrow Carl will "guide" them on a hunting expedition. He's so considerate of people's feelings that I'm waiting to see if he will come out in his worn work clothes, pick up his gun, and be ready to go, or if, knowing that they might feel foolish seeing how "real" hunters prepare and equip themselves, he will dredge up some obscure piece of farm equipment or broken harness and tell them he will use it to beat the bushes for ducks, or approximate the swish of a deer's tail. Or any other yarn he comes up with.

While I love few things more than the late-afternoon respite from chores that involve a great deal of moving about, and can sit peacefully to stone cherries or string beans or mend in the hour before dinner preparations are in full swing, sometimes it turns into a bit of heavy lifting of its own: wives can be bored and want to be entertained.

They ask anything from if I've ever met an Indian (I have) to whether I've ever been attacked by one (I have not). If their poor eastern faces then go a bit crestfallen, I cheer them up by telling them about killing rattlesnakes with a rake. That never loses its savor: the women perk up and chatter like magpies, wanting to know if it's hard (not terribly), how long the snake continues to move (depends), and if I'm scared (always).

But Kitty and Violet are lower of voice and calmer of temperament than many, and I sincerely enjoy our conversation during the quiet turning time of the day, when we move from still heat to the first soft stirring of the downcanyon breeze, bringing the buzz of cicadas to a higher level, and giving the children a second or third or fourth wind, sending them out for a last adventure before dinner.

Today, Kitty talked about her recent time in London, and her fascination with the Romantic era of literature. She rhapsodized about Samuel Taylor Coleridge, and I then recalled reading *Rime of the Ancient Mariner* in school, mostly for "water, water everywhere, but nary a drop to drink," and for a line I personally preferred, "He prayeth best who loveth best," because I think to love brings a longing to pray for those loved.

Violet was unfamiliar with that but had read *Kubla Khan*, which I don't recall. Kitty was most enthralled with Coleridge's idea that to be happy, one must have a soul mate, which she defined as the person who completes you, provides the missing half of yourself. Her eyes fairly glowed when she wondered out loud how she could have stumbled across her true soul mate in Monty, when the world is so large and full of people.

When asked, I said mildly that her guess was as good as mine—a line I've heard Travois use to good effect to avoid disagreeing with someone. But she and Violet both pressed eagerly to hear my views. I think they see me as very different from most women, as if by living in the "wild" I must also be less restricted, perhaps more primal, than they. Never mind that my upbringing included gas lamps and elocution lessons.

Anyway, it gave me pause, and I figured out that I actually do have a belief about love: it's not that there's not one soul mate, exactly. Maybe more like a larger number of partial soul mates.

The world is vast, and even in our small section of it we've met many people. But I imagine the odds of meeting the only single solitary person who is your soul mate, among the millions in the world, are slim. I posited that perhaps each of us is, in an unseeable way, like an island. And our shoreline can be as varied as every other aspect of us. So, for instance, the Island of Sedona may have one long curving shore, and then a sudden jutting-out section, and three horseshoe sections after that—it could be anything. And everyone else is an island of a different distinctive shape.

Suppose, then, that for the section where I have three sharp-curved sections extending out, Carl has a stretch of shoreline with three sharp-curved sections extending in. Were the two islands somehow able to be towed to sit side by side, those stretches would mesh perfectly. It feels like we do have that, on an invisible, unknowable level. He matches me so seamlessly and well and I feel so deeply loved.

But "soul mate" to me implies perfect accord; some mystical connection that's the stuff of legend. I've never understood Carl's habit of getting the last miniscule crumb off his plate, as if it's going to be judged to get him into Heaven. If I'd designed him to be perfect, he wouldn't ever snore. His ability to get lost in paperwork at his desk and emerge from it hours later can slightly annoy me.

So in my idea of shoreline, while that part of Carl and I match exactly, there would be other sections that don't fit together. Maybe some shorter lengths would align with someone I'll never meet. I guess as long as the person you marry matches the greatest length of the Island of You, everything works.

Further, if you are a very simple person, maybe your island has four straight sides. Which would mean all you need to be content and co-exist peaceably would be another person with a straight side. Conversely, if you are incredibly complicated, like a poet or an artist, you may have such wiggles and peninsulas that you could despair of ever meeting anyone that has corresponding configurations.

Kitty and Violet mulled this over with me, and all of us agreed it's impossible to know with certainty how much shoreline any two people share. But I've continued to contemplate it.

This evening I got ready for bed, and instead of writing downstairs in my chair, I've been writing this against my pillows.

Just now, Carl said he was going to go back downstairs and make one last check of things. I watched him leave our room and got an image of the two landmasses sliding gently, slowly together, and fitting so perfectly no water remained between them. I'm grateful.

Pearl

Pearl. Baby, darling girl, my Pearl, how can you be gone?
The only thing worse than thinking about you, my sweetheart,
is forgetting you—in a moment of putting out a grease fire or untangling yarn, I can be without thought about you. And the problem is that
then when I realize you aren't here, it's as horrible as if I am just learning it for the first time.

Your brother and sister are so sad. They see me cry, though I try to be
cheerful. They miss you too. Tad doesn't seem to want to do anything,
and I can't help him—one drowning man throwing another a rope just
makes them sink together. Genevieve doesn't seem as bothered, except
she cries out at night, and I end up holding her, crying into her hair
and watching over and over again in the darkness above her head as Pet,
that infernal beast, bolts. Carl shot her. I am glad. I know you loved her,
Pearl-girl, but she didn't deserve to live. She took you away. Then I feel
sorry—she was just doing her job, going after a cow, and I feel guilty we
ended her life. Then I envy her because she doesn't have to look for you,
and miss you.

You are not here; I cannot find you. Every time I'm in the kitchen,
I see that hated grave, the earth piled back over your little once-self. I
remember how you looked in the sweet white dress; tiny—the bruises
and broken places that made you not yourself, hidden. I know you
aren't in that grave. If I didn't know that, I'd be scratching at the
clay right now, to feel your little arms around my neck. But that is

not you. That is a shell; like the placenta that nourished you in my womb was no longer important once you were born. The body that carried you until you left is just casing that no longer holds you. So I know where you are not. But where are you, where are you? I walk, evenings, thinking I might hear your laugh on the breeze that comes downcanyon, that you liked to lift your arms and dance in. You aren't there.

You are an angel, I tell Tad and Genevieve. But what do I know? My girl isn't some classical creature with gilt wings and a beatific expression. You weren't big enough to get one arm around a harp. I say to them that God wanted you with Him.

But so do I!

And I can't have that, ever again, until I die. And that cannot happen soon enough. Don't tell anyone, sweet girl, but if it weren't for your father and your brother and sister I would walk out into the creek and lie down and drift till I got so tired I would slip under the water. As tired as I am now, it wouldn't be very far. I just want to find you, but I know if I did take my own life, you'd be denied me for eternity. Instead, it only feels like eternity.

Oh Pearl, how I wish it had been me instead. Or at least me with you. Are you frightened? No, I know you aren't. I know you are fine, held by God. I'm the one who isn't fine. I don't want His will to be done. I am so angry, and so afraid I can never feel anything but this raw, draining grief.

I just want for one minute to hold you on my lap, to see your bright eyes smiling at me. I want to answer one of your so-serious questions. I want to button your dress and kiss the top of your head. I want anything, anything but this huge dark place I live now. I want to forget. I want to remember. I want it all to go away.

Pearl. My baby. My girl. Find me. I need you, Pearl. Mama needs you so much.

1950

For years, starting in May when the days began to get longer, I would tighten up inside, as if my soul lived in my stomach and was trying to curl into a tight little ball. Because June, June 5, 1905 was when… it's still hard to look at closely. June 5 was when Pearl left us. Left me. Went on without her Mama. Left me here, to continue to breathe in a world without her in it. My little laughing reckless girl, my small girl, my first girl.

And the only reason I write it now is I think there's a confession that needs to be made, and maybe some understanding that needs to be given. To Tad.

How can the worst day of your life start so normally? There should be guns rumbling in the distance, birds flying backwards, something to warn you, to ready you. But there was nothing except flapjacks for breakfast and a double-yolk egg, which some say is good luck. We all went through the summer morning in ways I hardly remember. I haven't pushed at that too much. What difference does it make? Why would the color of the flowers she brought me matter? And that she wore her blue dress with the smocking on the yoke? (Genevieve's was like it, but yellow. Although not yet two, she would point at the smocking on both and say, "Same me her!" with such pleasure.)

I'd started the corn bread in a barely warm oven before we went to get the cattle. Carl was due home but I didn't know what time, and it usually wasn't until late afternoon. He probably hadn't left Flagstaff until late morning. So we set off to bring the cattle home, which I did when I was pretty sure it woule be dark before he got home. That meant Genevieve had to ride with us; that was usual when there was no kind guest to watch her, even though it always made me a little nervous. We didn't have a bull, or maverick stock, but any cow can get lively if the wrong thing happens—a rattlesnake, or a rider passing too close.

I had Genevieve sitting between me and the saddle horn; Tad would hand her up to me before he got on Racer. I held tight and kept an extra sharp eye for surprises, or thought I did. We were coming back from just up the creek a ways, where the herd often went. Tad was in front on the left, and Pearl in front on the right. I stayed at the back, and everything looked fine. Until Pearl saw something that we're sure was an arrowhead—she and Tad had such a collection. Tad thinks it was a crystal white…he thinks he recollects a glimpse of it before she bent down from the saddle to pick it up. But my good girl, my mostly good girl, did what I'd told her too many times (but not enough) never to do: she looped the reins around her neck. And that old red cow broke off for no reason I could see, and Pearl's pony, Pet, jumped after it. And Pearl fell. And the reins tightened. And then everything happened very, very slowly. I saw Pearl bounce, actually bounce, and tumble, on the ground as that pony ran, probably frightened by the sudden weight and drag. I remember Tad's shrieks. I remember Genevieve crying as I probably clutched her far too hard and started after that pony. I remember dust, and an unreal feeling, like a bad dream.

And I remember stopping at home, seeing Pet standing so still, sides heaving, head down. And Pearl, what was left of Pearl, there in the dirt, so still, so tangled, torn and broken like nothing's ever been broken before. Tad picked up her shoe a few yards away, and these low sobbing moans came out of him.

Maybe out of me too. How I got down and set Genevieve safe I have no idea. Maybe I was keening. Maybe I was calm. All I remember so well that I can almost still feel her, is gathering her into my arms—but not doing it right, it was as if she wouldn't come in any order, and talking to her. Telling her Mama's here, baby girl, everything's all right. When of course nothing was all right, nothing could ever be all right. Then Carl was there. Thank God. But Carl as I've never seen him: a strange, still Carl, saying, "Is it?" and "is she?" and I just looked at his face and saw the whole world go dark.

Somehow we got through it. I never saw Pet again. I know we buried Pearl in the prettiest little dress made from my wedding dress, and no one else in the house sewed, so I figure I made that. But I would never make her a wedding dress of her own. Or a dancing dress. Or a long dress. Any dress. There was a service, and soft voices and soft hands leading me to bed during the time folks came back to the house. And then black again.

I didn't get up. I didn't eat. I drank when Carl held the cup to my lips. But mostly I tried to…to just not be. I knew it would be a sin to die. People needed me. But living seemed out of the question. There was mostly pain and some external roaring, trying not to see her, and also trying to see her; trying not to think of her, and also calling her name. Everything and nothing. I know it was days, because when I finally got up I couldn't get a comb through my hair without a lot of work; I finally cut the bottom section off, maybe partly a Biblical mourning ritual. I felt like a ghost haunting my own life, seeing and even touching but not able to connect to anything.

Part of me wanted to run away. To be somewhere I didn't see Pearl, or the absence of Pearl: Pearl laughing, reaching under the front step where the kittens hid; Pearl on her knees, brushing crumbs into the dustpan; Pearl, rosy from her bath on the kitchen rug; Pearl asleep in her trundle. And especially Pearl in the raw red ground, just down from the house, where every time I looked out the kitchen window I saw that too-tiny grave and pictured my baby under the clay. Especially that.

Only finally when I'd been yanked out of my stupor, realizing how much I affected the children, did I see things again. The kitchen looked like someplace I used to know, when I walked back into it. I made myself use the pump Pearl loved to use to bring water down. The plates and cups looked forlorn, as if they knew Pearl would never carry them, so carefully, again; the spoons sad she'd never put them in her mouth. I couldn't look at her bed, and at some point, Carl must have washed her clothes and put them in the drawer (a faint part of me smiled to think of him washing; I couldn't picture it),

It took me longer to realize the change in Tad. My bright boy wasn't bright. Something had gone out. He didn't look up. He didn't run. He mostly sat, shoulders hunched, on the porch. If I spoke to him while we ate, he wouldn't meet my eyes. And I barely noticed at first. It cost so much even just to smile at Genevieve while I cared for her that I only just registered that Tad existed, on the periphery of what had to be done. We were still being fed off gifts, covered dishes left on the porch, brought in by Carl, stored in the kitchen.

But then once in the afternoon, I was going through Carl's shirts to see what needed attention and I heard some sort of pounding. I looked out, trying not to see Pearl's grave, and saw nothing but yard. And when I didn't see Tad, I went out and around the corner. He was kicking the house, over and over. Then he started talking with each kick.

"Take care of your sister. Take care of your sister. Take care of your sister!" He said it louder and louder, kicking harder and harder. "Take care of your sister, you bad big brother. You didn't! You didn't take care of your sister!" Then he started shouting, and stopped kicking and hit the house with both fists. "You didn't! You're bad! Bad! Bad! Bad big brother! You didn't take care of your sister!"

Then I got to him, and I pulled him into my arms, sitting down in the dirt and holding him, rocking him, even though he would never let me do that normally. But this wasn't normal. This was my curious happy boy very angry, and broken too, in a different way.

We both cried. I told him that it wasn't his job to take care of Pearl (although Lord knows I'd told him enough times it was) and that I was the one who hadn't been watching closely enough; if it was anyone's fault, it was mine. But not his. And he sobbed, and said, "Not yours, Mother!" and we both cried some more.

Eventually it stilled in us. I sat with my cheek against his hair and realized as if waking out of a dream, that the children left to me needed their mother, and I didn't want to cause any more hurt to anyone, ever. There'd been far too much pain, and it could never be made right, but I needed not to add to it. I smiled at Tad. I told him that as long as I had my big boy, I would always be all right. Him being there was enough. He looked at me very straight, with a new seriousness, and said, "Mother, I will always be your big boy, and I will never leave you." Then added, as if struck with new responsibility, "Well, maybe someday if I have a wife I might have to leave you for a little bit, but I'll always come back."

We sat. We were still sitting there, in the dirt, when Carl came looking I don't know how much later; Genevieve had woken up and was crying, he said, so he came up to the house to see what was doing.

That night, still feeling newly awakened and fragile, not sure how I felt about it, I told him about Tad, and how much it stung that he'd been blaming himself. Then both Carl and I cried, or I think he cried with me. I felt him shaking but I never looked. He wouldn't have wanted me to know for sure.

Over time, things took on a routine. It didn't feel strange to smile, and even laugh. I still dreamed of Pearl, feeling her hands on my face, seeing her crooked little smile. I still wept when I was alone sometimes. I'd start to think, "Maybe Pearl would like…" or "If Pearl wants to…" and then have to realize all over again that it would never be. But the biggest change was in Tad. He'd been so merry before, striding out like the world was a place full of things to discover and share. He became both quieter and harder, as if he was using a lot of energy trying not to care, or maybe even trying not to be happy. Perhaps he was afraid to think things could be all right and have them go so wrong again.

And really, after that…I never saw Tad the way he'd been before, ever again; running out into the afternoons with his sister as his partner and playmate. He became surprisingly sarcastic for a young boy. Carl would shake his head when he got too…well, he wasn't mean. He was just kind of…bitter? Can a seven-year-old be bitter? Whatever it was, it broke my heart all over again. The new Tad was all I had left of the old one, but he wasn't the same boy. In a way, I lost two children and got a changeling in the place of one: a watchful boy who looked like Tad but never smiled in the old way. I've wondered who losing Pearl damaged more, him or me. No parent should ever have to outlive a child, but I had a life of faith and some years behind me. Tad changed in ways that still make me sad to think on.

Oddly, though: he kept that promise. He never left me for long. Even when he did have a wife, and teaching positions all around, in Reservation Country and south in Arizona and hours away, he always came home, Sundays when he was close, and summers when he wasn't, bringing his own family back to Oak Creek. He may not have been the nicest man, but he was steadfast in his promise, made long ago in the dust that smelled of the creek. He never left for long.

Exile

We are sending Tad away.

That sounds harsh. It feels harsh. But we've realized his eyes aren't right; he doesn't see things we do. Also, he's seven years old, and there's no school good enough. We adore Ellsworth but he teaches all the grades, and Tad needs classics and access to good books. So we are sending him back to Gorin, where he will stay with Lillie and Loring through the school year. Carl will take him back on the train. It will be just Genevieve and me here. (Carl says he's already asked Ellsworth and Travois to look in on us.)

I don't care. We will be fine. We have food and a good roof. What else is there?

I'm glad, in a detached way, that we are doing what is best for our Tad. I confess I'm rather glad he is going. Every time I see him, I see him trying to be strong, and good. But he's broken inside the way I am. Better he be away from here, away from me. Most every day there are a few wildflowers on Pearl's grave that I didn't put there. He's mourning his sister, and maybe his childhood. He hardly laughs. Carl will drive the wagon to Flagstaff tomorrow, Saturday, so Ellsworth can go with him and bring it back. They will take the train. I expect it will be about ten days; I know Carl won't linger there, except long enough to see Tad settled in. He's such a good boy he will be no trouble to Lillie. And Carl is taking money to cover his board.

I just went in to kiss Tad good night (we moved Genevieve into that room with her bed on a different wall, leaving Pearl's where it was) and tell him I love him and am proud of him, knowing how smart he is and how well he will do in school. He looked a bit lost.

"But, Mother, I won't know any of the other children, and they will all know each other," he said. "And there won't be a creek. There will be city stuff, and I don't remember that."

I was starting to wonder if this was selfish on our parts and Carl should bring him back after they get his eyes figured out. But then he said,

"And there won't be anyone here but Genevieve to make sure you don't get too sad."

Dear God, I'm so blind.

"Tad," I said. "That isn't your job. You are not in charge of me being happy. You are my son, who I love. I want you to be happy! And maybe you can't be, seeing me sad. This is a very good thing we are all doing: you will be able to see better with glasses, which we don't have here. We want a very good eye doctor for you. Dad will be able to see his people, and Lillie will love getting to be around such a big smart boy. Dad and I are so proud that you are strong enough, and brave enough, to do this. A lot of boys your age couldn't do this. But you are very special, and we know you can."

He thought a minute, and nodded.

"I will be a big help to Aunt Lillie," he said firmly.

"I know you will. And we will write you every week, and you will know that I wrote your letter after lunch during Quiet Hour. You will know where I am. And you will know Dad carried that letter in his bag up the road he helped build, and that it rode on the train from Flagstaff just like you will do. You will feel how much we love you every day, because I will send my love for you up to God, and ask Him to send it on to you."

I held him in my arms, rocking back and forth a little.

"Want me to sing?" I asked. I used to sing to him every night, hymns we both liked, but we've fallen out of the habit during these disrupted times.

He looked surprised, then a smile burst through, making him look younger. "You won't stop till I'm asleep?"

"I won't stop."

And I didn't.

Grand Canyon

July 20, 1905

I can't believe where I am! I can't take in what I'm seeing. Truly, the Grand Canyon was rightly named.

We've travelled four days to get here, Carl and Genevieve and I. I don't want to think about the camping, the fire tending, or the dust, long enough to record them. Suffice to say if I'd known how fretful Genevieve would be, how bone-shaken we'd be, how long the days would be, I would never have come.

Thank God I didn't know.

I was exhausted, having not slept through the night even once on the way here. The party we came with, bringing wagons up from Verde Valley, are friends of Ellsworth's and kind, but strangers.

Weather had demanded my attention all that last day: wind whipped and tossed any branches brave enough to grow on the stunted crooked trees we saw, blowing in heavy dark clouds, and it took a toll by never ceasing. Like being on a ship, there was no escaping the sound anywhere.

So I was on sentry duty half the night on my pallet with our baby girl, watching the scud and shift of clouds, pale against a dark sky overhead, worrying about how to keep Genevieve from waking if it rained; feeling imagined raindrops and daring to sleep only when the moon had claimed the whole sky as its own. So an hour or so of sleep was mine. And I knew we had only a few hours of travel until we arrived.

When we first saw the Grand Canyon, we were coming through sparse forest—more like pine trees scattered across land than a thick, green, lush forest. At first it looked like just space, empty land. As I got closer I could see colors. Then, vague shapes. One is almost upon it (or should I say in it?) before it can be comprehended.

This is not a diorama. This is not a painting. For it seems like it must be, unrolled across the landscape farther than one person's eyes can see, when looking straight ahead; you have to turn your head in both directions to take in how far it extends. The buttes, slopes, shades and designs are impossible to comprehend at first. It's baffling to understand how it happened, was created, was carved out before an indifferent audience of flora and fauna. Nature's own artists—water, wind and time—have worked in glorious visual concert here. Patiently polishing and slowly grinding down stone, with the river and the breezes, gradually cutting deeper through layers of different rock so there are more hues and variations on the colors of sunsets and earth than I knew.

We will shortly go down a trail into this canyon. On mules. Carl laughed when I asked if it would be dangerous. "They don't make money by losing riders," he said. I suppose.

This is very different from Oak Creek. There, we're tucked into a pocket-handkerchief assortment of spires and sculptures. Here we are open, with the same kind of red rock artistry unfolding, more deeply than we can view. You can almost hear the ravens laugh with glee as they go sailing out on currents of air, over the rim: "One flap of my wings, and I go from ground to soaring free over the void."

I'm keeping Genevieve far from that edge. I probably over-protect her to a damaging degree, but as God is my witness, nothing will happen to this daughter. Occasionally, a wandering pebble goes skipping down off the precipice, rolling and leaping, reminding me what would happen to a falling child, and I have to stop walking and breathe carefully until I feel I can move again.

Squirrels are everywhere here, seeking charity with their bright, trusting little eyes. And more deer than I have seen in one place, apparently unafraid of us and our noise and equipment; surely we seem strange, clanging and thumping things that they can survive well without.

A beautiful hotel has been constructed here, by the canyon rim. (There's already the house perched like a nest, built by those photography brothers. The Lukes? I can't remember.) But this is truly the most splendid building I have seen since I left Missouri. The hotel boasts lightning rods and balconies, and a stately posture, like an elegant woman old enough to inspire respect but no less breathtaking because of her poise and authority. It's called the El Tovar, for an early Spanish explorer who came this way.

We walked about, and talked to some of the people working there. It costs most people a month's earnings to purchase a single night's rest. (They didn't tell me that; I just saw the rate card.) I will never be able to stay there, I doubt. I married Carl because I love how he thinks. Money is not important to him. Making people happy is. So he'll bring persimmons down from Flagstaff because Mr. Graham has been talking nonstop about them, and tell him. "Oh, they weren't much." We both know Mr. Graham doesn't have two cents to rub together. But I do the books, and I see how dear persimmons were! Then Carl won't buy his new overalls. "Maybe next time," he says when I ask him.

Anyway, we won't ever be financially rich. I will never walk up those broad front steps in a plumed hat and sashay through those heavy doors for a steam-heated room. But maybe, someday, I could come back for a cup of tea and a look-around. There's a women's lounge on the mezzanine above the lobby. Maybe my daughters or granddaughters will marry differently, and be able to visit this El Tovar as grand ladies. On the other hand, the Grand Canyon isn't any closer to people who stay there. And they probably wouldn't have a man as good as Carl.

I vow, that big stone fireplace will last 100 years.

We are at the bottom of the Grand Canyon.

That mule ride down the trail is something I'm glad I probably will not do again…although we have a return trip tomorrow, but somehow going up seems less frightening. Those animals have no fear of falling, not even a healthy one. Up at the rim, their handlers scrutinize all the riders to match each with a compatible mule, although that may be a contradiction of terms: try as I did, I could never establish much rapport with Bodie. We rode for hours, and every so often, one of the mules would receive an internal message to stop dead in his tracks and gaze over the edge of the trail, as if taking in the view. All the mules behind him, of course, halted, like a pattern of dominoes. They also seem less solid than the larger horses I'm used to; as if they are a three-legged stool instead of a solid chair.

While I felt a good measure of fear when Bodie took his turn sight-seeing, I would understand if they did want to stop and stare, even if this is their daily profession. What a visual feast! What views and vistas, turrets, towers, spires and slabs of colored cliffs. (I'm sure I'm not the first writer whom the Grand Canyon has driven to purple prose.)

I was never so glad to dismount at the end of a ride as I was at Phantom Ranch. It is an Eden, a sliver of civilization in a place as wild as Oak Creek was, when we first got there. There is the prettiest little settlement of buildings in a clearing, with tall cottonwoods dappling shade over everything. There are bunkhouses for men and women. And calling from just past them, water. Rolling, surging, singing water; a whole great gathering of water, if such a thing could be, compared to our Oak Creek.

Once we reached the Colorado River, everything felt infused with gossamer light and magic. The song of the waters kept constant company, and watching it was hypnotic. I didn't imagine there was so much water to be able to keep coming with such vigor, in this dry area of the state. It's so much more masterful and aggressive than Oak Creek, compelling in a different way. At home the murmur of the creek sounds like the voice of a friend. The Colorado River roars.

To wander about the camp, hearing parts of conversations, free and unencumbered, immersed in the wild beauty of nature tucked between soaring shields of rock, was an unfamiliar and wonderful feeling. I found myself reflecting that this is what "basking" must feel like.

We got to wash before the evening meal, such as "wash" can be in water that cold. We were all offered buckets and directed to a grove of trees, which afforded the women privacy to unbutton, lower sleeves, lift skirts, take off shoes. I took Genevieve and we felt much revived after a few minutes' efforts.

They served us dinner sitting around a big open room. Thick steaks, baked potatoes, corn, apple cobbler. We sat, guests, not hosts, and let others bring plates. Food that someone else cooks is delicious.

The stars are lush across the strip of night sky high above us, encased by canyon walls. More shooting stars than I've ever seen. We must be in a good time for them. Or maybe there is actually more sky here. Or is it deeper? We chose to sleep out, regardless.

I woke up because birds knew it was getting light before I did, and began taking attendance. I watched a small shape whisk by and thought, "time to go home, little bat." Then Genevieve came to, and clung to me, sweet and small and trusting. Moments like that ease the wound Pearl left, although they leave guilt as well. I shouldn't ever not miss her.

After a hearty breakfast in the sylvan surroundings of camp, getting back in the saddle was punishing. I felt sore down to the bone. But finally I could stop dreading the ascent. It took longer than coming down, but I was too tired to be scared.

Gratefully we handed over the reins at the South Rim. I kept a good hold on Genevieve all the time. Kolb is the name of the brothers who built the house, perched so precariously and delightfully on the Rim, and we actually purchased the photograph they took of our caravan. While we never spend money lightly, this is a priceless reminder of something we won't do again. (Also, I fear I have fewer photographs of Genevieve than I did of Pearl at her age, and I want her to always know she partook in this adventure.)

Kolb Brothers photograph at Grand Canyon, 1905: Sedona is
third from left, with Carl behind her holding Genevieve

Carl surprised me with train tickets for the trip back. It was heavenly not to have to face another camping expedition. We are weary,
dirty and content, and going in luxury. (Carl sent a telegraph message
for Ellsworth to meet us in Flagstaff.)

The train wasn't scheduled to leave for a bit. Carl fell to talking with someone, and as I was gathering our possessions before we went down to the train depot I heard Carl laugh delightedly. I listened.

Carl told me later he'd heard of Mr. John Hance from one of our boarders who had visited the Grand Canyon.

"This is someplace to be proud of, all right," I overheard Carl saying, "but you haven't seen my canyon yet. Oak Creek's smaller, but it's powerful pretty."

They fell to talking about wildlife, and Mr. Hance told Carl a story about a man asking him how plentiful deer are at the Grand Canyon.

"Very plentiful," said Mr. Hance, "I shot three this morning." The man said, "Well, you're talking to the game warden of this area, and you're in trouble." Mr. Hance said, "And you're talking to the biggest damn liar in these parts!"

If he'd known I could hear I'm sure he wouldn't have been so salty, but he seemed such a genial fellow: wizened like a leather boot, lean as jerky and possessing a whirl of white beard and hair. Carl told me later Mr. Hance is the unofficial ambassador of the Grand Canyon; that until two years ago, the little village at the South Rim was called Hance Tank. So now Mr. Hance tells stories and leads tours, having lived at the Grand Canyon for decades and learned more about it than any other white man alive.

"I'd like to do that," said Carl thoughtfully, once we were on the train, "get established enough to greet folk who visit and recommend what they might want to see in Oak Creek. I could be the Hance of Oak Creek Canyon."

"Well, I certainly hope you get to," I said, "And nobody would do it better. I don't think anyone has the love for that place you do."

"How could I not?" he answered with a twinkle. "It's named for the most beautiful woman in the world."

He does please me.

I am not this woman.

This is not my home, back at Oak Creek.

I have lied to innocent children and a trusting man: I have let them believe I am meant to be a wife and mother and caretaker. These lodgers, hungry for fried chicken and details of the trip, have no idea how hard it is to keep from hurling drumsticks at their benign and bobbing heads. I want to be back at the Grand Canyon. I was so unencumbered by nagging worries and lists of things to do. I felt free.

No planning meals. No changing sheets. No figuring out how long Mr. Graham should stay to make sure his lungs are truly clear. No fall clothes to cut out, no preserve jar seals to worry over. Just the day. The constant music of the water. Oh, I know Oak Creek sings, too, but right now to me it's a rhythmic song like slaves would sing in the cotton fields to keep their spirits up. It's a work song. The Colorado sang leisure and appreciation.

I feel so terribly guilty. How could I not glory in this life that many would give their eyeteeth for? I have the finest man in the world; my children are smart, dear, glowing bundles of health and joy. (Even if Tad is away, his letters sound very good; better than I had hoped for.) This house is the grandest around, we are blessed with foodstuffs no matter the season. This has got to be Enough. The only thing wrong here is me.

I have felt this restlessness before, but not since Gorin. There it made sense: trapped in a little smothering town with all its rules and wagging tongues, waiting for bug-eyed Donie Miller, as some called me, to make another mistake. I was fettered, so of course I felt it. But now I have no excuse. I could set off walking in any direction and not have to stop for so much as an outbuilding in my path (if I had hinds' feet and could scamper up the rocks). I have family of my own choosing and creation now, instead of family by obligation. So to have this urge to flee, be free, is heretical and profane.

Maybe someday I'll look back with more tolerance of myself. Maybe then I will think, "What mare, having run loose in the pasture, welcomes the bit and bridle?" Maybe anyone chafes under routine, after having slipped the bonds for a time.

Eastbound

Sept. 2, 1905

We are going back to Gorin.

I have felt somewhat better as time has gone on, but can't shake off this melancholy. Carl finally had the doctor come, despite me telling him over and over I'm not sick, just tired.

Just now I heard them on the porch after Carl walked him out: "You must move her, or lose her," he told Carl. Carl came in looking falsely hearty and said, "Dona, I've decided it's time to pull up stakes. We are going back to Gorin."

That was strange to me. He didn't ask. He didn't suggest. He just said it. Who can say if that doctor knows what he's talking about? How can Carl be so rash, by what right is this his decision alone? But I don't really care. If he wants to turn his back on all this, all the work he's put in, it's fine with me. It occurs to me that I won't have to see that grave all the time. But leave our girl? Oh, I don't know if I care. It just means a lot of packing up. Well, I have to be doing something. I don't want to go. I don't want to stay. I just want to stop feeling anything.

I must be the most selfish person alive. I don't know how Carl stands me. I don't know how God stands me. I can't stand me.

Travois came by, and I heard Carl invite him out onto the porch. My good manners must have died with Pearl; it used to be I never would have listened to their conversation. Now I don't even hesitate.

Carl told Travois we are moving. Actually, he said, "I'm moving Dona." That caught me up. We have always been a team, done things together. But now he doesn't see it that way. Travois said how sorry he is, and how he will miss us. I guess I'm glad I don't care much about much, or I'd miss him as well. There are no Travoises in Gorin. In fact, I doubt there are many anywhere but here. Carl took a deep breath in and let it out in an audible sigh.

"If it weren't the only choice, I could never leave here."

There it is.

How did I not see this?

He loves Oak Creek. He has given it two names: Sedona, and now people call the road Schnebly Hill Road. He has put his love and sweat and caring and effort deep into this place. He's only leaving because of me. Because I wasn't a good enough mother to keep our girl safe. Because I let her die. Because now I can't do anything right. Because, fool that he is, he loves me.

If I had the energy I would tell him to stay, and I would go. But he'd never let me leave alone, or with the children. I am costing my husband his dream. The one he's already made come true.

I'm even worse than I thought, and that's saying a great deal.

III. Gorin
1905-1910

Prodigal

When the Biblical son returns to his father after going off on his own and ruining his life, he is welcomed with open arms. Only in this case, the open arms were my son's, who was waiting, beaming, at the train station with Lillie when Carl and I got off the train.

I actually saw Tad from our seat; he was anxiously scanning windows. I began waving frantically, which I would normally never do—Tad! Our Tad! Our boy, in his new eyeglasses, standing so close.

He saw me. His face lit, he nudged Lillie and pointed, and we got to look at one another as we edged along the aisle, down the steps, and he was in my arms (therefore hugging both Genevieve and me), and then Dad's, who was laughing with joy.

During the time Tad was gone, I was too numb to think about him a great deal; then when I did, it pierced so deep I tried not to again.

But now the die is cast. We are here. And seeing him makes it so good, outweighing the feeling that we came back hangdog and defeated. Who cares what anyone thinks when we can see our boy?

This trip was much easier than the one going out, because now it was two adults and one small child instead of one adult with two small children. (Stab. A wave of pain about Pearl. Wait and write when it passes.)

Carl entertained Genevieve, and I cared for her. Also, Carl and I could together observe the scenery that seemed to unroll past our window, and comment to one another: Look how that woman is reaching out her window to hang laundry on a clothesline contraption that moves it to her; see the man way out in that field? You can tell where he's weeded. I wonder where that boy is running with such determination?

Now we are here. Lillie found us a place and Carl sent some things ahead, which she and Loring have kindly moved in for us. She was worried about how to place furniture, but I assured her I cared not at all.

Tonight she brought us dinner on elegant dishes, because Loring does so well. The old upset about him has vanished. I'm grateful he's offering Carl a business opportunity, a way to support our family. We're fortunate he wants Carl to invest the Oak Creek money Ellsworth paid him for our property in his menswear store. He didn't come with her; she said as a leading merchant, he has many evening obligations with prominent city and county businessmen.

She caught me up on how the family is doing, and I asked if she thought Mutter would be coming. That flashfire smile I've missed so much. "She won't be able not to."

Tad was allowed to stay up late; Genevieve was yawning even before dinner, her little head drooping. When I took her upstairs and began to sing to her, she knew she would miss the activity, and tried to cover my mouth with her hand.

"No song, Mama...no..." and then another yawn. She knew she would drift off to a lullaby. "No...song..." and she was asleep. I crept back downstairs.

Only after Lillie had departed did I turn to Tad to say it was bedtime.

As I tucked him in, he asked if I'd sing "Abide With Me," adding, "You know, like you used to when I was a little boy."

Only three months have passed since he left. (Only four years have passed since we all did!) But he does seem so much older than when I saw him last. He has grown tremendously in spirit, and some in body. When you see a child every day he never seems to grow. Absence shows it.

I'd never been away from one of our own like that before, and I still believe it was the right thing. But I am so glad he's with us! I hope we don't ever have to do something like that again. Well, we won't. That was one specific era in all our lives, and whatever comes, it won't be that again.

A Project

Other than planning to celebrate Genevieve's second birthday (Tad has been fueling her excitement by saying the words "cake and presents" so often she sings that phrase endlessly), I have found time heavy on my hands. It doesn't take any real effort at all to keep a house running smoothly with this much civilization around us. After having inquired about how I fill my time, Lillie brought a box over today, setting it down with a flash of mischievous smile.

"I never opened it, I swear I didn't. It's all your old journals; I found them up in the attic at Mutter and Papa's. I didn't think you would want these in their hands."

Tonight I told Carl about them, and he surprised me. He almost never tells me what he thinks I should do, so when he does I pay extra attention.

"Go through them," he said. "Put together things that will let someone someday know who we were, if they're ever curious about who named that post office out west. Or perhaps our children or grandchildren will grow up and want to know where they're from. I've no talent for things like that.

"You don't want to, I know," he continued with his usual gentleness. "You don't want to do anything, and I understand why. But this way you can be of use to our family without having to be out and about." Then he played his trump card. "I would be so grateful, if you're willing."

All right, Carl. You're right that I don't care about anything, so I can please you, even if that's all I can do. I will put together the journal entries that tell my, and then our, early story, and add them to this current journal. Having just flipped through them, I see things that are so foolish and self-centered I almost can't do this. But if there's even a chance that someone else might learn from my mistakes, I will put them here.

I really must love you, to bestir myself so much.

Age 13

*W*hy doesn't a girl have as many rights as a hound dog? It's raining, and I'm as trapped inside as if those were balls of fire instead of drops of water. Boys can go out in weather; "they have to drive the sheep, do the milking," Papa would say. And even dogs, which are not very high up on the ladder of life, are out right now, running in circles as the storm blows in. They're excited by the change. It's going to be a hard rain, wind whipping the leaves against my window under a whole sky full of grey clouds: a glorious storm. I want to be out in it, whirling and spinning, laughing and tipping my head up to catch the drops. But that would be impossible for a million tiresome reasons, so I sit huddled in the parlor until one of my sisters, Lillie or Pearl or Goldie, discovers me and bothers me.

Today I'm too impatient even to enjoy writing. I feel nervous, like an unbroken horse. I want to be out. Not just outside. Out in a bigger sense. Things feel too tidy, too constraining. Too comfortable. Dinner will be at six. The napkins will match. My shoes are the right size. Our nightgowns are clean. All just right. All predictable.

I know Lillie would say, "Oh, perhaps you'd like tight shoes and a dirty nightgown?" But it's just so organized. Everything's already figured out and done. There's no horizon to sail off toward. That horrible Edward Taylor poem we had to memorize last term: "Make me, O Lord, thy Spinning Wheele compleate. The Holy Worde my Distaff make for mee." And on about being a loom, and knitting His twine.

Why not His chariot, or drum? Or even His Almighty fishing pole? No. Inside household goods. So tedious a sentence. How unspectacular to be a pittancy little spool when there are so many more splendid tools! Even a plough would be better. Then you could feel the sun and hear birds.

It's probably horrible, and I'm not even sure I mean it, but I almost wish a war were going on again. I know it was terribly sad to lose someone on either side of the War Between the States. And then things got desperate for a lot of people afterward.

But to have someone standing by the gate, overcome with emotion, kissing my hand and looking searchingly into my eyes before he marched away with my Bible in his pocket. Or my handkerchief, but that wouldn't stop a bullet for him. And me waving bravely through my tears.

Then, getting letters and pressing them to my heart before I read them. And maybe, even, a black-bordered "We regret to inform you..." and swooning. Everyone telling Mutter in hushed tones, "Amanda, dear, give her my best," while I'm grieving upstairs.

Better yet—to be a soldier! To be brave and daring, running across the battlefield with my bayonet ready! Maybe a spy, sleeping in haystacks across enemy lines. It seems so unfair that never will I get to be a patriot or a revolutionary. Independence is already won. And the states are united (in name, at least). How can I ever be integral to something if everything's already settled and solved?

I made the mistake of telling Amiel this and he gave me that superior smile and said I must be a hermaphrodite, to want to go into battle. I had to look it up in Papa's big dictionary, and then I was so offended! Besides, it was plain cruel. I told Amiel he could go whistle up a rope for all I cared, but he has no idea how he wounded me.

I know I'm not pretty, and I'm terrified I won't ever be. But I also know I'm not part man. I'm soft, and my eyes are big anyway. I push on them before I go to sleep so I won't look like "that little bug-eyed Donie Miller." Amiel told me someone called me that. Maybe by the time term starts next year everyone will forget about it.

Dear God,

I know You understand the feelings I cannot explain. Please help me understand why I don't feel content here. Show me somehow, something I can do to get beyond Gorin's tidy peaceful civilized life. I want to be dared. I even want to be hungry or dirty, but alive, truly alive.

If I were in a war, I might die, but if I didn't, I would be so completely alive—each moment, thrillingly aware of the air and the sun and my own movement. I want that. I want more than my own house on another street with different wallpaper and a varied china pattern. It terrifies me to think I might never be part of some grand adventure, some revolution, some pilgrimage. A whole world out there, harsh and huge and powerful, and I may be sentenced to "one lump or two?" Never to say, "Stop in the name of the king!" or "No! I will be the one to go!"

And I know it's shallow of me, Lord, but could I be a tiny bit beautiful? Could I have haunted mysterious eyes instead of pop-eyes? (Thank You for my hair, by the way. No one else in this family has the same wavy dark hair. I dream that someday someone will compare it to a waterfall of ebony.)

I promise, dear God, that I will try to do whatever You want me to. I only so hope it has something big or dangerous in it somewhere; that I may not die of boredom. And that I don't die without ever finding out what I was capable of. What I am made of. What my limits are. Whether I can make a difference somewhere that isn't already all filled in and figured out and finished, like Gorin is.

Amen.

I remember when we got to take the train to Omaha to see Buffalo Bill Cody's Wild West Show. I was seven, perhaps. They had Indians someone had captured. For a penny, you could buy a picture postcard of a great chief who was there. I was fascinated, and I wanted so very much to see a true Indian—especially one who had been fearless, and

led his people into an impossible battle with our troops. What a noble man!

But when I saw him, I wished I hadn't. I didn't stand in line to buy a postcard, although at least he would have had one more penny. But he was like a bear in the old renderings of those poor creatures waiting for a barbaric fight with dogs in our history book. It was as if perhaps taking him out of the wild took the wildness out of him, and made him pitiable. I felt horrible, as if I had captured him, dragged him there and chained him myself: I felt ashamed to be American, and ashamed for him. I couldn't meet his eyes.

I almost feel that way again: regretful for what's been tamed. As though by making life so civilized we've taken the power and dignity out of it. I want to see the Indians all free, and ride on a pony behind them back to the great open land. But I know there were many battles, and many killed on both sides, and that I'm ignorant about the whole thing, like so many other things adults stop talking about when I walk into the room.

Maybe wishing I could know freedom and wildness is like a tabby cat wishing it could hunt like a lion.

Maybe women have to be merely vapid circles of ruffles with modulated voices.

But maybe not. Just maybe not.

April 3, 1892

Lo, what light from yonder window gleams! (I believe it was Juliet in Shakespeare who said that...) I can see so much, looking out from this quaint window under the eaves. I have a sanctuary! This is my first opportunity to write in my journal in absolute solitude, with no fear of anyone disturbing my thoughts. (That's exciting enough to warrant an exclamation point, but it's such a dignified sentence I thought it was better served ending in a restrained period.)

I do love this room; I'm glad Papa agreed I could have a desk up here. At first it was grumble and harrumph: attic too cold, stairs too steep. But right next to the chimney it's <u>not</u> cold. And if I've made it fifteen years without pitching down a flight of stairs, I guess he decided I was capable of even this perilous a climb. So I have a retreat; a place to muse. Maybe become a great writer. And I have this wonderful little window looking out over the back and the fields, which feels so much more romantic than the windows downstairs. I feel like a mouse in a Dickens story.

Although the cucumber patches are very visible from here. I may be vain, but it pains me that part of our sustenance comes from providing the pickle factory with cucumbers. There is just nothing noble or refined about a pickle factory. It has no grace. And when I grow up, I will never plant a cucumber. Wheat is fine; it waves like gold that's fluid and timeless. Bringing in the sheaves, the gleaners…wheat inspires literature. Cucumbers just inspire…corned beef, or some other coarse sandwich wrapped in brown paper. Cucumbers are pedestrian.

I've finished my lessons. Mutter is so proud that we can speak four languages. I guess I should be grateful. But mostly I wonder why that makes us better than we would otherwise be. What would be lost if I couldn't ask if the teacup was blue in French, or say I would prefer the apple on the tree in German? Of course, since Mutter is Pennsylvania Dutch, she loves that we speak German. She makes fun of people who think Deutsch means Dutch. She has always had us call her Mutter; I didn't even know it wasn't English until I was in school and friends called their mothers Mama or Mother. Italian isn't my strongest language so far. Mutter says all this indicates we are refined. The Gorin Academy: Where Ladies Become Gentlewomen. Elocution. (From the same root as eloquent. At least I think so.) Classics. Embroidery. Music.

Actually, music is wonderful. I could study music for hours. Sometimes at the piano, I feel so alive. Playing Handel can do that: fill me with energy, and make me feel a part of something stirring and free. And some pieces are so beautiful they are tragic. I don't quite understand how beauty leads to sadness. But it does. Maybe that's the opposite of laughing at ugly things like toads, or clowns.

I love our literature studies. Mrs. Dathel makes Shakespeare so interesting. Some of the girls laugh about her after class, because she becomes so excited reading and talking about the plays. She's a small woman, with fluffy dark hair all piled up, and spectacles. But when she reads the part of Brutus, for instance, she almost grows; she seems a large, stern man. She has a gift for making the words seem like real people are speaking them. I am too reserved to do it in class, but I've memorized one of Portia's speeches from "Julius Caesar," and I say it when I'm alone. I love this part:

"Dwell I but in the suburbs of your good pleasure? If it be no more, then Portia is Brutus' harlot, and not his wife!" I know that's a very daring thing for her to say, but I feel strong and glorious reciting the words.

Portia also refers to "my once commended beauty." Does that mean she is no longer beautiful, having gotten married and become fat? Or merely that Brutus is a man of such stature that no one would dare speak too well of his wife? In any case, she seems splendid. I want to be as indomitable someday. Maybe I'll even get to refer to my once-commended beauty. Except I don't think, outside of Shakespeare, you're supposed to be the one saying it about yourself.

How is it that even though we're sisters, Lillie gets to be fair, and so comfortable within her skin, while I'm all dark and glowering looking? I don't feel glowering. I think I'm just shy, but it doesn't appear that way. Lillie's so unthinking about being herself; just flows around humming and arranging flowers or whatever she does....and everyone thinks she's so wonderful. I hope she doesn't get a suitor before I do. But at this rate it will happen. I could be always the bridesmaid, getting older and prunier in pastel dresses while all my sisters take turns wearing white; me like Miss Havisham, only not even getting the romance of being a spurned bride.

The Phillip Millers

*M*y existence is so boring. Pedestrian. Things happen, but never to me. However, today's sermon was about how most of us are blind to all the wonderful gifts God gives us. I resolved to be more aware of them.

First, my family:

Papa (Phillip Miller) is the second-richest man in Gorin. I haven't the faintest idea who keeps track of these things, but someone must, because everyone says that about him. He was smart enough to start growing cucumbers when he heard a pickle factory was being built here. Mutter says, "We're comfortable," in a tone that implies we are a great deal better off than that.

Mutter, Amanda, is formerly a Shaefer, and as I said, Pennsylvania Dutch. Which means...well, I am not exactly certain. But she says it often enough, as if her audience will understand that explains a great deal.

And then there are the rest of us.

Edward, I feel I hardly know. He was nine when I was born, but he's always been off doing older things, and went to school back east. Papa said it's important for eldest sons to be given every advantage in business education.

Minnie is married to George; dark and pretty and affectionate (Minnie, not George). She's seven years older than I.

Noah teases me too much, but he's kind.

Phillip and Amanda Miller of Gorin, MO

Amiel is very different; sometimes I think I'm a little afraid of him. There's a look he gets.

Lillie, of course, is Lillie. My leader even thought she's yonger, my friend and companion.

Goldie is only four years younger than I, but she and Pearl, who is seven years behind me, are always playing together, so they seem like little girls.

Edna is not yet in school, and seems fretful a great deal. There was a baby Johnny after Pearl and before Edna, but he died very early. And apparently there was a John who died even before Edward was born. Don't you think it would be dangerous to name a boy John, since two have died in our family already?

So I suppose I am grateful for my family. I don't know what it would be like to be in any other family, so it's hard to judge. I hear Mutter boast a bit to her friends about how even though they could afford all the help she wants, the children all do chores and we sleep on camp beds. (Well, that sounds a bit rustic. But I guess if the alternative is huge puffy piles of pillows on four-posters with curtains, yes, that is what they are. Maybe all the ladies tell each other mostly-true things. I guess I won't know until I grow up.)

Our house is very nice. It's big enough that we're never crowded, and the furniture is quite carved and complicated. We must be rich. I say that because everything shines, and there's always more food than we finish in a meal, and every year in the spring there are new dresses and shoes, and every winter, new coats. It seems rich to me.

I am mostly grateful for my new attic space. I love being alone, able to think—and therefore write—anything I want without worrying someone will creep up behind me to read it and make fun of me. I hate being made fun of. I already feel like I'm not good enough. "Little bug-eyed Donie Miller." You only have to hear that once to feel not good enough, ever.

Gentleman Caller

May 24, 1892

*H*ow can the best thing and the worst thing have happened at
the same time?

*The best thing is that I've finally had a gentleman caller! A
Sunday suitor. A parlour guest. Someone for whom shortbread and
lemonade are brought out on the pretty painted tray.*

The worst thing is: it was Alf Boltz.

*Or maybe the worst thing is that it was Alf Boltz and I rather
liked him.*

*I would be spurned at the Academy if anyone ever knew. I'm not
actually certain why he became so unpopular...he's not unhandsome.
Tall, certainly, and that thick hair curving over his forehead. But he
doesn't talk much; when he does his voice cracks, and people laugh. He
always seems so uncomfortable, as if he knows he isn't good enough and
hopes no one else will notice.*

*He was sweating, waiting to see me, and it isn't a bit warm out.
He was still all dressed up for church, as he should have been, and said,
"Afternoon, Miss Dona," just as any caller would be expected to do.
But he was so nervous it made his voice loud, and he almost shouted it.
That's when I heard Goldie giggle. She and Pearl were hiding behind
the folding door into the study, the imps! (I was never so wicked when
I was eight or ten!)*

*I suspect Alf heard them, too, because he looked around almost
wildly, like an animal whose foot has been caught in a trap. I just*

smiled and said again to please sit down, and would he like some refreshment?

How we passed the half hour I have no idea. Too much repeating one another's last few words and nodding. I believe he was as relieved as I when the clock struck three. And just as I said, "Where has the time gone?" he said, "It's that late?" And that was the moment I liked him. We looked at each other, and laughed, and I saw someone I could be friends with. Maybe if I knew more about him. But I can never dream of being his friend because of people at school. I hate that I think about that. But I'm not that brave. I'm already so perilously close to being an outcast I don't dare.

After he left I descended on the study, but of course Goldie and Pearl were reading a hastily procured book of nursery rhymes and looking up as if butter wouldn't melt in those mouths!

"Miss Dona," said Pearl with a little lisping simper.

"Or is it Mrs. Alf Boltz?" asked Goldie, and they both shrieked with laughter. I wanted to say, "You're just jealous because you aren't old enough to have callers," but I knew it wasn't true. They were mocking me because Alf Boltz likes me. Anyway, they don't know that for a minute I liked him also. That secret I will carry to my grave.

This morning when I carried my breakfast plate to the kitchen I heard Mutter tell Noah that Minnie's family is in reduced circumstances. I guess George made a bad investment in some type of factory up north. She stopped when she saw me, so I didn't get to find out what that really entails. Are Minnie's children in rags, selling matches on street corners? (How shameful if they are—after all, those are my niece and nephews.) Or does it just mean each one doesn't get to take a candle up to bed? Why can't I be told more?

But I can't ask Minnie, because if I write her Mutter will ask to read the letter. Imagine—my private correspondence to my own sister! Minnie moved away when she got married and I was only thirteen, so she doesn't seem my sister in the same way as Lillie and Pearl and Goldie and Edna do. Edna's only five. She's still very cute. Not a scamp yet like Goldie and Pearl have become. I can't decide if begging them not to tell anyone that Alf came would only make them tell all the faster. Maybe I should make some divinity and let them help, on the strict condition that they keep my dark secret.

It's evening now…Lillie made some disdainful remark about girls being courted by outcasts not having any other choice than to be grateful for even unwanted attention. She said when we're grown, I can live in her house as a servant and tend her children while she and her husband go to balls and receptions. I was so angry, I said, "Oh yes? Well, if that idea were alive, it couldn't wrestle an old man's thumb and win!" And I stalked off. I am not exactly sure how stalking is done, but it felt as if that were exactly what I was doing. I cannot believe I am related to her.

Baby

W*ell, mercy me! Bless my soul! Gracious! Lawks, as Mrs. Haushalter says. Mutter is going to have another baby.*

I know because now she's wearing the funny dark blue dress again, and she seems out of sorts a great deal. Why would she want to go and do that? Edward is a big grown up man of 23. He should be the one having new babies! And John Henry, who Mutter doesn't want to talk about, was born in 1866. That means she will have been bearing children off and on for 26 years. That's longer than I can even imagine being alive.

Why did she decide to have another child? I wish I could ask someone. Lillie heard at school that the mother and father together decide together, but I don't know what part the father has in it, since the mother gets fat and then can't go about, and then has to suckle the baby hiding behind shawls and (worst of all!) wring out diapers. Maybe the father is involved because another mouth to feed will cost more. I want to know, but I am partly terrified I will find out someday what part the father plays. I don't mind the idea of being kissed (in fact it sounds rather wonderful depending on the book one reads) but something shivery and unpleasant happens in my stomach when I try to think about what it's like to be married.

I almost forgot the other exciting thing: I've been asked to play the piano at Sunday Service! Mrs. Bromwell's been poorly for so long

I guess she's giving it up. I suddenly feel both too young and also quite equal to it. I know the songs by heart, and I love that by touching the piano keys in certain combinations with the proper count and cadence, it makes the music so much richer than the singers by themselves. Sometimes playing hymns is almost like dancing inside. I wonder what my first song will be. We practice, the choir and I, Tuesday night.

Dear God, thank you for this chance. I feel like laughing, I'm so very pleased and excited. I hope that doesn't mean I'm a showoff. It just will be such fun to be part of the music in an even bigger way than singing.

Dec. 26, 1892

Well, Mutter had the baby!

Her name (not Mutter's) is Lola, which I think sounds like music from a faraway island. So including John Henry, who died before Noah was born, and Johnny who died between Pearl and Edna, Mutter's had twelve children.

That's a great many. John Henry was born in 1866, then Edward was born in 1868. Minnie in 1870, Noah in 1873, Amiel in 1875, I in 1877, Lillie in 1879, Goldie in 1881, Pearl in 1884, Johnny in 1887, Edna in 1888 and now Lola.

Miller family, left to right, 1888: Minnie, Edward, Amanda, Pearl, Goldie, Phillip holding Edna, Lillie, Noah, Sedona, Amiel

Mutter's funny about naming children. Some of us do have lovely names (I personally think my name is quite pretty) and others are— well, plain. Lillie Veronica is pretty all the way through, but Goldie Amelia and Minnie Lydia end better than they start. Pearl and Lola sound lyrical, but Edna and Amiel Otto are more of a thud than a trill. Noah and Edward aren't really one way or the other. It's pleasant (although I would never say this anywhere but here) to be the only one named a brand new name. "There's a first time for every word," Mutter says when people ask her if Sedona is a family name. Someone at a WCTU meeting said she'd met a French Creole woman named Sedonie, so maybe my name sounds French. Sedona Arabella is, I think, the most elegant of all our names. I guess it makes up, at least in part, for not being the loveliest or the most graceful.

I sure wish I knew for certain about the first John. He was born the year after they were married; I saw it in the Bible. But he's never been mentioned. The one time I dared ask Mutter about him, she shut her lips for a moment, then said, "Do you see any boy running around here that age?" It was a terrible voice, and I've never asked again. I know he died, but I have no idea how, or what he was like. Maybe when I am a woman grown with children of my own she will explain that to me.

Also, yesterday was Christmas, which was rather lost among all the upset of Mutter giving birth upstairs two days before; Papa made us light the tree candles, and I played for carol singing, but it was odd. We opened our gifts rather quietly, and dinner was over very quickly because hardly anyone spoke. I think we felt ashamed for being excited about presents, when life was happening over our heads. But I love my new pen, and Lillie gave me a nice autograph book. And of course, baby Jesus was born.

March Fourth

March 4, 1893

*T*oday is the most inspirational day of the year.
Our beloved Dr. Asin, who has cared for us all since I can
remember, told us he wed his bride on this date; he says, "March
fourth!" is like saying, "Move ahead! Embark!" (They've been married a great many years and when I see them at gatherings they always
seem blissfully in love, making one another laugh, and even holding
hands when most grownups never would.) I hope to do something stirring on March Fourth someday.

Other inspirational things...

My favorite Bible verse is in Habakkuk. It's an obscure little book,
after Nahum (who also is not widely read or quoted) with a beautiful
way of advising us how to conduct ourselves under siege of doubt or
despair.

It reads:

> "How long, O Lord, shall I cry, and thou wilt not hear?
> Shall I cry out to thee suffering violence, and thou wilt
> not save? Why hast thou shown me iniquity and griev-
> ance? Everywhere there is strife, and clamorous discord.
> And the Lord answered me, and said:
> Write down the vision upon the tablets, that he that
> readeth it may run.

For as yet the vision is far off, and it shall appear at the end, and it shall not lie.
If it makes any delay, wait for it, for it shall surely come, and it shall not be late.
Behold, he that is unbelieving, his soul shall not be right in himself, but the just shall live in his faith."

I love God Himself telling us to write down the vision. That is what this journal is: a place to write it down. And I like the idea that when I do not have faith, my soul shall not be right in itself, but that the just shall live in His faith. That says just about everything important.

My favorite Psalm is 120:

"I have lifted up my eyes to the mountains, from whence help shall come to me.
My help is from the Lord, who made heaven and earth..."

I love the idea of being able to look up to mountains and see a meeting place between heaven and earth. Of course, that does not happen much around here. Gorin and its environs are very flat indeed. But someday, I hope to see mountains, and I am as certain as I am of my own name that I would feel able to lift mine eyes and see God's strength.

It would be better if I had an idea of how and where that could come to pass, but maybe this is all I need to do right now. I am, after all, writing down the vision upon the tablets. My dream is to see mountains. And to feel God's presence there as if in His own holy temple.

There's the vision, Lord. I will be just, and right in my soul, and wait for You to show me the specifics of how to do that.

Lillie

Lillie was always my favorite playmate and willing to be involved in anything I suggested, as I tried to be to her. But she didn't understand me when I complained about how nice our life was.

"I like nice things," she'd say, complacently. "Like my new pearl ring. Don't you like my ring, Dona?"

I would tell her that I did. But I realized early on she and I simply didn't share the same nature. She liked nice things, true enough. But she didn't wonder. She didn't wonder what it would be like to live in dire circumstances, or not have clean water, or any water. In short, she didn't wonder what she was made of.

Whereas that was never far from my mind. Sometimes after reading a powerful book about a young boy or man who survived something extreme, I would slip out the back door and lose myself in Papa's cucumber fields, out past where I could be seen from the house. I would rage, I would pound my knees and jump up and down and cry. I would hate being a girl, being a girl from a good family, being well fed and stuck in a town with gas lamps.

All this was made worse by the fact that as a child, I was afraid of pretty much everything. Except bugs; I felt sorry for bugs, so small and vulnerable. Lillie would scream at a spider, and shudder. She'd take a wide step to avoid a worm after rain. But she navigated daily life without pause.

Thunderstorms made me shake. I feared waking to find the house engulfed in flames from lightning. Bad dreams sent me fleeing into my parents' room, at which point Mutter furiously sent me just as quickly back the other way. I was afraid of loud boys in school who sometimes chased us as we walked home. I was afraid of being kidnapped, afraid of someone fainting or angry boys getting into a fight.

I suppose another kind of girl would have pushed the boundaries of a nice life to find adventure. Another kind of girl might have gotten matches from the kitchen and set different things on fire to see how they burned—I was terrified even letting a match burn down too close to my fingers, lighting a lamp. I always wanted to be strong enough, tough enough. But I was certain I would be tried and found wanting. Still, that never stopped the deep desire to find out what I was made of.

I'd had no way of knowing about this aspect of life with Carl when I met him. But I believed, especially once we got to Oak Creek, that God wasn't asleep on His watch. He knew even before Carl and I met, that with him I would have a chance to answer some of those questions that had plagued me since I could remember. I would find out, in some ways, how strong I was.

Carl took a little getting to know, but I think I sensed right away he was different than Alf Boltz and certainly different than Loring.

Loring. If I could go back in time and change one thing about my life without changing the rest of it, it would be to return to Gorin when I was 18 and whisper in my young ear that Loring Johnson wasn't worth wasting a thought on, and someday it would all be clear.

But would I have believed me? Believed anyone? No one knows things as firmly as the young. And a girl's heart is stronger than any muscle a young man is so proud of. Loring may have been shallow and vain and fickle, but he was certainly charismatic.

Loring

I *feel I've been transported to another planet, and it's just like Earth, only perfect!*
Loring walked me home.

Me, dark-eyed Dona, the dolorous one. Except he didn't see me that way; he saw me as a sable-haired Madonna, an enigmatic woman who makes (he said) the blonde beauties of Gorin seem like mindless bubbles. He said that! He is so urbane. So polished. So unlike all the boys I know. He even is scented of tobacco. (Not that he smells of it.)

Loring was here again. He brought a book, with a poem he'd been telling me about. He had mentioned it when he walked me home from a tutoring session I'd done the day before yesterday. (Poor little Carole White has no gift at all for French, and her mewling pronunciation needs all my patience and fortitude.) Anyway, Loring had mentioned wanting to linger in the arbor with me, but said he would not dare... like the rogue in the poem about gambling.

I wasn't familiar with the poem, so he brought it by. It's a bit raw for a young lady to read, but of course I adored it! It's about a girl named Fanny with Cupid:

"...beneath the silent moon's soft beams,
in fragrant flowery arbor,
that noted gambling house it seems
where players love to harbor."

It unspools a tale in which Fanny wins from Cupid smiles and looks, and feels quite superior. Then the tone changes to warning:

"Beware sweet girl, and go no more to midnight arbors rambling,
But think how soon you may deplore the dreadful end of gambling.
Sly Cupid has but played the knave, and let you come off winner;
This is the way all gamblers have with every new beginner.
Some satyr soon will with you sport, by Cupid's malice sent hence,
Win all your winnings and leave naught but sorrow and repentance."

I think it's so noble of Loring to warn that men cannot always be trusted with maids. It only shows how good and honest he is. And he said two things that took my breath away. We were standing by the front door, and he was staring so intently at me I asked what was wrong. (I feared I had a string of spittle on my cheek or something.) He apologized for staring, then said, "I was just trying to see what you will look like when you are old. I hope I am with you to find out."

It was bold, but so sincere! And then, he said, as he was leaving, "Being with you, Dona, is like drinking from the Fountain of Youth. I could walk to Boston right now just to bring you a chocolate, I feel so strong and ready."

It was a whimsical thought, and he expressed it in that light tone with his blue eyes wrinkling at the corners. I feel so dreamy now, thinking of him so affected by me.

It's humbling, and yet it makes me feel so powerful.

May 10, 1895

Loring walked me home from the Harpers' house just now; it's their wedding anniversary and we had stopped to pay our respects. He was, as usual, the center of attention, but in a quiet way. He fetched punch for the dowagers, played with the toddlers, and even picked up a baby from the adoring mother's lap every so often, walking about as if unaware he was doing anything unusual. Still, all the men seemed to admire him. He has no idea what it's like to be the rest of us; how much brighter he shines.

May 16, 1895

Only now do I think I have the fortitude to examine what happened with Loring.

Has it been four days, since he walked me home from the Temperance meeting? I want to darkly surmise I should have known something dire was pending; I was floating on clouds of well-being and merriment, with a languorous belief in the power of youth and beauty.

Poppycock.

I was wearing my white tucked shirtwaist with a new skirt, and my spring hat. Some years I think a group of fashion conspirators in Paris snicker into their modish sleeves, trying to make us swallow hard and pretend enthusiasm for what comes out. But this year, the wide brims and delicate decorations have been pure pleasure. Instead of finding a hat that will do, it was figuring out which ones you could stand to live without.

Anyway, Loring was waiting after the meeting to walk me home. I didn't count on seeing him, but I was delighted, and felt clever, telling about the meeting in a way that made him laugh: describing the oratory fervor of some of the older members, and the impassioned argument over whether language was crucial. (Phrases like "small beer," "new wine into old casks" and such cause incendiary debate, between women who claim the First Amendment of the United States

Constitution allows language in any form, and those who maintain that anyone who permits even talk of distilled spirits or malt beverages in her presence defiles the group as a whole.)

Loring was at his most charming. He stopped under a gaslight to tell me that while he was waiting for the meeting to end, he was wondering what I look like when I sleep.

"I decided it was impossible to guess," he said. "I'll have to make sure I'm with you someday to see for myself."

I couldn't answer, but I'm sure my eyes shouted imploringly, "Truly? Truly so?"

Oh, to look back now and wonder where it began. Was I too demure? Too forward? Too eager? Too cold?

Loring kissed me. We got to our corner, where the hedge blocks direct sight of the porch and first floor windows, and he stopped and tilted my chin up. (Even now, writhing in the rest of the memory, that moment remains delightful.)

I didn't know what to do—all the foolish practice kissing one another's wrists we did in finishing school was a complete waste of time. But I kissed him as best I thought, and his arms came around me. I could have melted. I felt warm, liquid, dazed, utterly womanly and perfect.

But. I scarcely can make myself pursue this. I am not sure why I'm even bothering, except that writing is a cleansing kind of thing to do, and sometimes later on, looking back, angles and ideas occur. And it's a confessional.

Well, Loring moved his hands. Around my sides. At first I thought—I don't know, I thought he was going to turn me around in his arms or something, and I didn't pull away immediately.

But then I could tell he knew exactly what he was doing. Instantly, of course, I was sickened and horrified. I pushed him away, and fled inside. I washed and washed, and I cleaned my mouth. But I still felt upset, and tangled inside. I can never see him again. I'm too embarrassed, and I am furious at him for doing something that means I can never see him again. What was he thinking?

Mrs. Bettincourt had told us at a Temperance meeting about pictures in saloons; great murals of women without any clothes, just little teasing scraps of drapery. Loring must have been in a saloon sometime! Otherwise, how could he have known what he was even feeling for?

Doldrums

July 19, 1895

How terribly dull everything seems.

Oh, Loring, why couldn't you be the man I see in you? Why couldn't you strain just a bit, try a little, to be that glorious person? Instead, you're a bit too cheap, too fast, too involved in what feels good to you, at the expense of whomever has fallen under your spell.

I feel numb. I go through the motions of dressing, arranging my hair, with brief shooting memories of how it felt when everything was suffused with magic light; when I might see Loring at any hour. Now, that light has gone out, and in the greyness I can't find anything to take joy in.

I just want to be back in time, when he was still unbelievable, and I was the luckiest girl in Missouri.

I've cried, some, but mostly there's just a heaviness, a pall, a boredom that bleeds into grief. I don't know what I would do if I could repeat the past few months; I don't think I could have changed him. I certainly won't try now. If he'd wanted to be different, he would have. I'm just so disappointed that this was not the future intended to be mine. I was breathing moonbeams, feeling so precious and special. And now I am of no value, because I am of no value to him.

At least that's how it feels.

1950

Our friend Travois swore men never lied. By that he meant that whatever they said, they meant it at the time they were saying it. So if Travois was to be believed, Loring had not been maliciously playing games with me, shredding my feelings for sport; nor was he an evil rake and rapscallion. He was just a very young man, immersing himself deep in a feeling that was fairly shallow, like almost drowning in a two-inch puddle, until you turn your head and shake yourself off and go on to something else.

And of course, go on to something else he did. He went on to Lillie. Who naturally, instinctively, superbly knew how to handle him as she did everything else; she laughed off my fumbling and awkward warning that he might be brash or forward with, "Mercy, Dona, any woman can handle that!" Except me, obviously—again, not a worthy woman.

In any case, anyone would have preferred Lillie, or I thought so at the time. Lillie was me, only better; more comfortable in her own life. She put on a hat without even looking, somehow simply knowing the exact geometric angle the brim should cast against her shaded right side, whereas I would have to study my reflection, turning back and forth, pushing the hat an inch this way, a half-inch that, until I finally gave up and settled for wherever it was when I grew tired of the effort and realized it would make no discernible difference anyway.

Lillie Miller in Gorin, MO

If Lillie'd been in town when Loring first appeared at the Community Oratory Spring Program, I'd not have even had the weeks I had. But she'd gotten to go stay with Minnie, who then took her to St. Louis; Minnie, being respectably married to George by then, didn't require a chaperone. So my sisters were staying in a hotel with steam heat, and seeing "H.M.S. Pinafore" performed by a repertory company after an elegant tea somewhere. I'd been wistful when they left. But meeting Loring, his eyes brimming with both intelligence and merriment, I hadn't been wistful any more.

Loring didn't just court me; he courted my parents. After standing the respectful amount of time when introduced (I found out later he asked Noah to perform the introduction after he saw us come in together—what admirable confidence and quick thinking), he held my hand just a whisper longer than the appropriate amount of time and gave it up with a look of actual regret. We exchanged only a few sentences before he asked make the acquaintance "of the angels, or whoever, who brought you to this earth." And so I introduced him to Papa and Mutter.

Those first few weeks before Lillie returned were like living in Paradise. Everything glimmered around the edges. Instead of feeling like "that little bug-eyed Donie Miller," I felt like a different woman. I became the woman Loring said he saw when he looked at me. My eyes were dark pools of mystery instead of bug eyes. I floated rather than walked; my lips looked so soft he feared they'd crumble, his hands ached to wrap themselves up in my hair. And even my voice, which I thought unremarkable, registered in the bottom of his spine at the same time as in his ears. He recreated me, and in that image I was beautiful.

But maybe nothing like that can last. People describe the Northern Lights as unforgettable...their floating shifting patterns and colors in the night sky burn behind your eyelids so that you never forget them; they take your breath away and humble you. That's how I felt about Loring. And later, when it was even darker for those mystical lights having vanished, I would wonder: If the Northern Lights are so electrifying, but so fleeting and undependable, did maturity mean giving up the idea of that marvelous feeling? Maybe grown-up love was not like that. Maybe if Loring was the Northern Lights, I should instead look for a lantern.

The writing was on the wall even before Lillie came home; no one knew her better than I. And while I tried not to, I knew that just as she always had to be the first to pick from the new ribbons, the one to implore most vigorously for the icing rose from the top of the cake, Lillie would see Loring and Lillie would decide to get Loring, and I may as well try to persuade the wind to blow from the east instead of the west. Loring would be hers.

The details don't matter; how innocently she said she'd never try to take him away from me; how she resisted even looking at him except from the corner of her eye, then acted so surprised when he pursued her; how she nobly, beautifully, tragically assured him with a trembling lower lip she could never bring herself to hurt me. Loring fell hard. Only after I'd already seen them together did he send a quick note: "So sorry. We moved a little quickly. I know you're better off without me." That was it. He came calling for her and greeted me like an old friend. I would go upstairs after letting him in and look at the line of my neck he'd admired, and wonder why on earth he had to bother. It was a dull ache that never lifted, for weeks. I took a lot of walks that year. I prayed for forbearance. I kept remembering I wasn't the dark beauty Loring had made me feel I might actually be: I was just a diversion before the real beauty got home.

Say what you will about loving and losing—it's a hard lesson we all must learn. I lost more than Loring; also a trusting belief that good would be met with good, virtue rewarded. I found out Fate is a capricious creature who can't be trusted, and who can be bought with beguiling ways. (Not that Lillie was ever just beguiling. She was also vibrant, laughing, clever, loving, dramatic—she had every weapon in the arsenal when it came to anything on the field of love. If I'd been Loring, I'd have been besotted with her, too.)

What a taste of dust that whole episode left in my mouth. I thought getting away from seeing all the places he'd been associated with every day would be good, so I decided to put my teaching certificate to use. Even if I was heartbroken, I could still be productive. So I applied for teaching positions nearby and got one in Rutledge; six miles is just far enough away not to see everyone I know all the time but close enough not to be homesick. I boarded with the Paulsens and taught lower grades for the spring semester. It was like playing a part; like being someone else. Miss Miller has no problems; the whole town doesn't feel sorry for Miss Miller…or, the whole town isn't laughing at Miss Miller.

But knowing that the Northern Lights could never be mine—and that I was a fool for wanting them—made things almost unbearably grey. Why yearn for love, if it's a lantern instead of splendid skylights? So if the giddy floating feelings were wrong, true love must be dependable. But how could true love be dull? I now found girlhood fantasies naïve and pitiable. But without them, there was just a straight horizon with nothing interesting on it. The whole time I was teaching up in Washington County, I moved as if underwater. Then I came home because Lola was not well. Of course, I had no way of knowing what lay ahead.

Vigil

*W*ell, *I feel about as useful as a third eye on a sparrow. School has started, but I don't fit into it anywhere. I'm back home. Today I was the one who made the lunches and filled the pails, sending the younger ones off for their day. I didn't accept any out-of-town teacher positions.*

I don't want to leave right now, with Lola feeling so poorly, but I will fill in for any teachers here in town who may need me for a day now and again. I wish they could figure out what to do about Lola! She's been given oxblood remedies and tinctures of herbs and nothing seems to plump her up. She's a love of a girl, but listless. She watches more than she does anything else. It must break Mutter's heart not to be able to fix her. I hope I'm not always as superfluous to the grand design as I am today.

Tomorrow is the New Year, and I want to write tonight so that I can make a fresh beginning. I have not wanted to think, let alone write, for the longest time. It has been the most difficult month.

Little Lola died 29 days ago.

I can hardly bear to put the words down. Mutter was so quiet, so still, even when Minnie took the baby girl gently out of her arms and carried her tiny body down to wash her for the last time and lay her out. Mutter simply sat by the cradle (Lola never did outgrow it) where she'd been holding Lola, crooning to her. Lola seemed to breathe better on Mutter's lap. But she'd never gotten terribly strong, or pink. She smiled beatifically, at all of us, but didn't talk; as if it were too much effort. The doctor came every day that final week, and neighbors started gathering. They reminded me of vultures, waiting for an animal to die, even though I knew the women were being kind. I was not angry at them, but angry that Lola could die.

The sadness that followed was good because it put a blanket over my fiery jealous feelings. Lillie has been walking out with Loring since they met. I didn't know at first, because she didn't want me to. She and I have never talked about what happened, and I shrink to imagine what Loring may have told her: that her spinster sister got upset over nothing? Over time they became so constant I had to see them. Then at Thanksgiving he came for dinner.

That was bad. Just plain bad. No adjective will do. I wonder, with something like pride, how I got through that meal. But after that, somehow, it became easier. I suppose I accepted it. And by then, Lola was wasting.

So here we are, on the threshold of another year. I wonder what 1896 will bring. I will have a position at the school after the holidays, teaching the third and fourth levels grammar and spelling. Also included in my duties are grading essays for the older students' teachers, and helping in the office during the afternoon. I am proud I will be bringing home a salary.

Mostly I feel resigned. Patient. But not in a dried-up spinsterish way. There's actually some peace, some beauty, in not expecting more than the night will bring.

I have a warm bed, with clean blankets. I am living with my family, where love and courage and effort are prized. I am fortunate to be in America, I know.

It almost alarms me to be content. But I think this year, while hard, has been a good experience. When I was feeling so bereft about Loring, I was able to spell Mutter with Lola, and be of value. I learned that even if my heart is breaking, I could still be of use. Once I accepted the bad feeling *as inevitable, like a limp or smallpox scars would be, I learned to live with in. And I do believe scars fade over time.*

So tonight, Lord, I am thankful. Hold dear Lola always close to you, and help Mutter continue to mend. Thank you for Minnie's brood nearby to cheer her and distract her. Thank you for Noah, who stopped yesterday on the way out to tell me he admired how strong I've become for the family.

Thank you for another year. Help me, in the twilight of this one, to realize Your promise of new dawn includes what we cannot see, still in darkness. I wonder what I will be writing about at the end of 1896.

Feb. 24, 1896

Happy birthday, Sedona Arabella!

The third level class sang to me today—Edna must have told someone at school I'm 19 years old now. Mutter left gifts by my breakfast plate: a new shirtwaist, embroidered just in white, the way I like; a beautiful pen, and some combs with honey-colored bars on them.

Tonight we will have cake. I believe Edward and Minnie and their families will come over.

In the meantime, it's a fine thing to be 19: a woman grown, with health and noble work and sisters with which to share life's walks and meals. I feel I'm growing inside, somehow, getting more grateful. Like the bulbs that come up in the spring: one day there's that first slender green shoot, and we all exclaim as if it just happened, when actually throughout the winter that bulb's been turning, laboriously, in the cold hard ground, to push against the force of dark dirt so that it can reach light and air. I feel like the unseen growing flower; still in the dark, but knowing spring's promise.

T.C. Schnebly

1950

It was then I met Carl. I'd gone to a WCTU meeting, and there was a simmering undercurrent of excitement over three brothers who had moved from Kahoka to open a hardware store—the first two friends I met there started with, "Did you hear?" So when Papa asked if I wanted to go with him to pick up a few things there, I said yes.

"Schnebly Hardware" was on the raw new sign hanging over what had been Clanton's Dry Goods (Mr. Clanton having died and Mrs. Clanton having moved to St. Louis to live with their oldest daughter). We went in and there was a long pale wood counter, built almost all the way down in front of a side wall, and standing behind it, a man. I was going to say young man, but he didn't look callow. He just looked…nice. I found out later the other two Schneblys (and what an amusing sound that had to me!) were out on the sales floor, as they called it, helping customers.

So while the man behind the counter read the list of things Papa needed, I watched him. He seemed very calm, not overly anxious to please. Just friendly and interested. His eyes smiled when Papa said something, and then he gave a little chuckle; too deep to be a laugh, but pleasant.

This was Carl. Mel and Frank were the other two, but I wouldn't know their names for some time. I wandered among the few notions left over from the former dry goods store and covertly examined all three men to see which of my friends might like which brother. Frank looked handsomest. Mel was dark and taller. I didn't think Carl would be anyone's favorite. Nothing remarkable there.

It wasn't until school closed for the year that I saw any of them again, and that was at our church supper. By now I'd learned that they were on societal probation for being predestination, so they came to our Methodist church only because there wasn't a Presbyterian one in Gorin. People seemed to be waiting to decide if they were going to see the light and openly convert or not.

Carl behind counter at Schnebly Hardware, Gorin, MO

When we arrived at the supper, Mel was walking out with a girl who had moved to town recently. Frank and Carl were talking together, and I saw Carl look up when I came in. I was mildly pleased that he continued to watch me. There was a quiet strength to him, and I don't mean physically, although you couldn't move heavy things about and not be able-bodied. It was more of an internal strength. Like nothing confused him.

I suppose since I'd been teaching, he felt I was an adult and approached me without seeking an introduction.

"You won't remember me," he began, but I said, "But I do," and then realized I had no idea what his name was. "Except I don't know your name," I added.

"Theodore Carlton Schnebly," he said. "But Carl is fine."

"I'm Sedona Arabella Miller," I replied. "And Dona will do."

He bowed, courtly and also rather making fun of the gesture.

I've wondered since what we spoke about that evening. I have never remembered. What I do remember is feeling completely comfortable; I can probably count on one hand how many times I've felt that way speaking to a new acquaintance. And it continued, when Carl began calling.

Finally I realized something good about the whole Loring experience; it gave me something to compare Carl to. Loring talked. He was amusing, irreverent, ardent, certain. Carl asked questions. When I said I wrote every day after lunch, he wanted to know what I wrote about. He asked how my day was going, and wanted a real answer. He seemed completely at ease just being there. Loring always seemed to need applause, or at least appreciation. Carl needed nothing from me. Nor from anyone else, as far as I could see. Business wasn't brisk, and he even said he thought it might have something to do with the Schneblys being Presbyterian, but he didn't seem bothered. "People should shop where they're comfortable," was all he said.

July 4, 1896

What a wonderful Independence Day celebration!

We go every year; we have for as long as I can remember. But this one was particularly fine. The parade seems to have come into its own: instead of a few feeble floats with paper chains, today's had lots of decorated buggies, wagons with children in darling costumes, and of course, the veterans. God bless them. I always have to blink very fast when they come by, so proud, even though no longer so straight or so strong, many of them. I always end up wiping away tears. What they must have been through, I will never know. But we don't need to know the details to recognize the valor. The town cheers like a house afire for those gallant men, some in uniform.

The lemonade was cold and sweet; the ice cream velvety smooth and rich with strawberry. There were sausage rolls and egg salad and lots of berry pies. And Carl was by my side.

Courtship

*C*arl came to call!
   I didn't think he would because I didn't see him at church, but we were finishing setting the dining room to rights after lunch when Goldie came running in to say a man was here to see Miss Dona. I stopped in the front hall and made sure my hair was loose enough to be flattering. I wore a new waist today, intricately tucked all across the front, in the palest spring green. As I had hoped, it was Carl, looking at the portraits of Mutter and Papa in the parlor.

   "Do you feel like they're watching you when you're in here?" he asked when I entered. He smiles so gently. There is such stability in him. He isn't terribly tall, but he's strong, with a straight back and square hands and well-set shoulders. He looks like he walks balanced on the earth. I offered him refreshment, and asked why I hadn't seen him at church.

   Well, a little wrinkle in what could be a harmonious acquaintance: he isn't planning to become a Methodist. I don't know much about Presbyterianism, but I know it isn't Methodism. Papa would have kittens hearing I entertained an unrepentant Presbyterian this afternoon. (I will confess only here that I don't give a fig myself. Certainly it's important to believe in God, and to live by the Golden Rule and the Bible, but I think there's room for the idea that we make decisions in our lives. God knows what they will be, and gives us the intelligence to do so, but I think it's arrogant to assume we know exactly how much God plans. I mean, did He pick this color shirtwaist, or did I? And if I know all our necessities and luxuries are through His bounty, does it matter?)

Anyway, I was a little concerned, so I made him identify a few Bible verses, as if I were playing a game. He is excellent at it. He says being predestination Presbyterian just means knowing that since time began, God has known everything that is going to happen. Since it says in the Bible he's known every hair on our heads since before we were born, I don't see a problem with this.

He told me a bit about his family, because I asked him to. His great-grandfather, a doctor, came from Switzerland before the Revolution! Their family still owns the plantation Dr. Henry Schnebly built in Maryland, called the Garden of Eden.

"But you wouldn't think of that name if you were there during mosquito season," he said. He had malaria as a boy when his family lived there. He told me that he was partially reared by a freed slave, whom he admired greatly. "His name was Boyle. Washington County, where the family plantation is, was Union. At the beginning of the conflict, my father and grandfather freed all their slaves and gave them land." He said some of those who remained took the Schnebly name. (I told him my father had been wounded fighting on the Union side as well. He expressed his sympathy.)

It makes me happy to hear that a freed slave played a significant role in his early life. We all say, "all men are created equal," (which doesn't mention women!) but many people feel their equality to be of a higher status than some others' equality. So a man who saw many of his early smiles in a dark face truly does see all people as deserving of respect.

Carl has two sisters and four brothers (and more who died too young). He says he is closest to Ellsworth, whose first name is actually Dorsey, even though his brother Mel was born between them. Carl's first name is Theodore. I asked why they use their middle names, and he said he'd never thought about it, and doesn't know. Mel is actually Jacob Melvin. But then it changes—Will is actually William Francis. Why did they reverse the pattern on the last one? Again, he never wondered. I swear, men are so very different. He went to Kahoka College. He said it was fun, with all the other men in classes going on hunting parties, although some acted a little wild.

T.C. (Carl) Schnebly, center, with Kahoka College graduating class

But he has never taken strong spirits, or smoked. He doesn't like coffee. When he had malaria, the doctor told his mother to put the quinine they had to give him in coffee. "So now if I even smell coffee, I can almost taste the quinine." I was happy to be able to tell him I never make coffee. Then I confessed I don't drink much tea, either. I prefer hot water. A little lemon in it is nice if there's some around, but hot water is fine. I was surprised I was telling a man that. But Carl feels more like a friend, albeit a handsome one, than "a man."

It was so easy to talk with him. I didn't feel like it was a courting visit, very tense. I felt very comfortable, and made him laugh, and asked many questions. When he was leaving, he said, "You are the easiest person to talk to I have ever met!" That made me feel special.

I'm glad he came. He has a strength of character that is a combination of courtesy and courage. I vow, he would have wonderful children.

But he won't fall in love with me. That wouldn't be fair, because I won't do that anymore. Still, I will be curious to meet his sweetheart someday, and she had better be very good to him!

July 27, 1896

Each time I see Carl, I admire him more. I found out today he's a full eight years older than I am!

I knew he seemed more mature than most of my friends, but I didn't realize that until I saw some papers he was filling out for the hardware store. It had his birthday: December 29, 1868. I wonder if this December I'll know him well enough to give him a birthday gift.

Aug. 8, 1896

Saw Carl tonight. Sometimes I can go downtown for a bit of ribbon or on an errand for Mutter, and be nearby when he gets done at the hardware store. He walks me home then. It's a ritual I believe we both secretly anticipate, but we've never risked acknowledging it is more than happenstance by saying so.

I'm glad he is a college graduate. It's a fine thing when a family values education like that. He seems proud that I completed the Gorin Academy, and can teach. I do enjoy it. Although I don't believe I want to do it my whole life.

1950

This proves once again Carl is a very smart man. Reading these pages as an adult has been fascinating, and lets me see my upbringing differently. In the Miller house, everyone was constantly being judged. People were either like us, and we approved of them, or they did things we would not have done, and we didn't approve. Every action, every belief, was rated good enough or falling short. With Carl, I always felt good enough, merely by breathing. It felt wonderful; I wanted to keep that feeling.

Carl had told me during one of our early talks that he grew up knowing his first spoken words had been, "Mother's tired." He was apparently watching her move ceaselessly about, embroiled in all the tasks a young family demanded. She told him those had been his first words because she praised him for his thoughtfulness. "I guess if one of my brothers dropped their candy, I would give him mine," he said. "It was much more fun to see him look happy than to have a sweet."

That goodness, that essential desire to make sure everyone around him was happy, was beyond anything I'd ever seen. His caring for me seeped into me and healed something, until I never wanted to be away from him for very long. We saw one another every weekend all that summer. I felt my life was turning in a wide curve, focused on another future, in another direction. When I wasn't with Carl, I was often thinking about him; about how his eyes crinkled at the corners when he smiled at me, about how strong his wrists looked when he was unpacking something at the store. I thought about the scent of him: clean cotton, sunshine, and a touch of dust. And I didn't just think about Carl; I thought about me.

Because, as much as I found Carl himself a wonder, how he saw me made me see myself differently. I wasn't just shy and awkward and worst of all, Not Lillie. I was Sedona, or Dona, as he called me. I was no longer just defined as the sister who fell short, as I always had been in the family and in Gorin: I was an entire separate person who remembered quotations and liked words and had a nice voice (so Carl held). For the first time, I felt pretty enough. Carl didn't go on about my looks as Loring had. But the way he looked at me was even better.

Carl found out fairly early on about my writing; I don't remember what I mentioned, something he'd said that I'd written down. He swooped in on that like a bird, seeing movement in the grass from far away. He wanted to understand the process. I'd never really thought about it before, and his interest humbled and touched me.

"I guess...if something happens that matters to me, I think it deserves to exist forever. Maybe it has some value to someone else; maybe it simply gets honored by being recorded. I wonder if we are all given certain experiences and memories, like puzzle pieces that are part of the whole world's picture of itself. And if we don't contribute them somehow, share them—I don't quite know what I mean, but if we don't all contribute what we've learned, I suppose... maybe the picture is less complete."

He took my hand, and looked at me, and smiled a little, and shook his head.

"What?"

(Once I heard a woman describe her husband as a "Fire...aim... ready!" kind of person. Carl is the opposite of that. He can look at you, and think, unafraid of making you wait; just searching his thoughts and making sure they're lined up as what he wants to say before he speaks.)

"I just didn't know someone could see the world in so many ways I don't, before I met you. It's an honor when you share how you see it with me."

If I wasn't in love with him already, that clinched it. I can still hear his voice saying those words...and I think I've been able to every day since he said them.

So without even trying, surely and completely and easily, I got over Loring. I understood how infatuation and love might not always share space. I not only healed, I thanked God for what He brought me. And I realized I'd been wrong about the choices being between the Northern Lights and a lantern. There was a third option: the moon. Carl was the moon. As dependable now as in the earliest days of life, 28 days throught, no matter what. And also mysterious and beautiful and com-pelling—not ever mundane. It's powerful enough to govern tides, and also full of variety in how it appears: golden, silver, pendulous, fragile. Not a lantern, dull and dependable; not Northern Lights, fleeting and fickle: a constant, compelling source of light.

Then, just as I was starting to think about marrying Carl, Lillie radiantly announced her engagement, and Mutter was counting pillow-slips and serving pieces with her as if never before had a young woman wed.

So Loring wasn't done causing me trouble. Not on purpose; he never seemed to think about me at all, turning that dazzling but perfectly polite smile my direction if I passed through a room where he and Lillie were murmuring and laughing.

Loring had proposed to Lillie, which made Carl's and my relationship look all the worse to my parents. To them, Loring was perfect: bright smile, ingratiating manners (right down to just a touch of over-familiarity with Mutter, which she relished like a confection), sharp dresser, with dancing, language and joke-telling skills. Compared to him, Carl was…plain. Carl didn't try. Carl just was. That, of course, was why I loved him: he was sincere to his bones. He wasn't out to impress anyone; just working to be the best person he could and live the most useful and helpful life possible. How could Mutter not see that?

I think in part she had never gotten over the idea of being the belle, and Loring's sharp eye for seeing what people wanted gave him a golden key. He flattered her, he praised her, he compared her to Lillie. She didn't quite simper, but she came uncomfortably close to it. Carl wasn't a smooth talker and he didn't want to be. I remember early on after a discussion about a book (he was a reader, which pleased me), he said words had their uses, but judging people wasn't one of them.

"Words are good for explaining, but explaining things, not people," he said. "You can explain how weather works, or how to assemble a gun. You can even explain, sometimes, what makes a woman pretty. But you can't explain character; it's easy to speak high words, but getting up to meet them is another thing.

"A man's measure isn't taken with what he says he wants to do, but with what he does. Look at politics; those fellows can talk so beautifully you expect them to rise up on harp music. But look at their actions and tell me if you'd trust them to see you home."

So Carl wasn't competing to be the favored suitor. He cheerfully left that to Loring, and both Loring and Lillie basked in the status of being the Golden Couple.

Had Papa been married to someone else all those years, he might have seen it. But as Lillie and I were growing up, we came to see that Mutter ruled the household, and was wise enough never to point it out...as long as Papa let her rule it. (It's funny, because his long moustache and heavy eyebrows make him look so stern.) But he let her set the tone for things, and would disappear behind his paper if something touchy came up. It was interesting: if he came out with an opinion during dinner that surprised her, her eyebrows would shoot up and he'd look startled, then furtive, and stare at his plate. Later that evening, if you walked into the hall, you'd hear her low tones as she told him what they both thought about something. And sure enough, next morning he'd tell us all what he'd "meant" to say.

I was glad Carl had such convictions about doing right. I would never want a man who could be led or steered as Papa was. He actually seemed more comfortable talking to Carl than he was talking to Loring, but Mutter would have none of it. The united front decreed that Loring was good. And that Carl was lacking.

Then one day after Lillie and I had both announced our engagements, Mutter came home looking like a naughty child who just had to brag about what she'd done. She was elaborately casual:

"Someone downtown...oh, it doesn't matter who, so don't ask me... but someone said that Phillip Miller is going to be getting 100 sons-in-law." She widened her eyes as if to say, "how could that be?' and continued. "They said, 'Loring is one, and Carl is double zeroes.' Can you believe that? One and double zeroes is 100!"

And she made her mistake: she laughed. A proud laugh. As you would about something you created, not overheard.

I walked out of the room, and upstairs. That was the beginning of the end for me. It's one thing to disapprove; we can't always change our feelings. But to be so gleeful about calling my choice, my love, my future out as naught? Too much—far too much. From then on, I didn't feel guilty for letting her down. I felt angry. So very angry that I began to think we had to get away, Carl and I. Staying would be like trying to start a garden in a coal scuttle; the sun could never reach the growing things.

So it wasn't even really a surprise when one evening after dinner Papa asked me to stay at the table. He looked miserable. And Mutter said grandly, "Tell Sedona what you've decided, dear."

Well, this didn't sound good. But what had he decided—my left foot, he never decided anything that I knew about. So when he said, "If you really do intend to marry that young man and abandon our faith, I won't be able to keep you in my will," in a flat expressionless tone like he'd memorized it and just had to get it out quickly, I actually felt a moment of sympathy for him. We were both Mutter's pawns, Papa and I. Except for one major difference: Papa had lived his entire life this way. I had a second chance. I could leave. I was leaving.

After that it was easy to shut her out of wedding plans. I made my dress without consulting her; it was amusing how curious she was about it, but it would snow in the pantry before she'd let herself ask. Lillie was my attendant, and we married at the church on a Wednesday morning. Not just any Wednesday morning, but my twentieth birthday. Carl's brother Ellsworth had come home from his travels to stand up with him, and it was fun to spend some time with him. (He would become a very important part of our lives, although I didn't know how important at the time.) I did know that after the wedding breakfast, I simply wouldn't go home.

Marriage

*M*y *wedding day.*
My last morning under this roof.
And my 20th birthday.
Mostly, my wedding day.

I don't think I ever truly believed this would happen. Oh, I dreamed of the white knight and all. But I feared, because I am dark-looking, that if ever I managed to get married, it would be to some perspiring widower who talked Papa into a handsome dowry to take the embarrassing spinster daughter off his hands.

Instead...my wedding is my 20th birthday present.

So soon I will put on my new opal silk, and Lillie will button me up the back, and dress in her pretty lavender, and we will go together down the stairs, and to the minister's study, where Ellsworth will stand up with Carl and we will be united forever as man and wife!

I suppose it would be nice if it were the social event of the season, and buggies were parked for blocks, and there was a crab and ice cream supper at a grand hotel afterwards. But that isn't to be. And all of those things wouldn't mean a peppercorn if they didn't include Carl.

Did I even dream, a year ago, that this would be how I began this third decade of my life? That instead of being concerned with perfecting my white sauce or learning a new piano piece, I would be packing my valise and trunk to leave my girlhood home forever...to become wife? It's amazing to me.

I feel terribly anxious. Not about Carl—he is my ally. I am more at home with him than anywhere I've ever been. He is closer to me than my family, already. And we aren't even related yet! But this role of wife I am about to step into, I know nothing about.

What does it mean, really, to go together into that big bedroom at the top of Mrs. Bledsoe's carriage house stairs, and shut the door? Lillie helped do all the embroidery on the yoke of my gown and the light robe to go over it. I like them, so long that I say they fall two inches below the floor, and they are very fine and soft. They will give me confidence. I never felt shy or insecure with Carl, but this will be a very different experience than I've ever had, and it reminds me of my complete lack of coquetry and feminine wiles and all those other things that I suddenly desperately wish for. I know nothing about one of the most important events in my entire life.

I know I love when Carl kisses me. I just wish I knew what comes after that.

Now I actually regret not paying attention when more adventurous friends who had crept out to watch their father's stallion cover a mare and whatnot told us about it afterward in whispered tones. I never cared. It didn't apply to me.

I tried to ask Mutter once years ago, but she looked so uncomfortable I didn't press her beyond her answer that a woman belongs to her husband and nothing he does is wrong. (What does that mean: either that he doesn't pull her hair and make funny faces at her, or that she's supposed to smile politly if he does?) I've listened to her and Mrs. Allen talk when they didn't know I could hear, and they've said things like, "I just picture wallpaper patterns I want in the parlor." I admit I am curious.

But I'm also afraid. I guess as long as I'm with Carl, I don't have to be too afraid. I trust him more than I trust myself.

I've always been called standoffish. I don't throw my arms around every girl I went to school with like we're bosom friends if we meet on the street. I never liked being cuddled up on a lap listening to a story being read by someone; it makes me feel scratchy and nervous. I have been afraid it would always be that way. But it's not with Carl. Carl is like finding the other half of myself. I am very comfortable when he holds my hand and kisses me on the forehead.

By this time tomorrow, I will be Wife. I will know.

Dear God,

This feels so momentous. I wish I knew the best words to write on the last morning of my childhood; on the threshold of my new life. I want to be a wonderful wife to Carl, Lord. I want to give him olive branches around his table and joy in his heart. I want to rise to every occasion and make him proud of me.

But far and away the most important thing: I want to be good enough. I don't want him to be sorry he married me.

March 5, 1897

Carl just left, and I'm still in bed. I can't believe I'm not up washing and cleaning and starting the day. But this feeling is too delicious, and I don't want to step out of it yet.

I used to think women who got married and suddenly acted so condescending and removed were overreacting to a simple thing. A ceremony, a wedding band, and suddenly they were so patronizing! As if they had been included in a fairy ring of secrets that so outshone our meager little lives they could only pity us.

Now I understand. (I will still never act that way.)

To have Carl with me like this: to have our house, our bed, our time… and no one telling us what to do or how to behave. He tickled me last night, chased me all the way up the stairs, and we laughed and shrieked like wild children, half-waiting for someone to sternly rebuke us; for a grownup to come storming in demanding to know what this foolishness was about. But now we're the grownups. We can eat breakfast at midnight if we want to. We can put our shoes on our heads and pretend we're gnomes. And we can lie about in the morning and whisper and play.

Our first evening here, I didn't know what to do, how to act. I know he saw how nervous I was. He smiled.

"Get me your autograph book."

I blinked. Whatever words I imagined were spoken on the night of the nuptials, it wasn't those. I looked at him.

"But you signed it already, right after we met."

(Oh, yes, Dona…that's the most important thing right now.)

"And I want to see it again."

I could lay a hand to it quickly; my possessions were not many. I brought it downstairs, and he opened it and found the page he'd signed before. We looked together at his writing: "Compliments and best wishes, your friend, T.C. Schnebly"

"And now bring me your guest book."

From the same place, I brought down the slim brown leather volume that opened wider than it did tall, which I bought when I deemed autograph books juvenile, and turned it to the current page.

He sat down at the desk and picked up the pen, dipped it in ink, and wrote,

"Feb. 24, 1897

The greatest day of my life.

T.C. Schnebly"

I looked at his face, and shut the book, and then I wasn't nervous anymore.

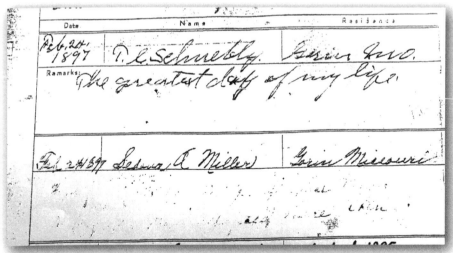

Carl's inscription in Sedona's guest book

I never knew how lonely I was before Carl. I always felt bereft;
even with my family I felt I didn't fit in, that I was odd, somehow.
Carl is my family. He is my ally. He is my exact fit. I knew, some-
how, the first time he held me that I was connected to him in some
deep way I can't even now put into words. He is my other half; he
completes me, and he enhances me. He makes me brave. He sees the
me I want to become, but don't feel I am yet. To him I am beauti-
ful. I feel beautiful with him. My body doesn't feel awkward. I feel
confident and supple. I feel like a mermaid, or some sylvan forest
nymph, purely female.

Why don't Mutter and Papa seem to enjoy one another the way
Carl and I do? (I imagine they don't; surely something would seem
different if they did.) Just too many years, too many disappointments,
too many children? Maybe it's inevitable. But I don't believe that in
my heart. Carl is too wonderful to ever take for granted. I will be
grateful every day for this gentle, strong, laughing man who calls me
his Dona.

Thank You, God, for Carl. Help make me a wonderful wife and
partner to him—a helpmeet, a source of pride and comfort.

I feel like rolling around in bed and just giggling. I guess I'll get
up and act like a wife for awhile. But tonight, he comes home and we
get to be us all over again.

1950

All my private storms leading up to the wedding made it hard to
feel the sense of girlish wonder and romance I had always supposed
would lead up to being wed. But I do want to write down Carl's proposal. I'd assumed, growing up, it would be in front of a parlor fire
with a plate of shortbread on the side table, where a young man (face-
less to my childish dreams) would take to his knee, put his hand over

his heart and declaim his passion and fealty, then ask very humbly if I'd consider making him the happiest man in the world. And I would sweep my eyelashes down and murmur something, and then the family would stream in for laughter and hugs and an evening of song around the piano.

But actually, we were out on a walk, one late afternoon just before Christmas, talking about the hardware store and how difficult it was to attract a robust clientele. Carl said Ellsworth kept writing him about this place out west and how much he wanted Carl to come live there. He described the rich soil making everything grow, blue skies and red rocks (which I couldn't quite figure) and a creek filled with fish. It did sound like a wonderful place. I was feeling a little envious, thinking how nice it must be to be able just to pull up stakes and live somewhere else, when Carl stopped and took my hand.

"Sedona," he said, very seriously; so seriously, I was afraid. He always called me Dona. I thought, with dawning panic, this is when he says he's heading out west and will never forget me. I just stared at him.

"Sedona," he started again. "I want to go west. I want to start something new. I want to see what I can do out there." I was starting to get tears in my eyes so I looked away so he wouldn't see.

"But I don't believe I can ever enjoy anything again if you aren't with me. So will you marry me? Will you come with me to Oak Creek—not right away, but soon—and make it home?"

I went from almost crying to almost laughing, so relieved and surprised and amazed to hear these words. I threw my arms around him (what matter did it make if we were seen? We were leaving!) and said, "Yes, yes. Yes." Then he held up a smooth silver band and said, "I let myself hope—I got it just in case." And we both laughed. And felt the future begin.

Sedona and T.C. (Carl) Schnebly, 1901, Gorin, MO

Expecting

March 7, 1898

*W*hat's the matter with me? This baby could be born any day, and I'm running around like the proverbial chicken— and I don't mean the one crossing the road. I am in a swivet, suddenly determined to have the front room curtains down and blocked and clean this morning. I have conserves bubbling on the stove, all the bedroom furniture pulled out from the walls to do the baseboards. There is an urgency to it that's absurd. But I guess after the baby's born I won't feel like doing any of those things for a while.

March 10, 1898

Ellsworth Miller Schnebly.
Our son.
Dear Lord,
Thank You for this tiny face, so small and perfect. Thank You for the way he flails, like a small innocent animal, and his little mews and stretches, and the shapes he makes with his mouth.

Thank You for how easily Carl took him for the first time, and how sure and large his hands look holding his boy. He was sober, worried about me; he said afterwards, he was sure I was going to die (I never thought I was going to die; I just couldn't believe something could burn so much). But now, here we are, safe and tired and tucked in for the evening, with my warm water to drink and my journal. (I didn't have a taste for milk or food; water is all I think I can handle.)

This baby. I keep wanting another look at his wee eyes, but they are open for so short a time. I am afraid. I thought I knew everything about babies, but now I feel completely blank. What does one do?

We will learn, together, our lad and I. Carl said he thrusts his legs like a tadpole. Little Tad. Our first child.

Tad

*T*ad *is six months old! We've continued calling him that,
because naming him after brother Ellsworth is a nice tribute, but confusing in conversation if our boy went by the same name.
(He's actually six months and nine days—I thought of it on the date
itself, but writing time is like gold.) Right now, our wonder is crawling around here at my feet (which they say is early; he's so smart),
looking so alert and curious, and delighted with himself as well as the
world he finds himself in: carpet with patterns, the fuzzy bear Lillie
brought when he was born—his constant companion he talks to and
laughs at as if he'd gotten an answer, and my skirts.*

*I still marvel that his existence makes me a mother. I wouldn't
have hoped to have a fine son so soon...I was never sure in my heart
I would even get married at all. So to have the husband (due home
soon to an unexpectedly fine meal of pork and wide noodles) and the
child—well, it's almost beyond comprehension.*

*Of course, when one is expecting and the married women are tell-
ing one what will happen, they certainly keep quiet about a great deal.
I will be different. I swear, I will warn my sisters, and anyone else
with whom I feel sufficiently intimate, that a dark discoloured line on
the skin develops down the stomach. Because of the morbid fancies that
come with pregnancy, I wondered if it was something gone horribly
wrong; maybe some literal bloodline carrying the baby's nourishment
away. (They also don't warn the girl approaching motherhood that she
will become a dervish, a viper, an idiot, an orphan, a blank slate and
a crowded attic all at the same time.)*

I will tell girls that after the joyous event of gazing upon that tiny face for the first time, there are weeks of leaking from every possible orifice of one's body. (I don't know how I would say that, but it would have helped me so much to know that I will try.) I will warn them that when sleep is scarce, it becomes a highly prized commodity, and that I have a constant abacus in my head. It tallies how many hours I have had to this point, and how many I can hope for before sunrise.

At the same time, no one could tell me of the wonder. It seems a magic trick performed by God: I ate eggs, and cheese, and preserves, and somehow my body took these rich, simple ingredients and performed alchemy far beyond turning straw into gold—my body, with no help from me, formed and grew miniature, perfectly functioning veins, bones and kidneys. I don't even know what those look like, let alone how to make them.

Then there's the birth itself. I was there, and I still don't believe it's possible. It would make more sense to me, somehow, if there were a garden of cabbage roses with baby faces peeking out of large blooms. That my body could become a hothouse to grow this—well, this person, is beyond me.

Tad. Little Tad. Our miracle, our joy, our proof God meant for us to be together. For if we weren't, he wouldn't live, and the world clearly needs him.

I wonder what he will do…if he will shape and influence minds, or discover great things. I wonder whom he will love. (I certainly hope he always loves me.) I want other children, but I am also afraid they could not possibly hold a candle to him, and might resent him, always feeling they are standing in his shadow. Could I love the second one enough? Would I feel the same breathless reverence watching the round sleeping curves of another child's cheek in lamplight? Would the delight of creeping in first thing in the morning, to see him smile up upon seeing me, be repeated with another baby? I don't know.

In the meantime, Tad is here, still mine to feed and hold. Sometimes I feel I could miss the entire present wonder, worrying about things like him dying as a baby. My mind, unbidden, unspools the whole macabre experience: a runaway pram, some accidentally chewed-up poison leaves, the wailing and black crepe and tiny coffin. Maybe it's the conceiving and child birthing still haywire inside me.

Oh, he's drooling. How can even that be cute? I have wiped, held, touched and smelled substances that would have shocked me before, with no more reaction than thinking of how best to wash the soiled cloths. Motherhood truly is amazing.

Ellsworth (Tad) in his christening gown with Sedona, 1898

That was when Ellsworth Miller Schnebly was born, and became our Tadpole, our Tad. The center of our world for 20 months, every new accomplishment of his heralded by us as if he'd invented gaslight.

But then, around his first birthday, I would get suddenly exhausted, suddenly upset, suddenly so hungry I felt I would have fearlessly fought a bear over bacon. Carl figured out before I did what it all meant. Another confinement, this one not as long and frightening as the first, with the midwife's helpful hands while Carl paced downstairs.

"This was wonderful compared to the first time," I said afterward. Carl saw it differently. "You yelled. There's nothing wonderful about you in pain." I held firm: "So much less pain. And we knew what we were getting."

Although who can ever know what they're getting when a baby is born? Even seeing her for the first time, we didn't know she would be the exquisite tow-headed Pearl Azalea, sturdy and impetuous and determined from her first bewildered breath and indignant cry. We had been able to stop boarding and afford our own place from the time Tad was born, a few doors down from Schnebly Hardware, so Carl could come home for lunch. As often as not, he'd feed the baby (and then later, feed a baby and talk nonsense to a toddler) while I made us lunch. That habit never broke. Everywhere we lived, east and west, grand and humble, whenever he could, Carl came home for lunch.

I did continue to see Lillie; we had been brides at about the same time. So happy with Carl and our children that I didn't think about the beginnings of her relationship with Loring, we resumed our old easy happy sisterhood. We compared successes with roasting pork and challenges with making lumpless gravy. We talked about cleaning sheets, laughed guiltily about things men did that struck us as strange, and sometimes giggled like children over aspects of marriage about which we'd not been told. It still stung that I had been so easily dropped by my parents, like an inconvenient or troubling acquaintance rather than a daughter. But I grew better able to shrug it off as my own life grew fuller.

"It's just that they have so very many daughters," the irrepressible Lillie said.

West

W*e are going west.*
How many people get to write that, compared to how many who merely wish they could? Ellsworth's been writing to Carl for months about his travels, and lately he's been absolutely insistent about Oak Creek again. It's in the Arizona Territorys. I can scarcely write that without getting a thrill! How exotic. Any place with a "z" in the name has got to be very different.

Anyway, Ellsworth's raved on and on—as he did before our wedding—about Oak Creek Canyon. He says the soil begs to grow fruit trees, the seasons are mild, only about five families live there (which makes his occupation as a schoolteacher rather lean, but he's getting by) and the scenery makes grown men weep at first sight. I don't know if Carl has been secretly longing to cry over a view, or if it's the fertile land, but we're moving.

Things are not going well here. My parents are barely civil to us when we do happen to meet since they still can't fathom that I wouldn't jettison my love, my husband, because they disapprove of his religion; my sisters who still live at home can visit only in secret. With no land to farm, and Carl working, there isn't that much to fill my days. The children keep me busy, but Lillie is my only companion among old friends; you are warned against defying the second richest man in Gorin. I feel as if our true tale has not yet really begun. I feel we are hamstrung, conducting our lives in this narrow-minded place. I don't want our children hearing whispers about their father being in any way unacceptable. They are too young now, but growing so quickly.

We had planned to head west, of course, even since Carl's proposal, but with the coming of each child our departure was postponed.

I had thought that when we did go, we would be setting out from a position of stability, not from resignation. I don't want to feel driven out; I don't want to be some wayfaring stranger. It seems most people who head west are those who for whatever reason don't do well here: iconoclasts, dreamers, misfits. Through no fault of our own, except religion, I now realize we have become those misfits. We are hybrid now, Methodist and Presbyterian, and Gorin isn't evolved enough to accept that. In the Territories, where Ellsworth writes that men even take Indian wives, who will care what church we attend? He says men from back here go out there, and marry Mexican girls or native maidens, and everyone seems to coexist. (In fairness, he said there's more revelry and tomfoolery out west, but it isn't based on race or creed.)

We will take the train. Carl will go first, to get our possessions there ahead of us, and I will follow with the children. Ellsworth has found 80 acres Carl can buy from a Mr. Owenby with his share of the hardware store ownership money. The land already has an irrigation system begun. It daunts me to think of the journey, but it also gives flight to my soul.

I remember the first time a train pulled into Gorin. The station was little more than a raw wood platform with a shed for tickets. Practically the entire town population stood, proud and breathless, listening. First, we heard the whistle. Then the clicking rhythm of wheels on the newly finished tracks. How proud I felt, holding my sister Goldie's hand, watching this behemoth beast of black metal and smoke roll in and lurch to a stop. It was bigger than anything I'd ever seen, and it came to our town.

The people looking out the windows seemed not to be real. I wondered what it would feel like, to actually be bound somewhere, looking out those windows, watching the world outside roll away like a player piano scroll. It made me excited and wistful and scared, all at once.

Soon, I will be one of them. I will be leaving Gorin. I am so ready, and yet so suffused with anxiety about going. But there is nothing for us here. By going to Arizona Territory, Carl and I have the chance to help build and shape something brand new, instead of being judged and found wanting in a small society's unforgiving system.

I wonder if the air will smell different.

Arizona Territory. Arizona. What an amazing word. I wonder if all the places out there have odd names.

Sept. 12, 1901

Alf Boltz just came by with a going-away present. He looked abashed, standing there as I opened it: a set of garden tools!

"I know Carl can get anything he wants from the store," he said. "After all...it's his." He laughed, a little awkwardly. But it seems endearing more than ridiculous. He and Carl have become surprisingly good friends; something in each of them just tickles the other one. They can get going on about something, and I don't really follow the conversation, but suddenly they're clutching their sides, gasping out one more line about a race or something, and then off again laughing.

Anyway, these are quite handsome garden tools, with heavy handles out of some pale wood, smooth and glossy. Alf said that they came specially ordered from England, which was where the genesis of gardening as a passion began. He told me that these are individually made with a lifetime guarantee, and that he just thought in a country where a lot of things will be very strange and difficult, that I should have a luxury.

"But I knew you would worry about a luxury like a china teapot, breaking and all," he said, "and you wouldn't use an ivory fan. So I wanted a luxury that you could use all the time, and feel genteel and like the landed gentry you deserve to be."

He's a very quaint speaker, and I sometimes see why Carl finds him so amusing. More than that, he is a good man: sincere, genuine, and without guile. We are fortunate to count him among our friends.

I must be on the waning side of the moon, or something. I feel melancholy about leaving Alf Boltz. But how many truly kind people does one meet in life? When I remember how lacking I used to find

Alf, just because he wasn't a classic silhouette ideal of a man, I'm sad. Children are mean, I'm certain of it. They mocked Alf because he lacked polish, and I said nothing. But patent medicine sellers are polished, and you wouldn't trust one to hold your door key.

In defense of us as children, Alf has also changed. He was so shy growing up, and seemed to have extra elbows and knees, all gangly. He clearly didn't like being who he was. To cover our own insecurities, I suppose, we didn't act as we should have. Now he's more comfortable, and that makes him more comfortable to be around. His self-consciousness was excruciating to witness. Anyway, he'll come around when Carl gets home, and he's invited to dinner. Maybe he'll come west and visit us someday. I think he plans to move somewhere he can attend a university.

I will pack my new garden tools in the boxes that will go on the boxcar. And I wonder where I will be, what I will be seeing, when I plunge the new trowel with the handle the color of honey into the earth to dig.

Oct. 6, 1901

What am I thinking?

Leave Gorin? I may as well leave myself.

Tad and Pearl are asleep, and our home is gone: everything boxed, crated, packed, or given away. Tomorrow I'll roll up the blankets and the ticking to return to Lillie. My brother Edward will come and help get us, and my very heavy satchel, down to the train.

Carl wrote from Oak Creek Canyon. He is as anxious for us to leave as I am—that's what keeps me from abandoning this whole misbegotten venture. I don't know if I can even exist outside Gorin. I have been here, or close by, all my 24 years. But I do know that I wouldn't want to bother existing without Carl

Still, leaving is more difficult than I expected. I just looked out the window, and even the street under the lamplight seems beloved. How often have I stood here without even noticing the tree shadows from the willow in the corner? Yesterday I walked past the place on the sidewalk where Carl first kissed me. We were married here. We became a family here. And now, without a fare-thee-well, I'm blithely tossing all that over my shoulder for some adventure, in a wild place with no family, no friends.

What will Carl do if another baby comes? What can anyone do if there's no doctor? We won't have a store; we won't have anything. (Part of me understands that the whole point of going is to be part of that creative process—to live on the land and make it blossom like the rose. But right now, it looms like an arrogant and careless decision.)

Even saying that, I know with a dead finality and complete certainty that it was the only decision to make. We are not of this place. This is stultifying and suffocating Carl especially. We are right and wise to move forward.

Still, I feel bound by ropes of tears and memories. My sisters and I, walking to school, doing Trade Lasts and spelling our words to one another on Thursday afternoons. The birthday tea parties on the front veranda, with lemonade and cakes. The scent of wet grass, the (somewhat) predictable eleven o'clock train whistle.

How many times have I heard that, and wished I could throw down my embroidery and flee? Become a vagabond, living by my wits, like a card dealer on a riverboat might. I sulked (I admit) that I was sentenced to live out a genteel life defined and bordered by French knots and blanket stitch. So I'm a fine one to be sniveling and moping now. Sure, Miss Fancy Talk. Adventure, courage! And right now all you want is a pillow on the parlor sofa and a good book.

It isn't only the people, or the places. Every thought I've ever had, every feeling I've ever experienced, has been here. My whole heart's and soul's contents come from roots that go deep into Gorin's soil. I don't know if I can be somewhere else.

And yet, like a sleepwalker or condemned saint, I will move forward. I recognize the tragic truth, which is that in order to grow I must leave. I am rootbound. I do not want our children to be stuck in similar containers. I don't want Tad and Pearl growing up where people think it is appropriate to judge other people by where they pray, or how they look. I can't wait to get away from the smug complacency of people who believe worth can be measured by the price of their china. I bitterly resent that I blindly accepted the standards and measures of this narrow little town.

There are people so vastly removed from even the most outré of Gorin's citizenry that I want to meet. I want our children to talk to Indians (even though I'm a little afraid); I want them to meet children who are not like them. Not cookie cutter classes, with the only differences being what color braids hang over the white collar.

All right. I feel better.

What I seemed to forget, momentarily, is that God isn't only protecting and loving Gorin. God made a whole wide world, and is giving us the chance to see a part of it many people never have. (It sounds so difficult to get to, probably few ever will.)

We will shake Gorin's dust from our shoes. We will not be bug-eyed Donie Miller and the double-zero son-in-law anymore. We will be Sedona and Carl, settlers in Oak Creek Canyon.

(That is the end of the early journals. Now I return to our life as it is unfolding.)

Mutter

I had wondered how long it would take Mutter to come.
Why is that relationship so complicated? Mutter seems so powerful: when I was a girl, she was the source of all good, and all wrath. I feared her anger above all else. I yearned to make her proud. I depended on her, and looking back, I resented that dependence. (Maybe we all resent those upon whom we depend.) She provided years of love and discipline and tending and instruction. A few times she wounded me deeply. Now we are once again near her, where I could be once again in her thrall. I mostly dreaded seeing her.

It took a week. We arrived on Sunday afternoon, and this is Saturday. When I saw her coming up the walk, I realized she wouldn't want to see us for the first time at church, in front of people. I don't know if it's because she was afraid I would freeze her, or collapse, or somehow embarrass her, but regardless I was pretty certain that whenever we met, it would be in private. I felt myself straighten my shoulders as I opened the door.

I thought she'd have to act very sorry about Pearl, and hide her glee that she was right and we were wrong about going west.

I could not have been more surprised.

Before I even shut the door, she pulled me into her arms.

"My poor little girl. My poor darling child. What you've been through!"

And I cried.

I've forgotten I was a daughter. I have been only a mother, and a poor one at that, to the daughter I let die, and to the two children left to me. But suddenly I was a daughter again. I wasn't in charge; I wasn't responsible. Mutter was here.

It's amazing; any anger is gone. She isn't the least bit superior about us coming back; only sorry for our loss. We are both mothers who have lost our Pearls. (How strange that is!) Of course, my sister Pearl was 18 when she died, the year after we moved away. But we both know that empty-hearted feeling.

She is full of plans; we will come to lunch tomorrow: "Papa can't wait to see you!"

I have a hard time forgetting about her repeating—or creating—the "100 sons-in-law" remark. But she has truly forgotten it, or pretends to. I want to.

It turns out Lillie has been taking Tad to visit Mutter and Papa regularly, so thankfully there's no awkwardness with him. ("I know I probably should have told you," she said. "But you were so sad, and it seemed just one more thing to worry you about. And it's all right now, isn't it?")

Tad gets more like his old self every day. He told me yesterday at some length about the differences between Gorin and Oak Creek. I rarely call the town of Sedona by that name, my name, especially to Tad. It keeps things less confusing and I still feel somewhat foolish about it, so afraid people will think that I think it makes me grand.

He said it took him some time to adjust to living here.

"Out there it was always quiet except for the water and the birds. Here people are all around all the time, so there is always their sounds. Do you remember how many arrowheads we found, and all the pieces of old pots, Mother? Here there's none of that. But I got so used to looking at the ground there, that here in town, I find lots of thing. Coins, mostly. And sometimes a little chain, or a button. Once I found a whole dollar! People are surprised at how much I find."

There's a lesson to that: if we aren't looking for something, we won't see it. I would have thought I would need to look for the good in Mutter. But it was all I saw when she came. I'm very grateful.

Nov. 1, 1905

It's not as if we never left...but it's close.

I market at the old store. I nod at many of the same people on the street. It's as if nothing has changed but me. Not on purpose, yet while we were gone, I did change. I learned a great deal about doing things without the conveniences of living in a town, certainly. Also, being the hostess, the person in charge, and rising to that. Welcoming strangers, learning to put them at ease. Not relying on Mutter and Papa, and even getting somewhat accustomed to Carl being gone for several days. But change occurred in my mind as well.

Before we left I always felt judged and found wanting. Actually, that part hasn't changed; I'm still Not Lillie, only the lesser sister of Lillie. But the difference is that I no longer care.

We have lived in the west. I have cooked for dozens of strangers, had lengthy debates with a man dressed in animal skins, killed rattlesnakes with a rake, watched my husband ride away and leave us alone in near-wilderness. I have given birth with no doctor, only an elderly (and very wise) woman present. I have washed in creek water. I have buried a daughter. There isn't much anyone here can do to make me feel bad.

Genevieve and Tad, Gorin, MO 1905

Sometimes I actually feel stirrings of unattractive superiority—although in someone else of whom I am less judgmental than I am of me, I would call it confidence—when people here ask breathless questions about the Wild West. I answer graciously, knowing I would have asked many of the exact same questions of someone, had I not been the one to go.

I suppose the difference is that I did go. I gave up everything they hold so dear: a china closet, a new spring hat every year, a calling card tray. I was willing to be very uncomfortable, and now I don't see comfort as necessarily a good thing. Maybe because it carries a heavy penalty: the price extracted is boredom. In any case, I don't hold much with comfort any more.

Give me a summer rainstorm, even if we're drenched by the time we reach the house. Give me the red trails of running water through the vegetable garden afterwards, rather than a paved street. Give me the scent of wet leaves turning ever so slowly into mulch, and then earth, instead of perfume from Paris. Give me rough hands because I baked for ten people today, rather than the finest gloves. In some small ways, we changed Oak Creek Canyon, and it changed me, too.

Oh, is that so?

Well, then, Miss Adventurous Spirit, what finds you back here?

You weren't tough enough for the west. You wanted to be, but then you lost a child, like so many others do, and you couldn't handle it. You tucked tail and ran. Just remember that, next time you feel stronger than someone else.

Dec. 28, 1905

Christmas is over. What a different five years can make!

This Christmas evening, we went for dinner at the old house after opening our presents at home first. I wanted the children to have Christmas memories where they don't have to be "seen and not heard," where all our attention could be on them. Carl got Tad a wonderfully impressive fountain pen called a Safety Pen that shouldn't make the mess most of them do. (Yes, I've tried lemon juice, boiling water, cold water, baking soda. No, they don't work. The sun does the best job, but it's never perfect.) Tad kept taking his new pen out of his pocket and looking at it, turning it in his hand. He felt like a grownup. Carl gave me tortoiseshell combs which are larger than most, and I know they will make it easier to keep my hair up; a thoughtful gift and also lovely. I made Genevieve doll clothes; she seemed quite content to keep changing her new dolly into one outfit after another all afternoon. It was a pleasant day.

So after we were returned home and the children tucked in, Carl told me that Papa had taken him into the study while the women were clearing up after dinner, and somewhat awkwardly told him that despite their early objections, Carl has turned out to be a more-than-satisfactory husband and provider. Papa said specifically that it must have been hard to walk away from the empire Carl built out west (of course, with no thought to the idea that I played a role in that), and that moving back here for my health is an admirable thing.

We are, in short, back in their will!

We laughed about that, a little ruefully. Who knows how much will be left at the end of their lives? And with so many children to divide it among, how much difference can it make?

But it does feel good that they finally hold my husband in higher regard, as he deserved all along. I guess Mutter and Papa just needed time to come to it. Also, since he attends church like a sober believer and doesn't make rude noises or strange hand symbols (who knows what they think a Presbyterian might do?), they must have finally decided to welcome us.

That is a good thing. And especially for the business. Carl and Loring have friends and customers, but if my father actually does what he told Carl he would do—come in to purchase his next suit—that will get the attention of a certain echelon of Gorin society.

Motorcar

What an adventure. Not only did I get to attend a WCTU conference again—something I thought had ended for me when we went west—but I got to ride in an automobile.

Papa, who is parsimonious to a truly impressive degree, has always taken his status as second-richest man in Gorin quite seriously. He believes that to reassure people that he has not slid farther down that scale, his prosperity must be visible. So he actually purchased a Model T in St. Louis and had the man from whom he bought it drive him home in it. (Once he'd gotten a chance to practice here, away from the busy streets of the big city, he drove the man back...and came home all by himself.)

I am impressed that Papa was willing to learn a new skill. As we age, we enjoy less and less feeling inexpert, and it holds many people back from embarking on anything new.

Anyway, he learned to drive, although he is still timid and hesitates to take the auto busy places. But when he heard eight of us had the opportunity to be taken in motorcars to WCTU, he knew enough about them to consent to let Mutter go. We had to get long sections of veiling to hold our hats on. The motorcars can go quite fast, especially outside of town. Twenty-five miles an hour is not uncommon. (Briefly I let myself think of how marvelous that would have been in Arizona Territory's vastness, but I realized there are no roads smooth enough to accommodate such a thing.)

We got up early and all met at the train station, where two handsome young men were waiting with their vehicles. Mutter and a few friends went in one, and I was in the second one with Joyce Barkley and two other women.

It was amazing. A bit like flying must be, the wind rushing past, and everything a blur out on the open road. I hadn't realized how nervous I was until we arrived, and when I got out my legs were almost shaking. And in a way, something is lost at that speed: you see everything so briefly it barely registers. I guess progress takes getting used to.

Motorcars bound for WCTU with Sedona wearing
large floral hat, center of photo

Old Friend

April 25, 1906

We have not leapt into society here in Gorin. Some people remember Carl from the hardware store, and those who met him, like him. But those who wrap themselves in the mantle of being Methodist don't want to give a Presbyterian the time of day. (How can that be Christian, when Christ always seemed to make it a point to spend time with the least among us, whether it be women of easy virtue or Samaritans?)

Well, when I saw Carl come up the steps for lunch yesterday, I didn't recognize the man with him; of a good height, well dressed, clearly neither farmer nor tradesman.

It was Alf Boltz. Upon my word, I'd never have recognized him on a crowded city street. He outgrew his awkward tentativeness, his shambling walk. He is quite distinguished looking. After a minute of conversation, I began to see the old Alf, eager to think and share those thoughts, perceptive and also kind. He and Carl therefore have a great deal in common. I barely spoke at lunch, enjoying listening to the two of them dissect and draw conclusions on the future of machinery in agriculture, the relative worth (or lack thereof) of sharecropping, the ideal system and rate of taxation, and even (apparently a discussion that began in the store) the best width of a cravat.

Carl, of course, has known almost from the day we met, that outside of my foolish and disastrous experience with Loring's attention, Alf was my one and only caller. He simply said it showed Alf to be a man of excellent taste. I was delighted to hear that Alf earned a degree in the law, and now works for important men. He is unmarried, but said whimsically that there always seems to be some young woman who thinks that should be changed. Currently, he is not interested.

"The law is a jealous mistress. Perhaps once I reach a certain level of success I can take time for hearth and home, but at this point there is always a meeting where I can gain introductions, a board to be of service on, paperwork, new journals published every time I turn around. This is quite enough for now."

Carl was beaming like a boy on the playground at his friend. We will surely be inviting Alf over for meals frequently. I am so pleased that my early lack of social skills didn't appear to damage his development at all. Indeed, he told Carl while I was getting dessert plates that I had been very kind to him: "When I was the least desirable among mortals, and any other girl our age certainly would have either collapsed with laughter upon seeing me at the door, or turned and fled, Sedona was gracious and kind."

I don't quite remember it that way, but I'm relieved he can. And maybe it's true; the screaming was only going on inside my head. I've been told often enough that I always appear calm and at ease. That is hard to believe, since inside I feel frazzled, frantic, bewildered and bordering on panic so much of the time. How do we manage to fool the world? What would happen if we stopped trying? I guess adults would be acting like children. There's quite enough of that already.

1950

I just came across this section and wish, so wish, I could have known then what I know now.

For years I thought the hardest part of the commandment to love thy neighbor as thyself, was loving that neighbor—some can be distinctly difficult to love.

But from here it's clear that for most of us, far and away the biggest challenge is to love thyself.

We don't love ourselves; how could we, when we know how truly unlovable we are?

Yes, but...now I understand what I didn't then. Love isn't merited. We don't earn love. We give it freely, not as an award for excellence. I've certainly always loved Carl just as he was; why couldn't I extend myself that same courtesy? I don't know exactly, but I do know that as years pass, it gets easier to forgive myself, knowing I've always done the best I could.

How much did I cost us all back in those days, standing in such stern judgment of who I was, of what I did and didn't do? I'd just lost Pearl, and had small children. I was still broken. Then I piled condemnation on top of that. It didn't help me heal; it probably slowed healing down.

Maybe if I could tell other people even just one small thing, it would be that: realize you don't earn anyone's love, not even your own. Give it, just because. And don't fear becoming too fond of yourself. Imagine, if we each woke up thinking, "I am good enough just as God made me. I don't have to prove it to anyone, or earn their admiration. I can just enjoy the gifts of this day, and be kind." We would be so much easier to get along with.

Why don't we get to figure things out sooner? I was admiring Patsy's hands the other day, so smooth and white. Mine are full of spots and scars and veins and knobs. But I know things now. I guess each age has to have its own privileges. When our faces and hands and hair are looking much the worse for wear, we get peace.

Papa

Papa has died.

What an odd, displaced feeling this is.

We were cordial, visiting back and forth just often enough to feel fine about everything without having to talk about anything deeply. I feel no sense of unfinished business, just slightly bewildered...half an orphan.

Mutter said when we went over, "that war wound finally got him." She wouldn't say more. Where was it? How did it kill him? What on earth happened?

Carl and I surmise it must have been somehow embarrassing; in an unmentionable location, or the cause of something regrettable. I can't imagine keeping something as significant as the reason for a parent's death from the family, but there you are. Poor Papa, not able to discuss something as important as an early injury. Ours was certainly a family of secrets.

We went to the laying-out, although Mutter had already washed and dressed him, I believe with Noah's assistance. Papa looked as stern as ever, with his face in repose, between the flickering candles on the dining room table. I didn't take the children; they should remember him alive. Death comes to everyone, but they have had quite enough of it for a time.

Carl's parents still live; we've both lost siblings at young ages. This is different. Papa was always there. Now he's gone. I feel sad, and also I feel sad that I don't feel sadder. Had we been close, I would.

Christmas

We made it through another holiday. This was the third Christmas without Pearl, but Hank is four months old. We named him Daniel Henry, for Carl's father and grandfather. Our Genevieve is four years old, and Tad, at nine, reminded me recently he will be two digits on his next birthday, and never one digit again.

It was also another Christmas without Papa. Mutter seems to have adjusted fairly well. Maybe by the time you're in your 60s you've seen so many things, you know you just keep going. But she actually seems rather more lighthearted than she did when he was alive. She could be: she is no longer responsible for another person. Mutter cared for Papa their entire married life, and it always used to be her job to be aware: is he comfortable? Does he need anything? Now, she openly jokes with Tad and sings little songs to Genevieve I remember from my own childhood. Genevieve adores her, and loves to be called her big helper in the kitchen.

Tonight, I find myself wondering how things are in Oak Creek (I could say "in Sedona" but it sounds too odd). Maybe that means I'm healing. I can afford to think of the good times there a little longer, before the memories of the bad ones engulf me and wash the pleasant memories away.

Schnebly Ranch

I don't know why I even care.

Carl just showed me an advertisement in the *Coconino Daily Sun* (the paper out of Flagstaff) that Ellsworth sent him. It's inviting people to stay at Schnebly Ranch!

Schnebly Ranch? That's our home.

Was our home. Was. And it's my fault it isn't still. I thanked God when we left that Ellsworth had married Mary, and they were able to stay on and live there when we left. (Carl swears Ellsworth will pay him every penny for it...but we all know Carl.) Anyway, I know Mary was glad to become mistress of her own kitchen. She had been helping me out, but she clearly hadn't enjoyed it.

Mary is Mormon. I don't have any real knowledge of what all that entails. I'd heard it meant men could marry as many women as they wanted, so they could have more children, making more Mormons. I also heard that before they came to Arizona and Utah, they kept getting run out of wherever they tried to settle. People talk about special underclothes, and different levels in Heaven. But no religion can be understood in a few words. Unfortunately, I never reached a level of comfort with Mary that let me ask her more questions, curious as I was.

Actually, Mary and Ellsworth had corresponded for years, having met when he was still in school back in Missouri. Finally the parents she'd been caring for both died, and she was free to marry. It was very brave of her to agree to become his wife, since they hadn't spent more than a few hours together in about ten years. Ellsworth was excited for weeks, getting her train ticket to Flagstaff, buying a ring he had engraved with her initials, telling people with shy pride he was going to be bringing his bride home soon.

I imagine most people were a bit surprised. Ellsworth's always been a bit of a rambler, not like many other people. He can walk for miles—when he taught in Cornville he would frequently walk up to see us in Oak Creek after school got out on Friday, and that's more than 20 miles! "I like being out in open air," he'd say, as if it were the most normal thing in the world. He is an indefatigable worker, even-tempered, easygoing, a voracious reader and debater. He and Carl can poke and prod and pull at a subject like taffy, both clearly relishing the exchange. Then suddenly, he acquires a helpmate. Although not sudden; more than ten years in the very quiet making.

Anyway, he took the wagon and went up to Flagstaff, and married Mary, and they came to stay with us. I was excited at the idea of having female company that wouldn't leave after a few days or weeks. I thought we would have a great deal in common. First, coming west takes a woman with some backbone, so I admired her before I even met her. And no one understands better than I how your hometown can become too small. But from our first greeting, there was distance. Maybe not quite distrust, or maybe so. Just no ease. She held her shoulders stiffly, didn't smile, and seemed easily upset if I suggested she do something a different way.

I confess, that got my back up a little. I'd gone out there knowing nothing about frontier housekeeping, and had figured out a great deal by the time she arrived. I was proud of being able to make things easier. But she seemed to take everything I said as a slight. I said less and less.

In fairness, she was wonderful with the children. Merry and light-hearted with Tad, giving him little rhymes I'd never heard for him to memorize, and praising him when he did. On a day he was able to recite one, he got to choose the kind of cookies she would bake. He loved that. Maybe I felt a little slighted because that had never crossed my mind to make choosing a type of cookie a treat for my children. And she would hold Genevieve for as long as I'd let her.

I think dogs and children see people more clearly than the rest of us do. I can't explain it, but we had a dog once that loved everyone, except one friend of Papa's he would growl at. We thought maybe it was because the man wore a tall stovepipe hat. But we came to find out years later that he had been rumored to have killed his wife and burned her body! Did that show, to a dog? And children instinctively go to some people, and hang back from others. I have always figured they can tell who feels comfortable in their company. And maybe Mary lit up like a candle for children, even if she didn't warm up to me one little bit.

Perhaps she didn't care for my company because I reminded her of someone she didn't like, or because she knew I was Methodist. I know I can be distant; I'm terrified people won't like me, and it creates a reserve. Maybe she'd been taught not to trust other folks not part of her own kind. Whatever the reason, she was pretty silent around me, giving me "yes" and "no" to questions like, "So, do you think you'll be happy in Oak Creek?" I finally let her be.

Carl had told me shortly after we'd arrived there that Arizona Territory had tremendous numbers of Mormons. I remember wondering why he mentioned that, and what it meant: I knew Mormons were a fairly new faith, but was he warning me of something? He said, no, no, they were fine hard-working people as far as he knew, but they could be a little clannish.

"If the person who created our faith was killed for his beliefs so recently, we probably would be too," he said, and told me about how their leader, Joseph Smith, had been shot about 25 years before Carl was born. Even though it had happened 200 miles away, folks still talked about it when he was coming up, and he developed a curiosity about these people who had become pioneers, somewhat like the Israelites searching for a homeland.

The gentleman from Prescott who installed our telegraph in Oak Creek told us the first telegraph operator in the Territory was a young woman named Eliza, up at a place called Pipe Spring, about 50 years before we came. She was Mormon.

Funny how remembering one thing starts a chain of other memories, like dominoes falling and hitting the next, and the next. That telegraph installer was named Herb. (His second name escapes me.) He had been to Pipe Spring, and said he had been curious to see what it was like. I guess Mormons didn't want help from outsiders, but they needed some cable they just didn't have, so someone had sent a letter to Sunset Telegraph in Prescott.

He said there was a huge fortress, completely enclosed. It was long building with two wings forming a courtyard closed by heavy gates, which had been built right over a spring! Not near it, nor next to it, but right smack dab over it. He explained it could be possible for an enemy to poison a spring, or cut off the water supply, but not this way. He described a trough running down the kitchen floor, cooling everywhere off as it passed through other rooms. I was fascinated. And yet, I couldn't imagine building our house over the irrigation ditch. I suppose that's different; things could float in. If the spring starts right under your floor, it's pretty clean.

I'd completely forgotten about Pipe Spring until now. It was someplace I would have liked to see while we were out there. Now I suppose I never will.

Anyway, the advertisement. Schnebly's Ranch. Am I such a snob that it sounds less than genteel? It seems to me like a ranch is a place for stock, not hosting people.

Instead of people fortunate enough to live in a big house that can take guests, I guess it reads like they've made a deliberate decision to become business people. Nothing wrong with that—Carl's in business. It just seems odd, rather common, to have an advertisement. And I reckon two things in it offended me.

The advertisement says in large letters at the top, "Schnebly's Ranch."

The schoolteacher in me already doesn't care for that. It is the Schneblys' Ranch: more than one Schnebly. The apostrophe where it is means it belongs to only one Schnebly. Then the text goes on, "Cool, Delightful Place to Spend the Summer on Oak Creek; Fishing and

Hunting. Fresh fruits and vegetables from our own ranch." (Wouldn't those be from our own garden? Ranch garden. Anyway...) "Cleanest and Best White Cook In the Southwest."

That really frosted me. Charles Rutlege is apparently gone. He was with us as cook from 1904 on. I was resistant at first, but Carl was right that it was too much, all those meals and the housework as well. Charles Rutlege had a nice touch with it, and we communicated just fine. We co-existed happily. We never had a single guest complain, or even look askance at him.

Then Mary arrived. If she wasn't sure about me, she was sure about Charles Rutlege. She was not comfortable around him. Maybe there was some reason in her past that I don't know, and I am aware it's wrong to judge. But this statement of a White Cook shows that he didn't last, and that they think they are better for it. I mourn for him. Charles Rutlege loved the children, and they him. He grieved when Pearl died.

Anyway, the ad goes on: "Positively no Guests With Lung Trouble Admitted."

That gets my dander up also. Carl never turned anyone away. Lots of what some folks called "lungers" came to Oak Creek from the east, seeking a dry climate. Carl knew it wouldn't be wise to have them in the house, but those tent houses were just downstream, and I would carry trays down to a table outside. Poor men—it wasn't their fault they were ill. This makes them seem like outlaws, unwelcome and unworthy. Then it says, "Address or phone No. 100 b," and "D.E. Schnebly, Sedona, Ariz." Well, they didn't change the name of the post office, anyway.

And a telephone. Aren't we high in the instep? And yet, how is that different from the telegraph? Sunset Telephone and Telegraph was in Prescott already when we got to Oak Creek. It wasn't much for Carl to get line run to the telegraph machine that was in our downstairs front room, so it was probably a similar process to get a telephone. (I still do Morse code sometimes in my head, just to see if I can. While most likely not something I will use again, I'm proud I learned it and was able to send, and read, telegrams. I don't want to lose it after the effort it took to master.) I suppose because that line is already in place, a telephone wasn't a huge expense. It just seems so commercial, somewhat craven. When we were there, getting guests felt as if friends we hadn't met yet were coming to visit. Now it's a boldfaced business, not a home.

Maybe I'm fooling myself. Maybe an advertisement is just good sense. Maybe I feel jealous that it isn't mine anymore.

I always held Ellsworth in high regard, and he seemed to adore his Mary. She must have just been shy. I hope this all works for them. And I will continue to hope that until I mean it.

First Grade

Sept. 7, 1910

M y little girl is in school now. Genevieve, so solemn as she came downstairs in her new dress, but also as if she were trying to contain a light and eagerness I rarely see. Carl caught it, and said mildly to her, "You look nice, Genevieve...is today Sunday?"

"Dad!" She pulled herself up, not sure to be afraid he was losing his mind or surprised he hadn't followed the preparation rituals of the night before more closely. Then she saw his smile and her own emerged.

"I'm in first grade now." She said each word very deliberately, as if hearing them gave her as much pleasure as saying them. She looked lovely; I'd taken the curl rags out and brushed her hair, tied the sash on her new plaid dress in a perfectly balanced bow. Her shoes gleamed from last night's blacking. She had her Sunday petticoat under her dress, which I had emphasized was a first-day treat only. Genevieve's a pretty girl; her hair is lighter than Tad's and she has even features. When she was dressed and I turned to come downstairs to breakfast, she was looking in the mirror.

"I'll just be a moment." Sometimes she speaks like an adult in tone and word choice. I think being so quiet, she picks up on more than most children. I surmised she wanted to behold the first-grader now in this room, where a non-student had gone to bed, so I smiled and left. This is important to her.

Even though she's five years younger than Tad, it distresses her that he can do so much she can't. School seemed such an injustice: she watched as he picked up his lunch pail, his books—those emblems of maturity and independence—and walked off alone, before she would come slowly back inside. Hank is only three. That implied to her that babies stay home. So now to be leaving when he does (and Tad will walk her to her class before going on to his own) lets her see herself differently.

Genevieve. I worry about her. She was so small when Pearl died, and no matter how I tried to keep cheerful for her, I know I didn't. She doesn't really remember her sister, I don't believe. And I say that because she won't talk about her. I think she keeps everything held tightly inside.

How much of us is formed before we're even born? How much difference does it make, what happens to us and what is said to us, after that? She's so restrained, so composed. I fear it stems from the tumult of those first two years, making her try not to whip up the atmosphere, cause emotion. But I acknowledge there's also a possibility that if she'd been dropped into a coyotes' den and raised by the pack, she'd be largely the same person.

Genevieve is not a cuddler, not a chatterbox. I see girls skipping ahead of their mothers and running back to throw their arms around the maternal skirts, and know that will never be us. She is never a spot of mischief or trouble. But she's also rarely visibly happy, which is what made this morning so special. Is hers simply an unusually tranquil nature?

How can I not know my own daughter? I know Tad almost as myself. Hank, while only three, is such a bright spirit that he seems easy. (The other day I told him I'd found the other sock that had disappeared from a pair on washday. He ran in with his big happy smile, said, "You're with me, pal!" to the sock and ran away with it.)

Carl seemed more interested than concerned when I wondered out loud to him if Genevieve's circumspect surface indicated she was somehow broken in the early years.

"Because the rest of us are so noisy and prone to dancing?" he asked, looking up from the money he was carefully sorting and counting for the bank deposit. "Sedona: heart on her sleeve and feelings all over the place."

"I know I'm not," I said, trying not to be huffy because I know he loves to tease, but as always wondering if I'm not good enough the way I am. Maybe great strong women are fire and ice, singing and shouting. "I don't care if Genevieve's quiet—it's the why of it. Maybe she likes to be calm. But if she's covering emotion so no one gets upset, that's worrisome."

"There's always something worrisome if you want to look for it," Carl said. "And it seems you do. She's who she is. Just love her, Dona. That's all she needs from you."

I hope he's right. And still I had to press my lips together to keep from saying to him, "It must be nice to know you weren't responsible for Pearl. It must be restful not to wonder if you broke your other daughter when you killed your first one. It must be grand, just driving in after it all happened, never having to tally the damage you caused your family members, from one minute of not paying enough attention." But I know none of that is his fault. And probably, if he could have arranged for it to happen on his watch to spare me, he would have. He deserves a kinder wife. I thank God that at least I didn't say any of that out loud.

Carl's started bringing coins home to sort and count because he's on the sales floor most of the time at the menswear store. He doesn't relish working there with Loring, but it seemed a good use of the money we got from the Oak Creek property, and Loring and Lillie were so eager for the two men to make a go of this, being their own bosses. Also, as Minnie said one time after a meal with us, "I think Carl could be happy in hell." He makes the best of everything, and likes not having to leave so early in the morning, and getting back before dark. In Oak Creek it was always can't-see to can't-see, as Carl quoted Boyle saying, and he was never done. Now when the two of them lock the front doors and leave, he's his own man until the next morning.

He doesn't act like he minds being back in the city, but I know if it weren't for me he never would have left Oak Creek. Sometimes he goes quiet and I suspect he's travelled across the night skies in his mind, back out west. He's walking outside, after dinner, hearing the ripples in the creek, breathing in that sweet spicy wet-leaf scent, seeing all those stars. He—well, we—created that homesite, literally from the ground up. I believe if he'd let himself think about what he wanted at all, it would have broken his heart to leave.

He swears I'm all that matters; if he's with me, he's home. I still deeply regret making him move, even if I know I couldn't have stayed. Maybe I should have come here by myself for a while. But I couldn't stand seeing that little grave outside the kitchen window. I couldn't stay in that house. So here we are.

I can't seem to get past melancholy tonight. I'll stop writing and sort coins with Carl.

Nov. 22, 1910

We went to Mutter's for supper last evening, with Lillie and Loring. The children were delightful, Tad so grown up in his Sunday suit, talking about how he's doing high school work at 12! Genevieve is sweet and shy, but answered questions in full sentences, and ate every bite. And Hank, irrepressible as usual, climbed onto Carl's lap when we were sitting in the parlor before dinner and began firing riddles at everyone, who kindly pretended not to have ever heard any of them. I could tell it was taking an effort, but worth it for his throaty chuckles when he delivered the answers in triumphant tones.

Dinner was the usual forgettable but hearty meal I remembered. I brought the children to sit with Mutter afterwards. She does seem to love having her grandchildren with her, and exhibits patience and interest I don't remember from when I was a child. But I suppose that's logical. When I was a child, she bore the complete responsibility of creating upright moral character in all of us, as well as teaching us every household skill we would need...and in addition to those things, making sure that we presented an attractive front to the world, schooled in elocution and music and languages and the gentle feminine arts. (And I am truly grateful—my crochet work was becoming known in Oak Creek.) So she was probably constantly worried when she was the mother.

With our own children, those responsibilities (and I didn't realize how heavily they weighed when I was one of the children instead of the mother) rest on me. She is free to simply enjoy Tad, Genevieve and Hank. She sat Genevieve and Hank on the piano bench and taught them one of the duets I remember from when Lillie and I were starting out. (I haven't done a great deal with them and piano, because they are clearly not at all interested, but they were very respectful, and paid attention.)

Carl came in with a letter from Will Jordan, a friend who lives in Jerome. Will wrote that our old house burned down, so we have no real ties to the area now. Ellsworth and Mary had sold the land to the Blacks, and promised me in a letter Pearl's grave will always be there, in its little fence. They joined her people in St. Johns, even though Ellsworth says he will never become a Mormon himself.

Part of me is heartsick whenever I picture the charred remains and empty foundation. It was such a wonderful home! It hosted our holidays, the hundreds of conversations among ourselves and with guests, some of whom have become beloved correspondents. Now that house is gone.

I wonder if the land misses the sound of our footsteps, the laughter of the children. I wonder if Travois still goes to check on the old place. Someone will probably build there again. I actually hope they do; otherwise the sound of the creek, the look of the light changing at the end of the day, will be wasted.

Embezzlement

Now it all makes sense. I'm sick. I'm furious. But at least I'm no longer confused.

Lillie came over earlier; a tremulous, trembling Lillie. I was just getting the end of supper cleared away, enjoying putting the still-warm china in the cabinet and knowing there was half a pie left in the pie safe, when I heard the rap on the back door. Carl got to it before I did, and invited her in, shooting a worried look at me. Lillie makes everything light, and we all enjoy being around her. But at this hour?

She stood, shaking her head when he invited her to take a chair, wringing her handkerchief—very unlike herself. Then when I asked what was wrong, she just started to cry, and kind of slid into the rocker. She sobbed, which brought the children to the parlor door, but I shook my head and smiled at them over her head, while I sat on the arm of the chair, holding my sister, indicating they should not come in. It frightened them to see something so unusual, so they melted back.

Loring. Again, Loring. Why, God, did You ever have to let him come to Gorin? Hasn't he been enough trouble? Oh, no—nothing is ever enough for Loring. He's stolen all the money Carl invested in the clothing store. He's gone. The money's gone. Our future is gone.

I looked over at Carl and he was as still as a person can be while still breathing. I crossed over to him and put my hand on his back. There was almost a vibration in him; a low hum of energy. But he moved not at all. I myself felt like I was seeing and hearing through a veil.

Lillie said that this afternoon two men came from the bank, to say that Loring had left a note with their clerk, telling them he left the last four payments he hasn't made on the store with Lillie. They added that before he left, he withdrew every penny from the store's account, and their own. Of course, Lillie had no such four payments, and thought he was at work as usual. But he'd never gone to the store today.

Carl never fails to amaze me. Despite the fact that he was as shocked as I was, and that this was his livelihood stolen, he moved. He walked over and soothed my sister by patting her shoulder.

He's always reminded me of the Matthew Arnold poem that begins, "Come to me in my dreams," for the line, "and be as kind to others as to me." Because of Lillie's way of beguiling men, I could feel edgy when Carl is so solicitous, except that it is so pure in him that it reminds me of why I love him so much. She kept trying to apologize.

Carl said, "Well, Lillie, if you had a gun on him making him do all that, I guess you'd have something to be sorry about," and smiled gently. She's in terrible straits, as we are: Mutter can take her in for a time, but something will have to get figured out. Papa left Mutter with enough to get by, and the house is plenty spacious, but there's nothing extra.

Loring. What was he thinking? That's easy, I guess: he was thinking about what he wanted. He must have gotten bored and decided he wanted to be a gambler or a desperado or God only knows what. Poor Lillie. I couldn't help but think if I had married him that would be me.

It explains some things: he would never let Carl take deposits to the bank. He got sharp when Carl would ask how their books looked, asking if Carl didn't trust him. Carl, who wants everyone to be happy, didn't push the point. For all we know, Loring could have created a second set of books, if he'd feared we would be suspicious. He probably laughed, thinking us such rubes he didn't have to expend the effort.

So that was all our Oak Creek money. There is the menswear store, of course, and the merchandise to sell off to cover debts. But then what? Of course, all the Sunday Christians will blame Carl for not taking more care. The old cluckers, anyway! I hate this town for its smug judgment. People who have never had an original thought, or tried anything new, somehow think themselves better than those of us who take chances. I'm livid at Loring, but a little bit upset with us for trusting him. Like that old story about the snake who takes the frog halfway across the pond and then kills him saying, "You knew I was a snake." Or whatever it is. Suffice to say we should have known.

Carl gave Loring free rein, letting him order those velvet waistcoats and fancy hats, even though Gorin has never been a magnet for dandies. He let him swan around, taking bankers to lunch and inviting them into the store, giving them handkerchiefs and such. I guess we all believed Loring because he always sounded so certain of everything he said. But now we find out the payments haven't been made—probably other bills not settled as they should have been. It's all gone, and him with it.

Carl said that tomorrow, he will get in touch with the Pinkerton Agency, to see if they can track Loring down. Tad was excited to hear that—at 12, he loves crime stories out of the paper, and this seems to him a real-life detective case. Of course, we haven't explained to any of the children that it's our money Loring lit out with. And that we don't know what we will do now.

Rats! Rats! I can scarcely take it in. We'd finally gotten our bearings here; the children enjoy their cousins, and we have a nice home. Maybe we need to go back west, Carl is saying. Maybe this is an invitation to change.

I am back in my parents' will. Maybe someday there will be some money from that. Ellsworth still owed Carl; maybe he will be able to send that. Would I have advised Carl to do differently if I'd been in less of a state about Pearl?

I don't know. I only know if Loring walked through that door right now I'd love to twist his head off his neck like the chicken he is.

Resettlement

Dec. 6, 1910

C arl and I just had one of our rare difficult conversations. We will need to leave, to start over somewhere else. He's pitied here, probably judged for letting Loring get away with what he did; now all the town leaders who bragged on how much they liked Loring are scurrying like mice to put as much distance as they can between themselves and his mess. I have feared for several days the question I sensed Carl was working up the courage to ask, and tonight it finally came: "How would you feel about going back to Arizona?"

How wouldn't I feel? I yearn for Oak Creek, miss it, dream of it. And equally I hate it, fear it, mourn it. It's where Pearl lived. It's where Pearl died. How could I be there again without searing myself daily on memories?

For the most part, I'd say I've achieved equanimity. Hank, Genevieve and Tad—and mostly Carl—deserve me to be whole. They fill my time, if not every tiny corner of my heart. So we are all right. Here. But there? To be back where it all happened? I'm not sure I could do it.

Carl could see probably every bit of that work its way across my face.

"I hate to ask," he said. "But I sure did love it out there. I wonder how our place is doing. I'd love to get back on that land. It felt more like home than anywhere I've ever been."

"I understand that," I said. "And you deserve that. I want to be able to give you that. I'm just not sure I could. I feel like I can walk on this land, but I fear what might happen if we go back. I'm not certain I would be able to walk there."

He looked away. He didn't want me to see his face. I suspect he was angry, or quite possibly frustrated with me. His will is iron: anything he sets his mind to do, he does. I'm sure part of him wondered why I couldn't give him this one thing. Why couldn't I be like him; just decide to do it, then follow through? I wonder that as well; I'd love to forget the way it felt after we lost our little girl. But those memories are part of me I can't excise. I started to cry, also turning away from him. I didn't want him to think I was playing on his sympathies. I almost said "yes," but I couldn't. I simply couldn't.

We were silent for a hard minute. Then I heard him clear his throat.

"Never mind," he said, putting a hand on my shoulder. "Just a thought. Maybe someday. I've heard a few times about some Gorin families going to Colorado. Apparently there's plenty of land to homestead or pick up at a place called Boyero. I'll see what I can find out about that."

IV. Boyero
1910-1931

Starting Over

W e now reside in Boyero, Colorado. A state, not a territory, like Arizona to the south. A big square state, where people can still homestead, so we were able to use the meager funds we had to buy a few head of cattle and live under a roof. The land itself is spare and joyless compared to Oak Creek. But it was free.

Carl has built me another house. I don't know how he finds the enthusiasm for all the work, but he puts so much of himself into it. This house makes the one in Sedona I thought so grand seem plain in comparison. The craftsmanship Carl's done here is so meticulous, and there are so many things I'd never even thought to want: pocket doors, windows on two sides of our bedroom, a whole area just for dressing! And the moldings, the carved doorframes…it's truly a thing of beauty. The children love that the downstairs rooms all connect so that they can run through them in a circle. (If I'd thought I might have suggested he not build it like that, but surely the novelty will ease.)

Last night he was standing on the front veranda (which is far too long to be called a mere porch) and I came out behind him and put my hand in his. "Thank you," I said. "I never deserve what you do for me, but how I do appreciate it."

When Carl says something flowery it always takes me unexpectedly; he's mostly a plain speaker. But this time he turned and said solemnly, "I don't deserve any of you. I don't deserve your love. I don't deserve your hair, with nature's own permanent wave. I don't deserve how good a mother you are, how you play and sing, your good meals. If this makes you feel appreciated, it is worth every nail."

My cup runneth over.

Hank

Feb. 3, 1912

My little Hank! What a true piece of work. He's working with modeling clay that I made from flour and baking powder, and pounded it to a flat piece with a wavy edge.

"Look, Mama! I made a dead ostrich by a lion." He says this with a face brimming with good cheer, and a happy countenance. Carl said the other day, "I don't think I ever sang just walking around, like Hank does."

One day, while we were returning to the house from some errands, I said a little impromptu prayer, thanking God for the children and our health, and such; then I asked Hank if he had anything he wanted to say to God.

"Dear God," he began confidently, "Thanks for making the world just...so...great!"

To Hank it is. He exudes pleasure, relish in what's going on. He expects to be delighted on a regular basis, and he is. He is deeply amused by nonsensical ideas that come to him. With a hearty chuckle he once said, "What if a baby dinosaur snuck up on a big plated dinosaur... and he burped?" It tickles him. He's been fascinated by the discovery of dinosaurs since Tad told him about them; Tad having gotten to see a plated dinosaur exhibit at the World's Fair in '04 in St. Louis, when Carl took him by train back there for that adventure.

Another day, Hank came running in: "Mama! I've been watching ants, and how they all go in a line. They are having a parade! So I clapped and cheered for them." I've seen ants for years and never had that thought.

I tend to ruminate, contemplate, evaluate. Carl solves, reasons, perseveres. But Hank enjoys! Not that he's frivolous. He sings an aimless little tune walking next to me, with an occasional skipping step that makes people pause on the church steps to watch with kind eyes. He answers any hello with a cute, awkward little wave repeated over and over. He is good, he believes life is good and people are good, and is rarely disappointed.

And there's something engaging about his demeanor. He has Carl's stocky legs and broad shoulders, with a little boy's stomach that rounds out in front when there's anything more than a chicken leg in it. His eyes, that clear light blue, meet yours straight on. He is a smile personified.

When I stop to watch Tad, I feel almost awe, that this intelligent, honorable young man is our son. Genevieve, beautiful self-contained girl, makes me feel grateful, soft, tender. When I catch sight of Hank, making his sturdy, certain way, I just laugh. He is all fun. He is joy. Strutting along, leading a chicken and talking all the way, or humming as he acts out a drama between two toy soldiers, there's just something touchingly humorous about him. His earnestness, his unconsciousness that he is worth watching. He has no self-awareness; his sentences never begin with "I." He doesn't need any applause.

"Guess what!" many of his sentences begin. Right now he's telling me about drawing a dragon, and a cave for him, "But I also drawed animals in the cave. But only nice animals. Fish, too. They're right in the cave. So that makes it nice."

Not that he doesn't have a temper. If he's sure I'm wrong, or someone has treated him poorly, the windows slam shut. He folds his arms and turns away with a "humph" that would do a Scottish recluse proud. If he's pouting, and I ask what's wrong, he won't tattle if someone has hurt his feelings: "It's a secret."

And now, he's writing a note to Tad.

"He'll have to use his eraser to read it," he says. "Because I'm covering the words with more pencil. Voila! That means 'ta-dah!' That's what it means."

When I ask how he knows that, he says, "I just know it."

His diction is clear, if unusual. I would like to follow him all day with a tablet, writing down every phrase. But I guess even if I will forget most of them, at the time I hear him pipe them out, they all creep into my heart and shine like silver.

Statehood

Our little Clara Amanda is five weeks old today. She's such a happy, even-tempered baby. Hank, delighted to no longer be the youngest, but a very big brother at four, talks to her constantly. She follows him with her big eyes. (Tad, fourteen in two days, seems a bit embarrassed that I had another confinement. I don't know how much he knows about how all that works, but I still remember when Mutter had Lola, that I felt there was something unseemly about it. So I leave him be.) Genevieve is eight, and loves bringing me things, holding Clara, even changing her. I can tell she yearns to be a mother. I hope she gets at least one child.

Carl came from town today and jumped down from the wagon seat so fast I was afraid something was wrong. He still moves as spry as ever, even though he turned 43 his last birthday.

"Dona! Dona! Guess what Sedona is now," he said as soon as he saw me. "Our little town is part of a state."

He had the newspaper, and there was an article about the United States getting a 48th state: Arizona. It said there were even moving pictures taken at the White House when President Taft signed the papers; they'd never taken moving pictures there before. We don't have any moving picture houses near here, but maybe someday Carl can go watch that somewhere. I know he still feels deep tenderness for "his" town (he says it's mine, not his, since it bears my name, but I counter it's his because he named it.) Anyway, there were fireworks and a parade in the new state. So now the "Territory" won't even be a letter on the cancellation stamp. Carl thinks it will be AZ instead of AT. I wonder if that same postmaster general is still at his job, or if Carl were to apply now, could it be named Schnebly Station? But I suppose you'd need a pretty good reason to change a town's name.

I think about going back from time to time, like touching a scar, or a place where a tooth was pulled, to see if there's any sensation. I'm not eager, I confess. We're happy here:—our lives are full, the children are blooming. But I also know Carl yearns a little bit, as much as he lets himself. He misses it. And certainly Boyero can't come close to Oak Creek in looks. Out here is flat and plain. It's grand for seeing who's coming, but not much for your eyes to catch on. They sweep all the way across the horizon without anywhere to rest.

Carl milking a cow outside Boyero house

Arizona, a state! I suppose we might eventually go for a visit. Although with everything going on here, I can't imagine how we'd get away. A young man, a girl, a small boy and a baby make for offspring who each need very different things.

Idylls Of The King

After re-reading *Idylls of the King*, I was so surprised by my reaction to it that I'd suspect the book of being altered, if it wasn't the same copy I read before I left Gorin the first time.

I remember so well Lillie and I being devastated at the ruin of Camelot, thinking Lancelot and Guinevere the unluckiest of all lovers, met too late and therefore trapped from ever enjoying to the fullest their perfect and unique feelings. We mourned for this golden couple denied the simple sweetness of meeting and marrying.

Of course, Lillie's visions of love have been smashed to flinders. She has burned every letter Loring sent to Mutter, looking for his wife. She won't divorce him, but he has ruined her belief in true love, at least in the realm of romantic love.

Anyway, upon this last reading, I found myself completely out of patience with Guinevere and Lancelot. Mercy, what a whining and weak pair they were. Oh, they felt an attraction. Oh, it must be lived to the fullest. Oh, life is so unfair to us. What stunted souls, thinking that merely because it was felt, it must be indulged.

Attraction happens in life. It can feel intense. And like a fire, it also burns itself out in time. But because those two thought themselves so special, so removed from the rest of us, they ruined a good man's trust (twice, once from each of them), a kingdom, and a dream. Seems a high price to pay for a bit of yearning fulfilled.

Love. That puts a pretty face on it. Love, my foot. Love is what happens over time. Love doesn't flourish by feeding off the broken innocence of another person. That would be lust or passion, false gods indeed.

I'm sure anyone under the age of twenty fell under the spell of the story. (Perhaps some people older than that as well; Loring taught us that some adults are actually just much older children.) But I thought this time I read it that the tale spoke to impetuous selfishness, and the consequences of not considering other people, more than actual love.

See someone when they're sick. Hold the basin, bathe the face. Bear witness to discouragement. Behold every weakness. And then—then—if you can still look at that person and be humbled by the force of your feeling, call it love. But not before that.

Healing

Jan. 30, 1916

Today we took Hank up to Hugo to get the cast off his leg. That broken ankle was the result of him deciding to jump from the barn loft, wearing wings made out of some baling wire with sections of the unbleached muslin I use to dry fruit on. (He's a good boy, but children don't think: the fruit is spread to dry on the muslin for a reason: piling it on one small piece of cloth won't do the same job.) It was a pretty mess—Hank shrieking in distress and pain, and maybe outrage that his experiment was such a spectacular failure, the cart he fell on crushed to bits, and (my insult to his injury) the fruit itself possibly ruined.

He's been in the cast and using crutches for eight long weeks. It didn't hinder him as it would have me; he quickly learned to get up and down stairs, navigating flat stretches nimbly. And of course, he isn't constantly carrying things from place to place as I am, so his hands are free to crutch. But the girls fussed because he couldn't do some of his chores, since collecting his share of eggs, dumping pails of dirty water, other things fell to them. Hank was as blithely unrepentant as only a sibling can be. I told him to thank them, but it was a poor effort—his glee at being able to duck the chores couldn't be disguised. We are all glad to be able to get beyond this chapter. Carl and Hank and I went, leaving the others home with a mostly free day. I felt they'd earned it.

I savored the ride, with wildflowers already from the rainy winter. I count us so fortunate that the county seat is large enough to have a good doctor. You hear horror stories of quacks preying on a luckless population.

I stayed with Hank while the doctor cut the cast down the center, scored the back side and opened it like a book. Carl took this time to get the shopping done. It was perfect because I don't think he wanted Hank to know he's not good at medical situations. I didn't know it myself for probably the first ten years or so we were married. He's so stoic, and practically fearless. But one day I noticed he had a rag wrapped around his hand, and asked what happened. He jumped as if he'd been caught doing something devious.

"Nothing, nothing," he said. "It'll be right in a day or two."

I left him to it, but kept my eye on him without comment, and after three days he was starting to support that hand with his other wrist. I decided respect ran out where good sense began. I sat down at the table and held out my hand.

"Carl, I need you to come here."

He trudged over like a dog anticipating punishment. But he saw my resolve, and slowly settled into his chair. I unwrapped the cloth and he took a deep breath in, turning his head away. I felt his heels begin to jiggle under the table, a sure sign of upset in Carl.

It appeared to be a splinter, but I wasn't certain because the site was puffy and red, angry and oozing.

"What on earth happened?" I asked.

"I don't even remember," he said crossly. "Just picked something up in it the other day, repairing the axle. It's fine."

"Clearly it's not," I replied. "Hold still."

He sighed, as if I was inconveniencing him for nothing, but I noticed his shoulders settle as if he released some worry, so that gave me confidence. I got the kettle, which always has hot water, and some soft rags and witch hazel. I cleaned the puffy red wound, tied it in wet strips of cloth, and said I'd check it again after dinner.

It took a few days, but the splinter surfaced with no further infection. It was because of that I realized that things to do with physical processes upset Carl in a way he didn't want to let show. So it was easy for me to take over that role. I love the wonders of the body, almost to the point it feels indecorous. Taught growing up that women didn't let their bodies make any noise or emit any substance (and if they did, pretend they didn't), I felt like something was wrong with me. But to me a scab, shrinking as it darkens, finally falling off to reveal tender skin, is as much a sign of new life as daffodils pushing out of the soil in springtime, or baby birds pecking out of their shells to me. All are rejuvenation, rebirth.

So watching the doctor, it came to mind that I would watch a surgery if I had the opportunity. To me, that is interesting. But I wouldn't want to carefully observe the entire process of a carcass gradually decomposing.

Which makes me conclude we each have unseeable spectrums. They include what is interesting versus what is horrifying, in terms of the human body healing. Other spectrums could be what is humorous versus what is silly, what is cautious versus what is cowardly, what is cultured versus what is pretentious. So my fascination-with-body spectrum includes surgery, but not decomposition. Carl's is even more limited.

With all that, it was just as well Carl wasn't there when Hank's cast came off. Because it had been a number of weeks since his leg had been out in the world, the skin was white, puckered and shredding. It was old dead skin, we discovered, and Hank and I started pulling it gently free when the doctor excused himself to go attend to something. We looked at each other like we'd discovered a fun but slightly unacceptable game, carefully loosening longer sections and sheets, competing to see who could liberate the larger continuous strip. Parchment thin, fragile as a butterfly's wing—this was Hank's skin: a part of him, but a part of him no longer. We were fascinated. It was such furtive fun to play with this gossamer aspect of science and creation.

But I knew Carl wouldn't see the beauty of it. So when Hank asked if we could take the old skin to show Dad, I said mildly that I thought the doctor should probably keep all things to do with his broken bone together in one place. (Parents can sometimes say things with sufficient certainty to convince a child it is true.) Hank nodded, holding his legs out straight to compare the ankles.

"That one's so much smaller," he said of the newly hatched left side. I explained about muscles, and how when we don't use them they seem to go away, but reassured him it would soon be back as it used to be without him having to do anything particular. The body is a wondrous healer.

When we left the office to meet Carl, Hank was walking with a little hitch, trying out the freshly released limb, getting used to it again.

"I'll miss my crutches," he said. "They were fun. They could be so many things: bridges and rifles and clubs and other stuff."

"Well," I said, "it's a good thing you have such a fine imagination; you'll find something else that's fun in no time."

Sure enough, some of the supplies Carl had picked up were in a heavy cardboard box with wire handles ingeniously installed on both ends, which Hank immediately saw as a potential boat. He had his promise from Carl that it would be his once we were home, before he casually mentioned taking a ride down the canal. I glanced at Carl, and saw him smile. At this time of year the canal is low and mild. I said, "That sounds interesting."

I once heard a teacher say, "Intelligent children are never bored." Hank doesn't have Tad and Genevieve's bookish curiosity. But his mind is so active; he turns things sideways in his head to see them differently than most of us do. I'm glad we didn't bring the dead skin home with us, but I'm equally glad we shared the odd, but wonderful (to some, anyway) experience together.

Holiday

I love this time of year.

Carl had to go all the way to Colorado Springs, but he brought us back a pine tree! And things to add to our decorations: cranberries to string, and colored paper to cut into strips and glue into chains. It was a good harvest, and he said he really wanted this year to be special. Genevieve has turned thirteen! Hank is nine; Clara is four. Margaret doesn't really care about any of it, at a year and a half, but her eyes grow big looking at the tree in the house. Tad is eighteen, a grown man at the Teachers College in Greeley, but writes that he cannot wait to come home. He looks forward to the fondant, and the gingerbread, and all of us singing carols by the piano. He wrote he thinks about waking up to hear Dad breaking ice on the water buckets. Funny—I'd never thought of that as something you might miss. But I guess it is certainly a sound associated with a person and place; no one at school does that. They have water inside there, and steam heat. Which would be nice, but this says "home" to him, hearing Dad's early morning gift of industry and service to his family.

We will have a turkey, and there are gifts—such gifts! Clara will get a big china doll, and I have made some exquisite clothes for it. Genevieve is getting a dress of real velvet. Hank wanted trucks like the ones he sees every time we're at the store in Hugo, and Carl outdid himself making an elaborate painted set with wheels that turn on axles from wire he had. (It's actually finer than the store's set!) Margaret is getting a huge soft doll I have made in secret, with her own wardrobe. I suspect she will adore it. Carl and I don't exchange gifts anymore; we have all we could want in each other. I love waking up, hearing, "Another Merry Christmas, Mother." I touch his cheek and say, "Another Merry Christmas, Dad." We are so blessed to have this big, healthy, happy, family.

War

I don't often question God—not on purpose—but I have to wonder why He, in His infinite wisdom, had to make men such blockheads in some areas. Even the good ones. Carl could not be a finer man, nor a more pleasing husband, and I admire most things about him. But he tried to explain to me Tad's frustration at not being shipped overseas to fight. And I won't have any of it.

Our firstborn, our son who is only twenty, already in uniform in a munitions factory in Ohio where explosion is a constant threat, wrote how unhappy he is that he can't be on the front lines. And Carl, handing me his part of the letter we would both send back, had been sympathetic. I said not a word after I read it; I just handed it back to him and came in here to write. I didn't dare say what I was thinking.

What don't men understand? That every single one of those uniformed soldiers is someone's son. That they each, on one unforgettable day, smiled a wet wobbly smile with the gleam of a first tooth showing through the gum. That they each said "Mama," and each learned to tie shoelaces, and each broke out in pimples. They are flesh and blood and bone and love, not just cheap machines for carrying guns. Each is his mother's very heart, and is being mowed down for some abstract ownership of power.

I've long held that men are somehow wired for wide views, large concepts. Land, exploration, honor and country. Women's eyesight is much clearer on small things: who likes honey instead of sugar in her tea, the uncertain downcast look of someone feeling awkward in a large gathering, the hesitation that comes before someone shares something secret and difficult to say. So war means very different things to us than to them.

Well, Carl is a man. I'm fortunate he didn't get called off to fight; born right after the Civil War, and already a father during the action in Cuba that took Pauline O'Neill's Buckey. Carl could have gone, I suppose, but fortunately his sense of duty to us far outweighed whatever lure that might have held. If I remember rightly, he was unsure it was a noble cause.

I suppose there's nothing wrong him with extending understanding in a letter. I just don't want that to encourage Tad to do anything foolish; stow away in a munitions shipment to the front for one glorious charge that places him within reach of the enemy guns.

Sometimes I wonder if the world is like a human body. If you have a hangnail, your tooth doesn't hurt. But if you are actually diseased, I think everything can be affected. Look at a woman after a long illness; her hair is dull, her skin is pale, her lips are cracked…even if it was a kidney that went all wrong and laid her up in the first place, all kinds of other things are affected. (Funny—you can be laid up and laid low, and they mean the same thing.) Could it be that so it goes with humanity? If enough mothers and widows are mourning their losses, can the rest of us truly go blithely about our days, smug and complacent? Don't we almost owe those sorrowing women our diminished enjoyment of a good breakfast? Isn't it perhaps toxic to the whole, when one part is in such pain?

The Great War. What a misnomer. I know they mean great as in vast, but it still sounds wrong. So many countries swept up, sucked in. We kept watching and praying we'd be left out of it, but as Carl explained from the paper, then the Kaiser decided the Sussex pledge meant nothing since we were supplying arms to his enemies. (Some of which might have actually been touched by my boy in Ohio.) I remember well our outrage in this country when German submarines torpedoed and sank the passenger ship, the Lusitania, causing more than 1,000 innocent souls to perish, including at least 100 Americans.

We've been protected from the worst of it: not living in a large city, we don't see the banners with blue and gold stars hanging in windows on every street where we walk (blue for a son who is serving, gold for one who died in that service). The food restrictions which we honor out of loyalty to our country, wheatless and meatless days, are to us more about teaching the children how to care about others than any actual privation. Since we grow more than we buy, we don't face the shortages city residents do. Carl reads us news out of the *Hugo Range Ledger* from time to time, but nothing that he senses might upset the girls.

Hank just sees the war as a reason to engage in more fighting play with his friends. And actually, he did finally complete one pair of knitted socks for a serviceman. Clara, bless her, has been a small six-year-old factory of one, diligently bent over her needles whenever she's not actually moving. It takes a long time to make a pair of lopsided socks, but they will be warm, and the yarn I buy for this is the thickest I can find. It delights me how she cares for others; her little heart is full of compassion. I do as many sweaters as I can, and Carl takes our bundles into Hugo when he goes to pick up mail or purchase something he can't either make or do without.

Mostly, I pray. I pray for mothers not as fortunate as I, whose sons are not in the Army in Ohio, but in the Army in France, enduring the conditions we read about and try to forget. I sometimes grow tired of this prayer. I started praying when President Wilson began to grow our military. I kept praying while we were supporting other people's soldiers. I continue praying while we send our own. And I pray Tad doesn't get blown up in an accident, and instead will come home to teach somewhere close by.

I know that I'm no more worthy, no more deserving of a living son than mothers who have had to receive a dreaded telegram. I am certainly glad not to be one of the telegraph operators receiving and forwarding all those sad messages. Sometimes, trying to fall asleep, I convert words into Morse code to give my mind something specific to do, so it keeps me from getting in a frenzy about something else. Clara: -.-.- .-.. .- .-. .-, and so on. I suppose it's silly, but it's comforting to know I could still transmit or receive a telegraph.

I've always subscribed to the idea that the End Times are known only to God, and I suspect that each generation has felt itself the first to live in so perilous and dangerous an era: never have there been so many young men—I can't even picture millions—maiming and killing one another with horrid new machines to aid in their destruction. I understand the Socialists who preach against the government on this issue. I wouldn't say it out loud. But I understand.

This is why I write, I suppose. To work through something without doing any damage with it. As I look down, my lap desk catches my eye. Carl made me this. It's only plywood, but he shaped it to curve around and rest on the arms of my rocking chair, so I can be comfortable while I write. He stained it a handsome cherry, and polished it smooth. He takes care of all of us. Me, by making something I'd never have dreamed to ask for; Tad, by understanding what it's like to be a young man who wants to be part of big things. He's always so patient when I get in a mood, and never seems to get in one himself.

I'll go and see if he'd like a dish of cobbler and cream before bedtime.

Food

If food just fell from the sky like manna, I don't know what I would do with myself all day. But it seems like I'd have all day to do it.

We just finished setting up sauerkraut in the ten-gallon crocks, layering the cabbage and salt, over and over. And Carl is butchering, so pig squeals abound. The children are eager for cracklings, which are the reward for frying down skillet after skillet of meat, which then gets layered in crocks and covered in lard to keep it from going rancid. It lasts all summer in the basement.

My back hurts already, and we aren't finished by half. The smokehouse is ready for the hanging pork, which is good. But it will be well past dark before I get the last skillet scrubbed out.

And even once we're done cooking, and laying in our stores, there will be soap to make from the lye and bacon fat. It makes Clara so sad when a pig has to die, but right now I feel it's the pig that gets the good end of the bargain.

Then, of course, today there had to be a rat. I saw him run for the door when I came into the kitchen. How Carl could tell me to let it go is beyond me. Who could sleep knowing that at any second, tiny feet might skitter across your face? (You can tell me as many times as you want that rats have no desire to seek out our sleeping forms; you can't prove it.) So the children helped me tear the house apart, and one of the cats found it, finally, under the hall tree seat.

How do people who don't have a store anywhere near them get by? Here we do get to buy 25-pound bags of dried apricots, and crackers. (I so miss Oak Creek's bounty of fruit.) We are constantly going through the apples stored in the cellar to ferret out the soft and brown ones before they spread rot to the others. I make so much applesauce I think I could do it in my sleep. I wish I could do it in my sleep.

But boredom must be the mother of creativity—I came up with what I call "apple pie dessert" which is the opposite of strudel, in that it takes almost no time. (I didn't think anti-strudel as appealing a name.) I mix dark and white sugar, a little flour, an egg and baking powder right with diced apples and a few nuts, and it bakes into a lovely dish I can serve with cream.

I told the children we will do a taffy pull this weekend as a reward for all our work. There's a box supper next week, too. So it's not all work and no play.

I know all our neighbors would give anything for a real bathroom, which thanks to Carl we do have. That copper tub makes me the envy of every wife within a ten-mile radius of Hugo. I know some who have to just splash off in the creek, or an irrigation ditch; others with just the standard pan in front of the stove in which to stand ankle-deep with a pitcher. Of course, I still have to heat some water, even while I can pump cold water into the tub. The important thing is getting the scent of pork out of my hair without having to be outside, or standing chilly in front of the kitchen stove. Tonight, I'm having a bath. I don't care if it's Tuesday. And I'm not winding the girls' hair in curl rags tonight. I know we all like it; curls seem to indicate leisure, and polish, and beauty. But Carl will just have to avert his gaze tomorrow if seeing his straight-haired daughters reminds him he has a faulty wife who can't get everything done every day. Lord knows I try.

That's not even fair. He would never scold me for not doing enough. He's the one constantly saying, "That doesn't have to be done before bed, Dona." In my guilt, I'm trying to make him the voice of higher standards. It shows how tired I am to turn my hero into my villain, instead of making myself the taskmaster of my thoughts. I wish I could see myself as Carl sees me.

Justice

I believe it was the ancient Greeks who first said that the mills of God grind slow but exceeding fine.

Loring has been sentenced to Leavenworth Prison. Apparently we were not the last dupes who trusted him. Lillie wrote us the news.

He has been leaving her and coming back, for years, I knew that; and we have had countless conversations by correspondence about why she lets him return. But what else, she asks, can she do? He is her husband. She wouldn't divorce and find another. She lives in a constant state of between, of upheaval, of unrest. Loring there, Loring gone. Neither is good.

Anyway, she says, apparently he cheated another partner who got angry enough to launch a search even beyond the state borders. (Carl hadn't had the funds back when it happened to us.) Pinkerton agents ran him to ground somewhere in Kansas, and because his crimes occurred in more than one state (I won't even ask), he was sentenced to prison at Leavenworth.

My emotions are very mixed. I am not nearly as jubilant as I would have imagined I would be upon hearing this news. Revenge should be sweet. But I'm so very sorry for Lillie. And so much has happened since he stole from us.

Although actually, now I realize I am furious. I have been since it happened and we had to move. I see from this surge of fury that I just don't let myself reflect upon it, or it would bring me to my knees, rob me of the will to do what must be done. I am filled with white-hot rage. How dare he! He stole our success, our future. That we have rebuilt to some degree doesn't excuse what he did.

Well, now he's in prison. Now I know that he won't do anything to any further trusting innocents. But Lillie is worse than a widow: she can't move forward and find love, nor is she loved or provided for. She writes that she had salted some money away during the fat years, and thinks if she is careful she won't have to work in a restaurant. But she's afraid, and rightfully. She is back with Mutter.

The only funny thing: Loring isn't his name. Well, it is, but not his first name.

John. John Loring Johnson. Lillie didn't know that until she received the notice that he was being imprisoned.

That's rich fare. What a masquerade. A plain, common John, acting like a Loring. And this is where it brought him.

The tragedy is that he dragged so many others along, bruising and breaking them, on his sorry path to perdition.

Armistce

Peace! The war has ended.

Men will return home to the fortunate families who didn't have to read telegrams that their boy was buried overseas. Some who do march in hometown parades will be broken in ways seen and unseen. We are among the most blessed, with Tad uninjured and still in America.

Even though for all practical purposes our lives will not change, it feels sweet to know the fighting is over.

I'm grateful, and yet I'm still feeling grim about the war happening at all.

Jan. 16, 1921

I just looked at the calendar and realized that since this is January, 1921, it's more than ten years since we came to Boyero. A decade!

When we came, Clara and Margaret weren't even thought of; Hank was three. Now Tad is a great grown man of 22 (thank God he's able-bodied and back in school while so many lie in foreign graves), Genevieve sixteen, Hank almost thirteen, Clara's eight and Margaret is five.

Just this morning I was thinking about how much I love this house. Carl gets better at building with each home. I still love the wainscoting, the special shelf above where he knew the piano would go, to hold my sheet music and books, the niche in the entry wall for the hall tree seat. He put beautiful details everywhere.

But because everything is both good and bad (I've always told the children, "Fire, knives and money can each be very helpful or very destructive, depending on the circumstances"), Boyero itself is my least favorite place to live. So wide, so flat, so spare, Carl and I have joked we could see the Four Horsemen of the Apocalypse days ahead of the Second Coming. The eye gets tired, having to go all the way to the horizon when looking in any direction, without any feature of either canyon or town upon which to stop and rest.

Schnebly family in front of Boyero house, left to right:
Genevieve, Sedona, Margaret, T.C., Clara, Hank, Tad

We came here because several families from Gorin had come. But we never see them. Everyone is scattered, and unless you chance to meet someone in Hugo, or at a church gathering, you toil away as a family, on your own land. They were right when they told us that the land is good; fertile and flat. But we've learned the hard way that when you're growing crops, the ground makes up less of the whole picture than one might think.

Our third year, it was grasshoppers. Everywhere. Speaking of the Apocalypse, it felt like a plague of Biblical proportions. Those creatures came, covered, chewed, and left us barren and baffled, stems picked to slivers. It was heartbreaking.

The next year was fine. God let us catch our breath and pay our bills. The year after that came the hailstorms. Poor Clara—we sent her out to rescue the chickens with a bucket on her head, but she came in with bruises all over her arms, that hail was so big and fell so fast and hard. The storm was short, so the crops survived. Then, the next hailstorm flattened every field before harvest, wiping out our hopes of any money from the year's harvest.

I remember that day. It felt as if there were no reserves left. Nature had not only won, but was standing on our necks and laughing at us.

Carl came in from surveying everything, and I caught the slightest shake of his head, telling me it was as bad as we had feared. But he saw us all sitting around the table, tense, nervous and still, and said, "What's with these long faces? There's a whole field of ice out there. Go fetch some buckets so we can collect it and make ice cream!"

Which we did. Thank goodness the cattle kept us in milk and meat and butter and cheese. And because it's an ill wind that blows no good, that was the year Hank decided fresh vegetables weren't so bad. We eked through on what I had canned, pickled and preserved, but after subsisting on so many things spooned out of glass jars, you yearn for something crunchy. (Popcorn. We always had popcorn, but that doesn't prevent scurvy.)

It was also so rainy that I felt the mudroom, full of wet boots, slickers, hats, and socks, would never again be dry and smell of sunshine. And the children would get restive, cooped up inside. I would play the piano and make them march. I doubt Carl did it with this in mind, but building the downstairs rooms so they each open into one another is perfect for helping the children get some exercise in bad weather. I play marches and they are supposed to keep time in a circle through the rooms. Since I love to play under any circumstances, they could get some of the wildness out without swinging from rafters or jumping off the staircase. While the songs I choose are measured to the beat of marching feet, I hear them scramble to run the second they disappear from view, then the muffled giggles as they compose themselves behind the kitchen door to pretend they weren't all bent-for-leather until reappearing. Solemn as a judge, I keep playing. Children need to feel power. And it's not malicious, just teasing.

I'm less comfortable when they tease me by changing steps. I never thought much of it, but apparently not everyone has to have people walking with the same feet at the same time, left, then right, always in step. Carl has always humored me and walks in step, but the children love to take a hopping skip step to alternate so we're all out of step. There's probably something wrong with me for caring, but I also feel that it doesn't ask too much of them to indulge me. Whether I let it go depends on how much patience I have on any given day.

Generally I'm patient, but when I do run out, I usually take it out on Carl, no matter who exhausted the end of what I had. Clara asked me recently why I want to live in the barn when our house is so much nicer. I felt bad; I didn't know she had heard that. Sometimes when Carl exasperates me, I say to myself, under my breath, "I'm going to go live in the barn." But she pays attention.

I told her it's just something I say when Dad thinks some foolishness is funny that I think is just foolish. She looked startled, as if she assumed that all grownups thought alike, simply by dint of being past the age of 30. She will learn.

Poor Clara—Carl never runs up charges at the store. I found out a few months back when she came home from town all downcast, that fathers who do that and then go in to settle the bill, get a piece of wrapped hard candy for each child upon payment. We live too carefully to do anything on credit. So this year for her birthday (good thing we didn't know how lean things would turn), I asked Carl to take all the egg money from the cup in the china cupboard and buy her hard candy. Her eyes were like stars on her birthday.

We are fortunate that there haven't been any prairie fires here. Maybe the railroad tracks and the stream would protect us, maybe not. I have no idea how far a prairie fire can jump—and I guess there's not one standard measurement—but when it comes to the unexpected, we have not had the best luck in Boyero so far.

Carl says farmers believe in God because Nature is so fickle that they have to think Someone who can rule the seas and command the clouds will look out for them. We've known hard years for other reasons in other places, but Boyero puts us most at the mercy of harsh elements. When there's lightning, I always work very hard not to voice my concern over a lightning strike starting a prairie fire that rain won't quench. I can almost feel that strike somehow, a quivering sensation in the back of my neck: a bolt of electric fire to something nearby that takes off and burns, growing and gobbling everything. We would run to the ditch and stay in the water until it passed over, so I don't fear for our lives. But our livelihood is precarious here. At least our cattle are strong, healthy, compliant animals. Nothing to fear there.

Silver Anniversary

Feb. 24, 1922

Carl and I have been married 25 years.

"Our silver anniversary, Dona," he said this morning. "Want me to buy you something silver?"

"I have my wedding band," I said, holding up my hand. "Even if it's white gold, it looks silver. This is quite all the silver I need."

But it does make one think. That's a quarter century. I would have thought I'd feel older, being a woman married 25 years.

It seems now as if life before him was something I only read about, or something that had happened to someone I knew, rather than someone I was. But at the same time it feels like it must have been only eleven years, or perhaps twelve, that we've been married. Twenty-five years? If we'd been married that long, we'd be old...we'd be dim...we'd be pale copies of our former selves. And yet, here we are, enjoying our walks, laughing at his silliness, holding hands under the table. I'd have thought being married 25 years would bleach all that out.

Margaret, our baby, is a big girl of seven. Clara's ten, Hank is fifteen. Genevieve is nineteen, and Tad, 24. He will be coming home for dinner this Sunday, as he does most weeks. He's teaching in Genoa, just past Hugo, and boards there. I miss him, but I am glad that he's an educator and loves his work.

It seems to me Genevieve might want to be going out on her own, but she says she loves being here. She's a tremendous help to me, mostly with the other three children. She will do any chore when asked, but because she loves to read, she will spend hours telling her siblings stories. That's worth even more. She also spends a fair bit of time alone. Unlike Clara, Hank and Margaret. Genevieve gets used up being with people in a way they don't.

Hank can get wild, but Carl is wonderful with him. Sometimes I hear him explaining something in a way that just sounds like conversation, about why it's such a good idea not to try spirits, or tobacco. Carl's so mild about everything, his comments just feel like observations, not advice. Hank respects him even more than Tad does, I think. Tad values education, and white shirts, and status in the community. Hank is more like his dad, and loves mucking about, getting dirty, fixing things. Tad lives up to the Miller that is his middle name. We can be a little bit snobbish about education if we aren't careful.

Surprise

August 22, 1922

I can't believe who came today. Travois! I didn't ever think I would see him again.

Carl was in town, and I heard a knock. I figured one of the girls needed something they'd forgotten for school, and hurried to the door, wondering as I did why they would knock.

There he stood, even darker, finally wearing a hat, but with that same great smile. For a moment he looked older, softer, with more spaces between his teeth. Then, suddenly, he hadn't changed a bit, and the force of his personality and his presence almost took my breath away. He swept me into his arms, and I held on so tightly. It was as if I was getting back something I'd thought I'd lost forever. I was crying and laughing, which I've done maybe only three times in my life. It was that big a shock.

He had heard we were in Colorado somewhere, and I guess in his travels up this way, kept asking around if anyone knew the Schneblys. Finally in River Bend not long ago, someone knew that Carl comes in occasionally. So he found us!

He has a pack mule now: "I don't travel as light as I used to, but I'm not as weighed down," he said with that old slightly mischievous quirk to his lips. I sat at the table, just drinking him in as he drank lemonade, to which I'd added some tutti-frutti syrup. He said he's been thinking about that treat for fifteen years...

When Carl got back, he looked once, and twice, and laughed out loud! They clasped hands and slapped backs, but then abandoned male etiquette and hugged one another like brothers. Their smiles were so broad it made my heart happy. I put lunch together and the men talked: where all have they been? What's changed? Travois didn't know anything that had happened after we left, assuming us to be still in Missouri, but then a second cousin of Carl's visiting Oak Creek had told someone we were back out west, and in Colorado. So since then, he'd been asking. (I suspect it might have made him trek farther north and east than he normally would.)

It's taken me years to realize this, but now I'm certain of it: when you're in the company of someone you met earlier in life, part of you feels that age again. Seeing Travois, I'm aware of how it felt to be the young mother, newly come from the suffocation of society, experiencing independence and developing resourcefulness I'd never have developed otherwise. I could feel being her so strongly. Travois' voice, the easy way he pronounces big long words, even though sometimes his demeanor is almost uneducated, was something I'd forgotten.

Carl laughed more during these three hours than he has in ages. He, too, seemed transported back to a younger age, and there were so many great memories: Billy Wallace, the elections, certain visitors from back then. The time the creek flooded from snowmelt (a story which, burnished by years, has changed from harrowing to humorous). Travois seems less restless, more at peace. Sometimes I used to detect in him a need to be admired, or wondered about. That's gone. I suspect a woman plays a role in that, but being himself, he didn't mention anyone special. Yet, I think so.

Travois said he had been through Oak Creek within the past month, and Carl hung on every word about it as if Travois were describing the Seven Cities of Cibola or the Lost World of Atlantis. He didn't say, "Can I touch you in case you still have Oak Creek dust on you?" but I bet he would have liked to. Travois says so many people live there, we might not recognize it if it weren't for the rock formations. He says there are dozens and dozens of families, and sometimes rich or famous people come to see what all the fuss is about.

I don't know if we will see him again. But my heart is happy knowing he didn't spiral down into some dissolute lifestyle, or end up mauled by a grizzly and dying alone in a snowy wilderness. He's still moving about being Travois, and the world is better for it.

After he left, I carefully touched the place in my mind where Pearl is, wincing in advance. But there was no pain. That's interesting.

Shingles

Our poor Genevieve—she has shingles. None of the other children ever did, although all had chicken pox, which somehow stays inside the body and re-emerges as shingles. I'd grown tired of seeing her fuss with a spot on her eyelid, and finally took over with tweezers and hot cloths. It was a stubborn little whitehead. For the next four or five days I kept hearing about how much I'd hurt her, until blisters appeared on her nose. When bruising around that eye followed, I took her over to Aroya. Mrs. Burns knows a great deal, having birthed 18 children and raised 15 to adulthood. We were barely through the door before she saw Genevieve and said, "Well, it's a good thing we all had chicken pox."

It was both good news and bad: shingles go away—relief. Until they do, there's little to treat them—disappointment. Genevieve has such serenity, and insists it doesn't hurt that much, but she looks so tired, and Mrs. Burns said it could be a month or more before she has much energy. I've fixed up an aerie on the second-floor sleeping porch because it's so lovely out, and Genevieve has always seemed to need to see outside (she gets that from me—I never want the windows in the bedroom covered, so I can see out at night). She's appreciative when I bring in simple syrup to help her sleep, or honey for the rash, or willow bark tea to keep the fever from getting above a simmer. She reads, and she rests.

I will never know what's going on in that girl's mind. I do know she likes visiting the Cox family, although not who there makes her look extra alive. I had to send word for them to stay away unless they've had chicken pox. I hope they have, and someone visits.

Hank's been such a good brother. Those two always get along. I feel solicitous and sorry for her, and tend to just sympathize, but he goes in every evening after supper and I hear her in gales of laughter. He doesn't poke fun, and he doesn't pretend she's not sick...he just turns things sideways and makes them funny. He also has a quick mind—last evening I heard him making up words to some song or other. I think it was "My Wild Irish Rose," but there were noodles and chicken in the lyrics. Our boy...he was brought to this family to make sure that if Carl didn't remind us that the time to laugh is whenever you can, Hank would fill in those cracks. And even Carl's not as quick with the nonsense.

I am still wondering how it affected Genevieve to be forming her world when we lost Pearl. She was only two years old, and they say that by the time a child is five, he or she is pretty well cooked. So the last half of the time her character was forming, I was in grief; trying not to be, but I know it must have slopped over on her some. People would sometimes say well-intentioned things about how she could replace Pearl, and of course that's like saying your hand could replace your eye—other than being part of you, they really don't overlap.

Just to make sure I never made the mistake of trying to fit Genevieve into Pearl's place, I gave all Pearl's clothes to the Armijos before we left. I knew they took care of relatives, and someone would be able to make good use of them. I'd done such careful smocking and crochet work around her waists and collars, they were beautiful dresses. Of course, her shoes were always as scuffed as Tad's, the way the two of them careened around, getting into every place they'd fit. But her pretty little light blue coat, the white Easter dress...all those gone.

So, I put extra energy into Genevieve's new clothes, vowing she would never feel second best. I still do. Her corduroy jumpers that look almost like velvet she wants very simple, but I get to do pearl buttons and crocheted button loops on the cuffs of the blouses that go under them, and deep crocheted lace collars on those. Sometimes I weave ribbon through eyelet on her new petticoats just so she feels special when she gets them. Clara shows no interest in such things. But Margaret seems to think the sun comes up just to see how she's getting on, so I'm sure she'll want the same things in a few years.

Genevieve...she's such a still, deep pool. Hearing her laugh with Hank eases my heart. I wouldn't say this aloud, even to Carl, but I know shingles can last for years, and in some cases cause you to go blind. So I let them think I'm just extra nervous, fussing over her. This way I'll know that I've done everything I can.

Now Hank is declaiming "Listen, my children, and you shall hear," but it's not the real Longfellow poem. He's got cattle drivers as the "hardly a man is now alive" and Heaven knows what's coming next. Even worried about her, it makes my heart lighter to hear them laugh.

Joshua Cox

May 5, 1924

My oldest girl is being courted...and it's not what I would have expected. Tonight Mr. Joshua Cox came to call, and I am very proud that Carl assures me my face didn't betray my surprise when I saw him. Mr. Cox is much closer to my age than my girl's age: twenty years older than Genevieve, making him six years younger than I am.

They met in Hugo, when she was with Carl on a grocery and general re-stocking trip, in the rather grandly named Emporium. Mr. Cox is apparently a stock transporter and other things. In these times every man does whatever he has to do just to get by. And once I got past the initial startled reaction to his age, he did seem a kind fellow. Tall, leaning slightly forward as if to hear better, he is both merry and gentle with Genevieve, and makes her laugh in a manner I've never heard anyone do before. She is quite reserved—I blame myself for that; I've always been that way—and yet Mr. Cox seemed able to bring out something that has been dormant. For that alone, I am halfway to approval.

Carl was less favorably inclined when I asked his opinion after Genevieve had walked this first caller out and come back in to drift dreamily up to bed.

"I'm sure he's fine," he said briefly. In a flash, I understood: Mr. Cox was not being judged at all on any particulars of self, bearing, manner or education. He was a man who was outside of ourselves, and he would potentially remove Genevieve from her father's circle of love and protection. That's a new and uncomfortable feeling for Carl. Genevieve's never been flirtatious, or remotely interested in romance, even in the most general sense. Her choice of reading materials is daunting to me; instead of shallow penny papers or chapter serials, she reads Ovid and Marlowe and early plays I've not heard of. Talk of courting makes her impatient. She has said once or twice, "Why would I want someone to call? I know I don't like anyone, so he would just be wasting his time."

For the first time, her father may have to see another man touch her. I can't imagine that will be easy for Carl. But he loves his girls with his whole heart, and I know if he approves of this man, he will keep his feelings completely to himself.

It's that Matthew Arnold poem again which begins, "Come to me in my dreams," and always reminds me of Carl, for the line, "And be as kind to others as to me." He is so kind to everyone, and so protective of those of us he loves. He will be kind to Joshua Cox, if things go that way.

The first wedding in our family! Our oldest daughter will be a bride.

Joshua proposed, Genevieve told us tonight. (We maintained a properly receptive demeanor, although obviously we knew, because he had correctly come to Carl to ask for her hand prior to that.) She seems both matter-of-fact and delighted, gravely showing us the gold engagement ring, set with three small sapphires. My estimation of Joshua rose significantly; he values her enough to make sacrifices to buy that ring, not even knowing for certain she would say "yes" when he asked her. Or now that I think of it, maybe she made it very clear she would, somehow. She doesn't wax rhapsodic, or in any case, not to me.

They will be married in the New Year: January of 1925. She will be 21, a fine age for a young woman to become a wife. I think I'm a little relieved; I was always concerned her natural reserve might prevent her from knowing the joys of wifehood and motherhood. But she's giddy as a girl with him—odd, considering he's older. And he's boyishly charming with her. I'm delighted. And grateful to God for finding a man to bring her to this new stage of life.

She says she wants me to make her dress, something light yellow, despite the rush to white bridal gowns these days. "So I can wear it for church later," she says practically. She's always liked yellow, perhaps because she's Goldie Genevieve. I expect she will wear her usual crown of braids, and be decorous and lovely.

It's quite a reminder that years are accelerating.

Lucille

It never rains but it pours.

Now Tad is betrothed. I feel like we just got things back to normal after Genevieve's wedding.

When Tad came back from the munitions plant in Ohio after the war, he earned his lifetime teaching certificate from the Teachers College at Greeley. Since then he's been teaching at the Genoa High School, about fifteen miles away, for four years. He's also been the women's basketball coach, and one of the young women in his class captured his fancy.

Her name is Lucille, and she is nine years his junior, although an inch or so taller than he is, he has told us. He sounds quite smitten, bragging on her athletic skills, the reddish cast to her hair, her queenly posture. He says he first noticed her when she started as a freshman, and has been impressed with her for four years, but would have considered any advances untoward until this year, her senior year. He sounds ten years younger, clearly enjoying the anticipation of presenting her with her diploma in the morning, and marrying her that same afternoon. So their wedding date is May 15, which is a nice pattern when you write it down as 5/15/25.

Tad says Lucille hails from Missouri as we do, and moved to Colorado as a child. (Wouldn't it be fun to know if any of our people and any of her people ever passed in the street, with no foreknowledge of the upcoming marriage?) She has been staying with relatives, because her father had forbidden her to continue her education past the eighth grade. So her mother smuggled her out of the house one night with a coat on over her nightgown, bringing just a satchel in the wagon to put her with family. Quite bold! She's done very well in her studies; clearly a young woman who can flourish in arduous circumstances. I look forward to meeting her.

Little Tad. He's always been my boy. I think maybe losing Pearl made him more protective of me than he would have otherwise been. I am determined to be generous. They should live wherever they want. I'm glad Tad's seen how Carl has treated me over the years; what an excellent example of a husband. But even I see that Tad is not Carl. Hank is the one who got their Dad's humor, his easy nature. Tad is too much like me; perhaps feeling shy, he covers it up with a bit of authority, superiority. I used to warn him about not coming across as too stiff. Maybe Lucille sees those traits for what they are.

We met Tad's fiancée. Lucille is a lovely young woman, with a slightly lower pitch to her voice, an open smile and fine manners. She seems very comfortable, so Carl was able to tease her right off. Tad beams in her presence. She said the wedding will be small, with a breakfast afterwards. She plans to get a Sunday dress, nothing overly fancy. I like her tremendously, and I thank God Tad's found such a woman to be his wife.

Before dinner she came into the kitchen, despite my telling her to sit and talk with everyone. She looked around, saw Clara getting out the board and knife for cutting carrots, and said, "I'll do that," briskly. Clara flashed her a grateful look; carrots can be stubbornly hard and she's cut herself more than once.

I was impressed. Many people say, "Let me know if I can help" in a way that shows they hope you won't. And some do come in and ask what they can do. I've never before had a woman assess the situation so swiftly and act kindly, without being told a word.

She will be a wonderful helpmate for Tad. She's not at all retiring, seeming very comfortable in her own skin. Also, she doesn't require attention or admiration, the way many young women would. I suspect she didn't get much cosseting coming up. She told us she has a lot of brothers, as well as a sister. Maybe that made her stronger.

Lucille is not softly pretty; her features are strong. But she is appealing; her face has a nice shape, her eyes are blue and lovely, and her posture is truly elegant. She looks like she will gain in beauty over time as she grows into her features, instead of being one of those powder-puff girls who get too soft.

Lucille Finney

Now that she has her diploma, might she want to teach? I asked. She said no; she loves doing things with her hands more than standing or sitting in a classroom. She quilts, and enjoys sewing as much as gardening. "Although if I sew inside, I don't enjoy it quite as much," she said with a quick smile. "I think I would live outdoors if it were practical. Everything is better outside."

I really like this girl.

Radio

March 6, 1926

Carl came home two days ago with a big box and a bigger smile. "Look what we have, Dona," he said. "We have the world." He bought us a radio.

Money's eased a little this year, so I didn't fret about the cost. A radio will be wonderful. Carl gets the news usually several days late. I'm sure he will still savor reading longer stories in the papers he picks up when he goes over to Hugo. But to hear about things as they happen! There are also dramatic shows to listen to, and lots of music.

This radio is a beautiful thing: a light wood case polished to a shine, and large shiny silver knobs with numbers above them. Tad will be over the moon when he sees it. He loves gadgetry. That's funny—Hank does as well, but he mostly likes taking old things apart. Tad loves new inventions, sometimes just for the having of them.

In any case, we have listened both evenings so far, and it's amazing to hear so clearly something happening hundreds of miles away as if it's right here. In fact, Carl says late at night there's a program you can listen to coming all the way from England!

The names of things are odd: Fleischman's Yeast Hour has nothing to do with bread. Apparently the company just pays for people to come on and sing or play music. And Blackstone Plantation has nothing to do with the South or plantations; it's a man and woman talking, and other people coming to sing. But it's all entertaining. I asked Carl the other day at dinner if he wanted to turn it on, and he said no: "If I did,

I wouldn't get another thing done this afternoon. Only at night after supper." It's a wise man who knows himself.

Feb. 10, 1927

I realize as I look back over these pages that I'm writing more letters in that precious hour after the noon dishes are done, and less here in my journal. And I think I know why.

When I first began writing, it was about my life and thoughts; some things concerned my parents or siblings, but a child doesn't pay much mind to that. But now, so many of my thoughts and mullings center around Carl and the children. Children, who are mostly adults with lives of their own. It feels disloyal to say something about them if it's anything but happy facts. So I don't write.

That sounds like I'm hiding dark opinions, and I'm not. But why write anything down that might be hurtful?

Maybe it's also that I'm less breathless about most events. So many things happen: startling, lovely, terrifying and funny. And then we move on. Such things happened for centuries before I was born, to someone, and will continue to happen to someone else when I'm gone. Nothing feels as urgent or as remarkable as when I was young.

And yet. This reminds me that someone said the truly big questions can only be answered with, "Well, yes and no." Who came calling, what someone said, what I wore, have faded in importance. The things that are most important now are what I would have called small things when I was younger.

When Clara and I smile at one another because we say the same thing at the same time; a smile of recognition and delight that someone shares a thought that closely. When I hear Carl laugh uproariously at one of Hank's jokes; proud that his son can tell a story so well, and surprise him. Seeing one of the cows being tender toward her newborn can bring tears to my eyes. Yes, it's just a cow. But that caring and nurturing has also been repeating itself in beast and man since time began, and there's something important and reassuring in seeing it play out again.

While I'm about it, my favorite times of day are the very first and very last moments. Waking up, realizing that the night has passed and I get to see sunrise again soon, and feel the warmth of the fire once I've stirred the banked coals and added some kindling; that soon bacon will send out a breakfast scent and Carl will come in with his, "Well, Mother, you're as pretty to look at as you were yesterday," and for a moment place his hand on my cheek. When anyone is around, I feel foolish and odd as he touches me, but when we are alone, I can look in his eyes and let that love fold around me in the sweetest way. The other best time is getting into bed, in a crisp clean white nightgown, or one that's a few days in, worn soft and scented a little bit like cotton and pillows. It's stretching my feet out, knowing I will get to read for a time while Carl putters around "putting the house to bed." He checks the doors...truth, I'm not sure what all he does. But there's some patriarchal instinct to make sure we are protected and things are as they should be, before he can take himself off duty and come to me, and rest. We hold hands when he comes to bed, and generally I'm asleep before he moves his away.

Grandmother

Many things are cyclical; seasons turn, everything and every-one ages. But while I know that, I still keep stopping, arrested by thought, whatever I'm doing: wiping the table or drying knives, struck again by the fact that Carl and I are grandparents. How can that be? I remember my grandparents; while kind, they seemed almost a different species than us: all folds and wrinkles, dry and rather musty, like they needed to be hung on the line and worked on with a carpet beater to bring back vital color and freshness. Yet here we are, somehow 51 and 60, with a grandson. Lucille has given us all a boy! Tad's son.

We got the telegram early this morning. Lawrence Wilbur Schnebly. A whole new person. Lucille is fine, by Tad's account. I so wish we were in Colorado Springs to see him, but I know they'll come when they can. Tad insisted the birth be at the Crestone Heights Sanitarium, with actual nurses and all. I am both touched and somehow a little ruffled that home birth had been plenty good for him and all his siblings, but not for his son. Still it's nice he wants to take such care of his wife, and now his family. A grandson. I guess it's time. Margaret is thirteen; she and Clara are wild to be aunties.

It seems a grand and momentous thing: an exact time and day that another generation was launched by the birth of a person who doesn't yet know he is one. Gradually he will become aware.

Someone said every birth is like watching the human race get started all over again: first walking, then learning to use tools, to talk, sing, figure, and perhaps even come up with new ideas or inventions. I loved the involuntary arm waves and stretches of a newborn, the sagging skin like the baby hadn't grown into it yet. The squeaks and squints that gradually turned into awareness and a wide wobbly smile. All of that lies ahead for our family.

Could anyone have a baby and not believe in God? In my own body it seemed impossible to figure: I knew nothing about growing a tiny set of lungs, how to form the littlest bones and muscles. But I would eat (and savor each bite with a kind of greed and almost ecstasy I'd never known), and somehow the eggs and bread and cheese and fruit also fed a potential person who was taking shape. Then the first time I felt them each move; a secret greeting from someone who didn't know me yet. I felt like a fort providing protection for a population of one, guarding someone so important and special, keeping him or her shielded from the world.

Being pregnant didn't bring me down much; I knew women who were constantly grinding their fists into their backs, sitting down pendulously. I moved almost as spryly at the end as the beginning. And even when I felt a little ungainly, a little too big, I also felt very strong and powerful, a type of fierce femininity. Carl wasn't the kind of man to croon about a woman's glow and beauty, but he was always even more careful with me when I carried, urging me to lie down right after dinner.

I thought I didn't get emotional like some women do, peckish and fretful over small things. And then I said that out loud at a Sunday dinner when Tad and Lucille were visiting us, a few months back. Carl, who wouldn't hurt anyone and especially not me, laughed out loud before he could stop himself, then looked so sheepish and sorry it made me smile as well. "Really?" I said. "I was? I thought I was always calm and steady."

It surprised me, and made me wonder what else I think is true that may not be. But regardless, I did it six times and now Lucille's done it once. He is another oldest boy in the family. We Millers started with Edward. Then Tad was our first, and now he's got a son to begin another layer of lineage. God, bless little Lawrence, I thought. Give him what he needs to make it through hard times; let the world be kind to him.

Jan. 1, 1929

Well, Larry—Lawrence Wilbur—was christened. He wore the long gown I made for Tad. It was such an odd collision of past and present. I could remember putting the stitches in something that was then on the way to becoming an heirloom, only I didn't know it. Little Larry has Carl's mouth, with that thin straight upper lip, and Lucille's lovely blue eyes, bright and curious and open. He was good during the ceremony; almost better than his Aunt Margaret, who had her new white dress on and kept fussing with it 'til I wanted to swat her hands. She isn't the baby any more, and even as a big old girl like that, I could tell she wasn't one bit happy about not being the youngest and adored center of attention. I spoke sharply to her after church.

I'd written Mutter that she was now a great-grandmother. It was too bad Papa didn't know—well, I suppose he knew, from Heaven. But we didn't get to see him know. And of course Carl's father is gone. But we are now Gramma and Grampa. It's amazing to take in. And wonderful. The light in Carl's eyes makes me happy. He's Larry's Grampa. The line continues.

Anthrax

Dec. 11, 1930

I'm so worried about Carl. He hasn't been able to shake the cold he got right after Thanksgiving; that cough just drags on, no matter how much Mormon tea, how much flaxseed I give him. And the past two nights he's not slept. He's burning cattle. Our cattle.

Our cattle. Poor creatures—they got anthrax. We aren't even sure how; it's been a hard winter, and Carl had brought water when the ditch wasn't running. Maybe it was in there. But whatever it was, the first two died a few days ago. He said Genevieve's favorite, Holly, was trembling before she fell. He was worried already when Ben came by to say he'd heard there was an outbreak. Carl looked up the symptoms in that ranching guide he keeps.

Sure enough, they seemed fine and then got very sick very fast. Most of them were dead when we got up the morning after the first two died, just lying on the ground. So now, as distressed as it makes me to write this, Carl had to go out to burn the bodies. I guess once anthrax gets into a herd it just gets worse and spreads, and then the carcasses have the disease. People can even become infected. I wish he didn't have to be out, exposed to the cold and wind. I can see the glow of the fire from here. God bless him! Carl has worked so hard, and he loves each one of those cows. (Well, not Trudy so much—she always tried to kick him when he milked her.) But to have to deliberately, willfully, obliterate all traces of these animals you've tended and coaxed and nourished, is especially painful to him.

It's a cruel cold out there. I keep sending Margaret with hot tea. "Dad's really coughing," she said when she came in last time. I have bricks heating for Carl's feet…if I can ever get him to bed. I don't know what we're going to do. It looks like a hellmouth out there, with the glow of those small individual fires and the shadows shifting as Carl moves from one to another. I'm glad I can't see his face. He never weeps. But this is bitter.

Night after night, Carl is out in that cold. Horns and hoof, hide and hair, everything has to be completely burned or the anthrax just stays in the soil, he says. So he's out after every long day's work. He's coughing a lot, which makes me worry he's also inhaling anthrax. But when I say he should stop, I'm lucky he just shoots me a look that clearly says, "Who, then?" And I know he's right. It worries me so.

It's been two weeks since the anthrax burning.

I finally sent for the doctor. Carl's fever won't stay down. It breaks, and I start to hope, and then by nightfall he's shivering again. He coughs constantly, shaking his head in irritation and despair. I'm actually thinking we should maybe get him somewhere warmer. Truthfully, as much as I love our house, I honestly don't see how we can stay here. No cattle. Poor harvest last year. It's just not adding up to anything good. And there's no one home to be of much help. Carl's brother Will is in Phoenix. I keep wondering if we should get on a train and go down there. (I'd have to keep him from jumping off as we went past Oak Creek, but he's so weak I could probably do that with one hand.)

It seems like life never gets…settled. You think you're done with all the big changes, and another comes. Carl is 62. That's pretty old to be starting over. But we can. We should. We may even have to. I will write Will a letter tonight and take it into town tomorrow. And then probably begin packing things around the edges of our life.

Arizona

It looks like we're going to go back to Arizona. Will says he'd love us to stay with them until we figure out what we want to do. We will ride in a caravan: Tad and Hank will both drive the biggest trucks we can find and we will camp on the way. I have loved this beautiful home; I doubt we will ever live in one as fine again. But Carl must get well. And that's all I need. We left Sedona when my health was in peril. We will leave Boyero now for his. I hope we never move away from Arizona again. Carl keeps saying he hates cities, and when Will wrote that 50,000 people live in Phoenix, Carl almost refused to go. I know it's a dry climate, but I let him think that maybe we will go back to Oak Creek from there. Anything that gets him out of here.

Do many people start over as often as we have?

Tomorrow morning we leave. Everything we are taking is crated, boxed, and loaded onto the two trucks. It's melancholy—the lamps throwing shadows all the way to the walls, with no furniture or pictures to break them. I so wish we had a barge or something so we could take this house. I love this house. But I hate everything around it; especially the black swirls out in the melted snow where Carl had to reduce every carcass to ash. Those were animals; not friends, but acquaintances. Now not only are they all dead, but eradicated as if they never breathed at all. And it cost Carl his health.

I've wondered over the years if that malaria from when he was a youngster stayed inside him, making his lungs vulnerable. But he's so sturdy and stalwart, going everywhere and doing everything, it never seemed a problem. He's thin now. He coughs too much. I've even let myself wonder if he's gotten tuberculosis on top of the bronchitis. Or could it be pneumonia? I fear that as well. I make flaxseed tea, Mormon tea, compresses, steam kettles. He's obliging with all of the remedies. He knows he's too tired, and I'm too determined, for giving me guff to do any good.

All this is what leads to the uprooting. This chapter is over; we will leave. Again. It's sad to write that Clara is not coming with us. She's 19, and going to stay and teach; she just earned her certificate. Hank is already working for the Union Pacific Railroad, and doesn't want to uproot his newly established career. Only Margaret will come with us. Tad and Hank will return to their homes once they get us settled in. That feels odd, too.

Tad had to leave his little family down in southern Arizona to come help us. Lucille and Larry are still in Willcox. Tad brought a photo of Larry; a merry-looking little soul. Lucille sends her best. I'm grateful it's summer, so Tad isn't teaching right now; otherwise, we would have had to hire help.

Will's place in Phoenix is small; we will find somewhere to store our things, I reckon. And I already dread the heat. But it's dry, and it will save Carl. So nothing else matters.

Jan. 18, 1931

This is not going to work. Carl is miserable.

Will works at a beverage company, driving a big truck that follows a route taking deliveries to stores. He said he could get Carl hired on, but Carl's too weak and tired to work yet. Which makes him so upset;

he deplores being idle. Mostly, he hates this place…and Carl never hates anything. I think the fact that Oak Creek Canyon is 100 miles away makes a mockery of being this close. He's already talking about going back.

On the one hand, I know this is dryer air. And hotter. But at this age, I do put a great deal of stock in being where you're happy. Like a sick child eating what sounds good to him. So I'm not saying no.

It amuses me to remember when I was young, and the elaborate process of simply dressing every morning: chemise, petticoats, drawers, stockings, garters, stays, dress, jacket, gloves, hat. Right now I get up in the morning and three garments later I'm set for the day, even at this time of year. It reminds me of when I used to wear Carl's overalls in Oak Creek. Of course, then, no one was around to see me. But here, this is what women do. A good dark pattern on a housedress—with one slip underneath—keeps it from showing anything. What's happened to civilization? What's happened in people living in a desert where only animals should. This place is unrelentingly, mercilessly hot.

While I'm writing about dressing, Margaret was looking at my clothes recently, on the nails that make my side of the "closet," and asked, "Mother, what is it about you and blue?" I had to think for a moment to understand the question; I wasn't looking at her and thought she meant I was melancholy or something, But she was being literal. When I followed her gaze, it made me smile: all my dresses are blue. Not all the same shade, and not all plain; one is flowered, one is figured, one is plaid. Dark, medium, pale. But blue they are.

"I guess I like the sky," I said. But now I wonder. People with big blue eyes would want to bring out their color. But my eyes are as brown as they could be. I certainly don't want to wear brown. Pink seemed frivolous to me even when I was young. Red is bold. Yellow shows every bit of dirt. There's nothing wrong with green…I just must not be drawn to it. Well, I won't waste more time on this. I like blue and I'm allowed.

It's the same with the way I embroider and monogram, always white on white. Yes, there's an array of lovely colors I could use. But I like white on white and that's that.

V. Sedona
1931-1950

Schnebly Hill Road

Jan 28, 1931

We are here. We are arrived. We are back, we are home, we are in Oak Creek. We are in the place that still shares my name.

I have both dreaded and yearned for this, and even as we pulled in, I felt an odd mix of fear and excitement. But then, seeing familiar outlines of rock formations I recognized against the sky, the longing for Pearl didn't outweigh the joy of reunion. This is really where my life as I know it began. It's where I, as I know me, began. I feel more a sense of Pearl smiling down at us than I do any emptiness, when I think of her.

The other children have always known about her, of course. Margaret, the only one to come with us, has asked where her older sister is buried and if we will visit her. I've said of course, but we are holding off: Carl is going first, to move her to the actual cemetery that came to be during our absence.

I believe that will make it easier. Before, buried outside the kitchen window, she was still laid where her death had occurred. In an actual resting place it may be easier to remember our daughter without reliving that day when she went from being my living daughter to my missing daughter.

As for the rest, I can't believe how much has changed! I knew our home had burned, and the Blacks have built a lovely low stone house on the site. I knew that any place would surely change in 25 years. But it's more extreme than I could have visualized. There's a whole actual downtown between our old property and where the Jordans have built. (These are the sons of Will Jordan, boys who Carl knew and liked very much when he met Will, a grower near Clarkdale.) There's what people call the Lower Store at the corner of our former land. So there's an upper store more toward Grasshopper Flat, going west toward Cottonwood. There are automobiles everywhere, as well as some wagons and horses. Far and away the greatest adjustment is the number of people. It feels odd not to know many of them, but Carl assures me we will soon. And the way he's always brought strangers home for lunch, I'm sure he's right.

We have moved into a small place across from our old land near the foot of Schnebly Hill Road. It's a rectangle with floor and walls and a roof, and not much room for anything. But it's close to the creek, and if I've learned anything, it's that the size of the house doesn't determine the level of happiness inside. There's no room for my piano, but Carl is storing it with the Jordans for now. Walter was a year older than Tad, and Carl loves seeing him and his brother George all grown. Carl and their dad have written back and forth for years. Just last year, Walter married a friend of his sister Stella's—a sweet girl named Ruth. She has a lilting quality, like she's half fairy, with a very high light way of speaking. I swear sometimes it seems like she's seeing something magic the rest of us can't. George's wife Helen is more definite; loves art and music. I felt comfortable with her right away. Anyway, we went to Walter and Ruth's directly when we arrived. They'd found us this place, so close to where we were before. I could tell Carl was deeply moved that his efforts to get that road built weren't forgotten; people call it Schnebly Hill Road. He beams every time he says it; he can't help himself.

Amanda

Feb. 10, 1931

Mutter is gone. I just read Lillie's letter (she dated it Jan. 22, the day after the death, but it had to go to Phoenix and then find me here). I can't imagine what to do: I want to either do something terribly important and significant, or something absolutely frivolous and foolish, but can think of nothing that qualifies as sufficiently close to either end of the spectrum. I feel I should say a prayer, or tell someone. But I don't know what to say.

Her life did not end the way it should have: in comfort, cherished and cosseted. She died beholden to the charity of her children. Don't get me started on the greed and ignorance of the bankers who let the money that was supposed to protect her vanish in the Great Depression. She never got to see Oak Creek. She didn't get to cross the ocean. She didn't get her portrait painted.

Now she never will do any of those things.

Who will I ask, the next time I don't know something? What should I have asked her before now? Do I know enough about getting stains out of laundry? Etiquette? Canning? Treating toothache? How on earth can I live out the rest of my life without being able to ask her things?

I know I'm a woman grown, but right now I feel like a baby who just woke from a nap and can't find Mutter. I feel frantic and bewildered, and so deeply, deeply sorry for the time we weren't in harmony. I don't know how it could have been circumvented or shortened, and I'm glad we mended things when we did. But any day I could have written her, and didn't, now seems like a glaring sin of omission.

She'd been widowed for 25 years; long enough for anyone. I'm sure Papa was delighted to come escort her into Heaven's gates. Lillie said the children and grandchildren in the area made their goodbyes, and she did read Mutter my last letter. So those things are good. But I should be there! I should always have been there. She lost so many others; her second-born son Edward two years ago; Amiel more than ten years ago, little Lola as a toddler, Pearl as a young woman, both Johnnys at young ages. Why did I move so far away?

I'm afraid I will forget the sound of her voice. I'm afraid I will hear it constantly. I'm afraid I can't be a good grandmother without her example. (I'm also a little afraid I'll be a better grandmother without her.) I don't have a map for the world without her in it, and just feel so terribly lost right now.

Amanda Shaefer Miller. That's what will go on her headstone next to Papa in Gorin. Did she get back to Pennsylvania enough? Did we make her happy? Did I resent her too much for trying to control us if she just wanted our happiness?

Mutter. My Mutter. I know you would want us to have faith above all, and perhaps second to that, to have decorum. I will comport myself in a way to do you credit once anyone is around. But right now I just want to curl up on the floor, and whimper, and not have opened the letter, so you could still be in Gorin, as far as I knew.

That's what I'll do. I'll not have opened the letter. You're at home, back in our big house. You're putting the kettle on for your four o'clock, checking the tin to see if any of the lemon biscuits are left, shaking your head a little if they seem too hard. You're winding the clock; the light is slanting through the front room blinds, and you're humming. You're there. I'll decide that, even if part of my brain knows it's not true. The front of my brain will picture you talking to the cat, and eventually it won't seem so strange if it isn't true. You're home, Mutter. Just waiting for a letter. Wearing your cameo and looking for your thimble before you start mending; straightening the edge of an antimacassar with a slightly impatient twitch. You're right where you belong, being you. We're all fine. I'll just finish the ironing this afternoon and not say a word. Or I'll go find Carl, and not tell him, because nothing happened today. I'll go find Carl.

Feb. 18, 1931

The best news is that Carl has gained 13 pounds in the first three weeks here! "That's what comes of being happy and contented," he says. He is constantly busy at our little home, making things more secure. Right now the walls let in a lot of the outside, but Carl brought home pink and blue construction paper that we will use for insulation.

But the piano is safe, and we are together, in our same white iron bed, with the same pillows and quilts we had in Boyero. So if this new home isn't as grand as the last, with my dressing room and all the chair rails and wainscoting, Carl isn't outside in the snow. He's breathing quiet and deep next to me at the end of each day, and almost always smiling. I want no more than this.

Ruth has a charming and well-built rock house up from here, and she seems a bit bewildered by what domestic arts require. I've been going up each day, once my brief housekeeping is done, to share with her the ways I manage things; you don't live this long without figuring out some shortcuts; things like getting the red dirt out of white tea towels. (Which of course men stoutly swear they never dry their hands on until they are completely clean!) Carl is working with Walter and George Jordan, since he doesn't have orchards of his own and theirs are new. (While the trees mature they're growing pinto beans—a good idea we never had—and other crops.) It's fun to hear him come home full of talk about the day. I hadn't realized: he'd become so lonely with Tad and Hank gone, working mostly by himself out there in Boyero, except for trips to town. It's good we're back.

Pearl's Grave

Mar. 31, 1931

Well, Carl did it. He moved our baby girl up to the cemetery. I didn't want to go with him. I want to remember her alive and in motion, and doubted time had been kind to her earthly body. I didn't know if the little casket had held, and Margaret firmly told me it would be a bad idea to go. (She's like Tad, firm about everything, where Hal and Clara are light as a breeze about most things. Genevieve simply doesn't weigh in on much.) So I left with Carl, and at the old property he turned left and I went on up right toward Ruth's, enjoying the walk.

I wasn't wrong that the spicy wet scent of the creek is probably the best thing my nose has ever encountered. It greets me like an old friend. Every place has its own birdsong, its own feel of the ground under your feet. I realized I was smiling as I walked.

It's funny: I'm 54 years old! More than half a century. And yet when I walk I feel like I could be in my 20s. (I know I don't look it; my hair may still have what Carl calls "Nature's own permanent wave" but it also has a lot more silver when I take it down at night.) Anyway, when I got home from Ruth's, Carl was already here. He looked whimsically at me—I wondered if he would be deeply sad or not. "Our girl is good," he said, and then his voice cracked. I went to his chair and put my arm on his shoulder, and let him turn his head into my skirt so he didn't have to be seen weeping, or pretend he wasn't. We were like that for a while. Even if his sad act had a happy outcome, it would bring those events back too powerfully to just shake off. He took out his handkerchief and blew his nose and patted the chair next to his.

Mr. Black had already given him permission to move Pearl. I don't imagine they were sorry to see that grave go. It still had the fence around it, and I can visualize that would put a chill on a conversation with anyone new, looking about the place. Carl said he was a little concerned while he was digging about hurting Pearl, but he went slowly and felt the wood of the casket holding firm. So he worked carefully all around it, and was able to bring it up by himself—it wasn't heavy.

"I had to see her," he said. "It had been so long. I knew it might not be smart, but I couldn't just put her in the ground without looking. And you know? When I got that lid open, she looked perfect. Exactly as I remembered her, like she was taking a nap. Then, I guess the air hit her, and she was dust. Just like that."

What would be in the clay here to do that—keep a little girl just as her father remembered her all that time? Or did God do it just for Carl? I'll have to ask someone who knows about such things someday. But for now, it's enough to see the peace, even the joy, on his face. I almost wish I'd gone. But this way was better. He got his time to say goodbye, and I can remember how she looked in the casket all too well anyway.

Tomorrow he will take Margaret and me up to her new place, out at the foot of a mesa toward Grasshopper Flat. He's already talking about ordering a real headstone. It is good to be back with our other daughter.

As I write that, I wonder if we should have come here instead of Boyero; think of how much more progress we would have made. But I also know I would not have been ready. This is the right time.

The Wallaces

April 18, 1931

We have reconnected with the Wallaces. Ethel and I have corresponded for years, ever since we left here. Billy, of course, had been a good neighbor, and we'd seen the rest of his family in Flagstaff a time or two. They had come down here for picnics in the fall and spring, when it was still cold up there. Ethel is kind and unflappable; nothing seems too big for her to take on. I remember when she wrote about Stanton and his sister Elizabeth getting scarlet fever, she seemed to shrug it off on paper: "It's just one of those things children get."

So it was wonderful to be able to write and tell her we were coming back. The other day when I was settling in, there was a knock, and there was Ethel! She's hardly changed, after a minute. I guess we all have, in the 25-plus years since we lived here last. But she's mostly the same, and had jars of preserved tomatoes and apricots. "I know you can preserve circles around the rest of us, but you will have missed a lot of this year's crop," she said, giving me a hug. "Let me be the one to help you for once."

Margaret didn't take long to meet and become friendly with Billy Wallace's son Stanton. He helps his dad out down here, while Ethel lives up in Flagstaff. Stanton is as tall as Margaret is petite, and seems kind, and overall jolly, like Hank. She spends a lot of time happening to run into him. I'm fine with that. I'm sure there are fast crowds even in the smallest towns, and Stanton is very responsible. He is just starting work with the Forest Service.

I remember Carl talking about Teddy Roosevelt creating a Forest Service when we were still here the first time, chuckling about what kind of service a forest would need...the trees measured? Stones moved? But it turns out, as more and more people come to a place, things really can get forests at sixes and sevens—too many big trees taken, fires, and then animals leave and rain washes away the duff.

Billy Wallace has been appointed to be the first Forest Service ranger in Oak Creek. It wasn't much of a change; he was already taking care of the area, and seemed to know everything about it. I guess Stanton will have plenty to keep him busy; there are forests everywhere. (Apparently even desert areas can have "forest" around them; it just doesn't look like what I think of when I hear the word.)

Anyway, Ethel and I fell into the old easy conversation immediately. She was as pleased as I was that Margaret and Stanton are such steady company.

We looked at one another, and said almost at the same time, "Grandchildren!" And laughed.

Carl teases me about that. "As soon as a fellow catches a girl's eye, you start naming their children," he says. Well, women do. Ethel and I agreed it would be a fine thing if we had grandbabies in common. She would be related to me through Margaret and Stanton's children then, which is like friends, only better. We will see.

May 20, 1932

I wonder how many children you'd have to raise before the next one coming up couldn't do anything to surprise you. Margaret just left, to walk with young Stanton. I swear the very chair cushions look upset. She can pull all the air in the room into a tornado around herself, it seems to me. I upset her greatly; my sin was suggesting she might want a wrap because there's a stiff breeze.

You'd think I had said, "I'm contemplating shooting your father between the eyes." She huffed up her little back and said, "Mother, really! You'd think I was just born," and on about things like that, so insulted and negative. I tried to just watch her and not say anything to make it worse until she flounced out.

How I miss Clara sometimes. We should have given her Equanimity for a middle name. The steadiest of them all, she takes everything in cheerful stride; like Carl, I guess. I miss her, although I'm glad she's teaching and loving the work. It's good, especially for a young woman, to have something to succeed at like that. But when she came home, she was always cheerful and interested. With Margaret, I hear her open the door and then listen for a moment or two to see if I can divine who will be coming in: a truly sweet girl who takes delight in things, or a dramatic victim of a vast injurious world that's singled her out for punishment. She doesn't have much of a sense of humor when it comes to herself. Although I guess Tad doesn't either. And I hate knowing they got that from me. I'm always so afraid I'm doing something wrong, I can't seem to relax and laugh if I make a mistake.

It's a good thing children get two parents. When one falls short, there's someone else to step in.

It's fun to have Stanton in our lives. He works with his father full time, so he is around our house a lot.

Ethel has adjusted nicely to Billy staying in Oak Creek most of the year, and he frequently gets a ride up the switchbacks to Flagstaff when the weather is mild. He is the same industrious soul we met the first time. Often after it rains, you see him riding his horse to this or that section of the canyon, where he takes his telescope or looking glass or whatever that contraption is, and checks for fires that may have just started from a lightning strike.

Billy Wallace, lower right, surveying Oak Creek Canyon next to his horse

He's very responsible, and was caretaker of our canyon long before the Forest Service found out about him and made his position an official government one. So it's fun for me that even while we weren't here to see it, Billy and Stanton both stewarded the land, if that word can be used, seeing the spring runoff swell the creek, the quiet flat water barely moving leaves in autumn, watching trees grow taller, and some fall, during storms. Now he can watch Margaret storm.

Someone said years ago that girls are born with 100 angels, and boys with 100 devils, and every year one of them jumps to the other. So a woman would die at 100 with all devils. Margaret seems like she was born at half and half.

I don't know what that's about exactly. But it does seem Carl gets milder, while I get a little sharper. Maybe women are told to be good for so long that finally we reach a point where we just think, "I've been good all my life and what has it gotten me? I'm going to say what I think from now on." I don't mean I don't want to be good; of course I do. But I don't see that suffering fools is necessarily making the world a better place.

I'll try to have patience with Margaret. I do remember what it's like to be young; sometimes you feel so fragile it's like the air itself hurts when you walk. But also as if nothing could hurt you, and it offends that parents think you might be fragile. Then confused; fine one minute, and the next it takes everything you have not to cry the next.

And she doesn't have Clara anymore either. Clara was always so swift to see how Margaret was feeling and be like a quilt padding between her and the world. Like Hank could for Tad. Even though he's nine years younger, Hank was always able to jolly Tad out of a mood. Life sits so lightly on Hank's shoulders, and practically bows Tad's down. I thank God every day for Lucille. What a helpmate. Such a capable young woman, and so strong, and so kind. She works from the moment her eyes open each day until they shut at night, and never complains.

Because Tad is so industrious with his teaching and often principal's work, a great many of what might be considered men's chores fall to her. She can build brick planters, lug heavy containers, and still sew and cook without complaint. She must see the Tad I see, even when he gets blustery and a little bossy. I've thanked her several times for her goodness to him without saying those words, and I think she understands.

Delia

Yesterday I rode up to Flagstaff with Delia Hart (they own Hart Store down here, and need to do things up in the big city regularly). I love making that trip with her; we've done it several times now. Because they are prosperous storekeepers, we don't take a lunch. She insists it's more fun to eat at a restaurant or a café, and insists that part of the fun for her is buying my meal. I hate it, but I let her.

Carl swears it's just as much fun for him, because he can bring out his canned sardines, back at our house. Try as I might, I never have gotten used to that strong smell. I feel like I'm in a shipwreck when I'm around that old-fish odor. So he eats sardines for lunch when I'm gone, and then is delighted to see me come home. He says he made that trip to Flagstaff enough times to last him.

There's so much going on in Flagstaff since the old days when we were here. Trains are constantly coming through, and the business section bustles. Delia and I ate last time at the Monte Vista Hotel, and today at the Rose Tree Café, on the main street. It's a charming place with a large menu. You can tell it caters to ladies who shop as well as men who are working downtown; there are steak and oysters and such, then in another section on the page are chicken sandwiches, fruit salad, a dieter's plate and hard-boiled eggs with crackers. Flagstaff also boasts Hotel Weatherford, where Zane Gray, the author who wrote "Call of the Canyon," supposedly stayed, and we went years ago with Dorothea. Delia says we will go there next time.

She is easy to be with and enjoyable to talk to; one of my closest friends. Still, it's always nice to get home. I don't know why being around everyone except Carl seems to tire me. He's so restful. And it's good to be out of my city shoes.

CCC

Well, Carl has a new job. He's been working with both Walter and George Jordan since we got here, but now he has an actual paying position, managing the Civilian Conservation Corps camp. A lot of CCC men are working at the Grand Canyon, but it will be cold up there in the winter, and they've created this place as headquarters for them, in addition to housing workers for this area. Carl is in charge of the grounds and buildings. He joked he got it because they saw he already wears khaki. For years he's favored the pants every day because they are sturdy but can go into town, and his shirts are mostly khaki, light blue, or white. Being Carl, with his eye to what needs doing in any situation, he quickly saw an opportunity for me to have a new job as well. I will be doing laundry for these men, who are working hard and missing their families. This means we will be less concerned about every penny and able to do more. Unfortunately, it also means that we won't be visiting any of the children for a while—men can't just not have clean clothes if I'm away.

Since my washtub and wringer are always set up on the back porch, I can do most of it outside for some time to come. (Carl even suggested he put my ironing board out there...maybe I'll agree.) He has to lug the heated water out before he leaves in the morning.

Actually, I like doing laundry, because it's such an exact process. When I finish, I'm never left wondering if I should have stirred the load longer, rinsed it better. It's done, completed, without leaving room for second-guessing or uncertainty about outcome, unlike things that involve other people. I love the look of crisply pressed creases, and smoothly folded shirts and pants. I'll be sorry everyone will have to come to us for visits. We'd hoped to be with Tad's family, since they have come back up north. But they are out on the Navajo reservation, in the eastern part of the state. Tad writes that baby Patsy is growing strong and determined; well, she comes by that honestly.

I have been to the CCC camp already; I wanted to see where Carl will be spending the lion's share of his time. It's amazing how much building and smoothing of ground has gone on. And every single man we passed either nodded or tipped his hat. It's a courteous, earnest group. I'm surprised that some of them seem fairly old, but I guess every age has suffered from the Depression.

It always amuses me to remember Carl reading back in the 20s that because of modern inventions, some steel workers could cut their workdays from twelve hours to eight. That's half a workday for Carl, often as not. But now that we're a little older, maybe he'll cut back a little. And pigs will fly.

Today I walked over to the camp, which is short of a mile south of us toward Big Park, to take Carl his lunch. It reminded me of when he was leading the work crews, building Schnebly Hill Road (everyone around here calls it that, and it pleases Carl immensely to know his role in the construction wasn't forgotten). I would go up to where they worked on their lower-down days to take him a bite during the noon break. Generally he'd work straight through, and either eat it on the way home at dusk, or sometimes say a little ruefully, "I didn't have time to eat, but (whatever man looked hungry) sure praised your cooking."

Someone directed me to where he was when I reached the camp, and he was helping the men—even though, as caretaker, he is responsible only for upkeep. I found him by his voice, telling stories of the early days here while they worked. No matter where they're from, the men seem to enjoy hearing about when there were only five families, or when Mantle Rock was formed. Carl is at his happiest and best here: surrounded by the land he loves, with a cadre of good men to talk to. I hate what the Depression has done to the country, but this is one of those things that prove that the Lord can use anything to His good. Men have work, areas like national parks get improved, and Carl and I are paying our way. President Roosevelt is a wise man.

Jan. 9, 1935

Several times since Carl's been at the CCC camp, he's brought one of his favorites home for dinner. William Walker has the loveliest brogue, having lived in Scotland until he reached manhood and began adventuring. He told us roguishly he "decided to make of myself a citizen of this grand nation" and applied for his passport listing a birthplace of Dover, New Hampshire. He talks sadly about "my lovely Rosamund," who passed away several years ago, leaving their almost-grown daughter to cook and care for William up in Flagstaff.

He's talked about when he worked as an Indian Trader. Hearing that job title recalled to my mind the man named Atkinson, who helped us find breakfast in Gallup those long years ago. I asked Mr. Walker if he'd run across such a person, and he said that he had: there are brothers and cousins in that family who have a trading post near the Grand Canyon. It was called at a spot called Blue, if he recollected correctly. I remembered stopping there by a bridge on our way back from the Grand Canyon, before we left Arizona the first time.

Mr. Walker also tells about going down into Mexico in 1916 with 2nd Lt. George Patton. "Imagine how proud I was, being able to help defend my adopted homeland against that bold rascal Pancho Villa!"

I well remember Carl reading to me out of the newspaper exploits of our troops over the course of some frustrating months. It was after Pancho Villa actually raided a town in New Mexico, on Tad's 18th birthday. That's probably why it lodged firmly in my mind; that and the puzzling outrage of a brigand actually daring to cross onto our soil and do such a thing. I say "puzzling" because I remember Carl mildly pointing out that in his opinion, Mr. Villa had done his own people a great deal of good. He was regarded by many as more of a Robin Hood than as a villain. Whether later telling regards him as a hero, or a goat, Mr. Walker was actually getting a front-row view of history playing itself out on that hot, desolate desert stage.

Another night, Carl and I were both fascinated hearing about Mr. Walker meeting a writer named Harold Bell Wright, a preacher back in Kansas. He then became the first author to have sold one million copies of a book, Mr. Walker told us. I've not read any of his works, but Mr. Walker told us Harold Bell Wright's mother died when he was young, and his father simply walked away from his children. ("Can you imagine that poor brood, grieving already, and then not even knowing how they'd get food into their wee bellies?") He said Harold Bell Wright "lived rough" for some years, meaning finding food and shelter by his wits, off the land. "Many a night he'd have to curl up under a bridge, faint from hunger an' despairin' of his life."

Then, Mr. Walker added, "Imagine how startled I was, when on the streets of my very own town of Flagstaff, I heard the voice that I remembered ringing out so rich and strong over the congregation of the good Reverend Wright's church, callin' me by my own name!" Apparently once he became a successful author, Harold Bell Wright left the religious life. He would travel about and live in a place before he set a novel there. Tucson and Prescott both hosted him, and he was visiting Flagstaff when he happened to see his old friend Mr. Walker. "I got a tremendous lot out of being in his company again, these many years later."

Listening to Mr. Walker's stories while I crocheted, for a whimsical moment I wished we could have moved across the sea to raise our children, and given them that accent. I love letting those rich rolling syllables of Mr. Walker's swirl around in my ears.

Tutti-Frutti

April 29, 1935

Today we had a fine Sunday dinner, joined by the minister, Tad's family and the Mr. and Mrs. Jordans both: George and Helen, Walter and Ruth. It was a lovely long table-sit.

I got thinking that I wanted to write about the tutti-frutti (which means "all fruits" in Italian). The crock holding the tutti-frutti sits just at the foot of the basement stairs on the platform I store the washtubs under, in the cool dim environs of that underground space. When anyone goes down there for something, I call out, "Give the tutti-frutti a stir, would you?" and whoever it is agreeably does. Myself, I like the sharp sweet scent that rises when I pick up the spoon from its saucer next to the glazed clay crock and lift the plate that serves as a lid. Then I gently push the spoon through the dark sugary stew: the peaches, apples, apricots, cherries, and berries all relaxing, losing their shapes and getting cozy, until they're virtually indistinguishable from one another in a fragrant and delicious new form. Hence, all fruits.

I guess the reason I think this merits writing about is that I didn't start doing tutti-frutti until we came west. Maybe I was still too narrow and too rigid, or too busy to make the time to start it in Gorin. No, I don't think that was it. I made time for what mattered.

The reason I waited to start tutti-frutti is that I wasn't quite ready to compromise my WCTU beliefs. Yes, I know what tutti-frutti is. I'm the one who began it: sugar, the bruised and softening fruit in my heaviest crock with the plate that seals it exactly. Then, darkness and time. Nature's alchemy does its work, and lo, meet the tutti-frutti. I know it ferments. But there's a lot of ground, to me, between some dissolute wastrel swigging at a bottle of poison, and this lovely dessert. I guess I'm writing to take ownership of it. I don't hold with hypocrisy. Yes, it 's almost edible spirits. And going back to that old saw that the answer to any complicated question is, "well, yes and no," I don't hold with overindulging in strong drink. Yet I make tutti-frutti.

We don't have it often. Days like today when we can ladle it over ice cream are the best. Once in a while, after dinner on an early winter evening, I warm up about two teacups' worth for Carl and me to enjoy. But mostly it's for company. Because when we have tutti-frutti, everyone has more fun. We laugh more. People relax enough to tell tales they might not another time.

Does it bother me that tutti-frutti is basically chewable brandy? Maybe less than it should. At this point in my life I think that good habits are useful. But being so bound to a good habit that it makes you tense and clenched and judgmental seems to me to be a much worse one, both on the holder of the habit and everyone around. So we still aren't drinkers, and we don't offer wine and spirits to visitors. But with a wink and a thank you to God for all the amazing things He creates, we can serve the minister tutti-frutti over ice cream on Sundays, and I don't feel guilty. I feel grateful.

Carl has never outright commented on my WCTU stance and this dessert. But he has a bit of a twinkle when he passes the dishes. I've wondered if Tad is aware, since he's as abstemious as we are. Maybe it's nice when any of us can let things be a little soft around the edges, instead of insisting on sharp corners on everything in our lives.

The West Fork

July 8, 1936

It was so unusual: Carl and I took a day to ourselves. Strange as it feels, since Margaret and Stanton married and moved to Flagstaff, we are the only ones to home any more; our being gone all day didn't impact anyone. It sounds mournful to hear someone say, "all the children are grown and gone," but it's not that bad. Besides, I tell people who are new to this state that it's the only road I know that leads to grandchildren, and that is a destination worth the journey. Genevieve and Tad have children and Margaret surely will soon. I so well remember Tad at the age his Larry is now. I can see a great deal more Carl in Larry than I saw in Tad; Larry has Carl's gentleness, and that curiosity. Tad has a bit too much Miller; we take all things seriously and worry about how people view us. It dims the fun. We feel ourselves to be deficient and in need of constant effort to improve. It always seemed like Tad studied because he didn't know everything already, and that made him feel less than he should be. Carl and Larry seem to find things out for the pleasure of it.

Anyway, we'd talked over breakfast and decided since we've always wanted to see the west fork of the canyon, this was as good a time as any.

That was near Bear Howard lived in a cave until he built his cabin. He died years back, but I remember seeing him the first time we lived here; very old by then, but still possessing the kind of strength that thinning bones doesn't entirely remove. He was about six and a half feet tall, and imposing, with a thick, white beard. As patriarch of the Purtymans, he was as intimidating as a man of almost 90 can be, with a very direct gaze. Cordial, but not overly so. We all heard (and perhaps even passed on) the rumors of how he'd been shot in the Mexican war and still had the bullet in his lung; also how he got on the wrong side of a sheep rancher whom he then shot by mistake. How his daughter Mattie Purtyman helped him escape from jail in California and he was our resident bear-killer from then on. He'd built a little cabin when he married Elizabeth James, but as full of his guns and his dogs as it was, there really wasn't room for a wife.

Anyway, when they made a moving picture about Zane Gray's "Call of the Canyon" on the old Howard land (which by then was Thomas land), one of the men working on it liked it so much he came back and bought it. Since his name was Mayhew, what was formerly Oak Creek Lodge became Mayhew's Lodge. That all happened while we were away. Every once in a while Carl will come back from the post office and tell me some famous film star was seen in town, while he or she stayed at Mayhew's. I guess if we went to picture shows we might know more about them.

This was the first time we've made the trip to see this part of the canyon. Walter Jordan said he was happy to drive us up the switchbacks and return for us four hours later. I felt very young and carefree, not like an old woman in her 50s. (Since we didn't figure on running into anyone we knew, I wore a pair of Carl's pants. They're really more mine now—I garden and do dirty work in them. Carl, surprisingly, doesn't think it unfeminine at all; he says a woman looks even more womanly in pants.)

No one was around, although we could hear someone splitting logs somewhere. The area is thick and green and lush, full of birdsong even at nine in the morning. The Lodge looks like what I think a Swiss chalet would, or maybe the home of a wealthy lumberman in the Pacific Northwest. It's very elegant, with stonework that makes one's back hurt just thinking about building walls that high. The timbers are decorative across the top; it's still rare here to see anything built more for form than function, and this place is. Outbuildings, and a garden with a lovely arched entrance and paths make it seem like a fairyland, a secret hidden hideaway. It's one thing to be in a luxurious building in a huge city, but to feel like one of the fortunate few who gets to come way up here and see it tucked into one of Oak Creek's deeper pockets, you feel even more privileged. There was a motorcar in front when we passed it.

Anyway, we kept going deeper into that west fork of the canyon, and after crossing a field and getting out of the sun, it's a different climate completely. The top walls have lovely lighter streams of desert varnish, laid down by innumerable rainstorms sending waterfalls pouring over the lip of the canyon (which were still running slenderly when we arrived, since a morning shower had ended recently, just mist at the house but apparently heavier up above). We even heard canyon wrens, whose exquisite little piping trills sound to me like a bird is delightedly tumbling end over end down the canyon, a descending "twee-twee-twee-twee" so musical and merry it surely can be sung only by happy birds.

We walked; the scent of the creek got deeper and spicier. Once after stopping for a drink of water I caught Carl giving me a look I don't often see—a frank assessment of me as not just his wife, or his helpmate, but as a woman, pure and simple.

I thought I ignored it but it must have started something simmering, because when we stopped for the lunch I'd packed, after we ate, we kept the chat running idly while we started holding hands. And then he kissed me. And then we did something we had not done out of doors in a very long time. Part of me wondered why I wasn't concerned about someone coming along, but the rest of me just pushed that away and enjoyed it. We were extra decorous when we got home—I could barely meet his eyes over supper. I wonder if my parents ever behaved like that. I rather think not.

There are parts of our lives I just don't write about. I suppose it's partly due to respect for Carl's privacy. This isn't just my life; it's his as well, and up to him whether anyone ever knows about it. But in this case, I determined it's worth putting to paper, because I have a feeling we're more fortunate than most to still be able to feel that way. And so feeling, act on it.

Maybe some of it is the truism that when you're with someone you have known for a very long time, part of you can still feel the age you were when you met them. When I look at Carl, I rarely see who everyone else does. I don't mean I'm batty-eyed and unable to process reality; it's just that this man with his sharp chin and long nose and thinning hair is overlaid, to me, by the man he was when he was fuller of face. I still see that youth sharing the body of this older man.

And apparently he feels the same. When I brush my hair out at night, he most times watches. (That's why I still give so much attention to my nightdresses, crocheting the lace deep in a border, with a nice square neck that shows the collarbones.) He generally doesn't say a lot, but he smiles. I feel like he's thinking he's the only man who ever gets to see me under those circumstances. And I don't feel wanton, or vixen-ish, or anything tawdry. I feel…lovely, I guess, although it feels foolish to write it. When we walk, he holds my hand. And even when he's not with me, I know that if he could be, he would be. Which is almost as good as actually having him there.

Marsh Pass

Jan. 17, 1937

Looking at your children is like looking through a kaleidoscope: each time the view is a little bit different. Some of the bright bits inside a child that shine out are inherited from relatives they've never met...the way a laugh trails off and swoops up strong again, or a walk with the right foot turned slightly out.

Hank has the same odd, quirky sense of humor my brother Noah does: once in a while either of them comes out with something so unusual you wonder how it ever worked into their minds at all, let alone stayed around long enough to be put into words. They must move through a world that looks very different than the one most of us see. It's surprising, and great fun, to see family members you love in your children. Genevieve has some of Lillie's flair; her instinctive artistry with her hair, with flowers, with placing furniture in a room, even though she is so very reserved compared to my sister. Tad has his Uncle Ellsworth's busy brain; it seems like he's always talking about one thing, doing something else and sometimes even figuring out how to solve some third thing at the same time.

And of course, Tad's got his dad's relish for being Very Busy At His Desk. I've watched them both, and it makes me smile. They seem to bustle in to sit down as if they've kept someone waiting too long; they're very intent, whether it's looking up something in a file, or putting a stamp on an envelope. It's like whatever they do sitting there is of great significance. I don't think I could write a will with as much intent focus as they have, just getting out a ruler.

T.C. (Carl) Schnebly at his desk

Of our children, Tad and Clara are the most constant writers. Even though all grew up under the same house tradition—that for an hour after lunch it was quiet time, giving me leave to write—it didn't seem to stick to Hank or Margaret; they far prefer more garrulous pursuits. Genevieve's always been a great reader; maybe with fewer children she'd have more time to write. But then I realize: we had the same number. I made time to write; I needed to write. It seems as far back as I can remember, something wasn't really done happening 'til

I'd written it down. Journal or letter didn't matter; it was recorded—available to more than just me after that moment. Writing makes something complete. And if anyone ever wonders what happened... well, I'm not sure they'd know to come looking here. But I need the writing part to make sense of things, and maybe remember them better.

Anyway, Tad and Clara are the ones who send letters every week, and one of my favorite times is opening an envelope with either of their handwriting on it. It's the moment when I'm about to be with one of my children. There's no time better spent.

Sometimes the letters leave me with an image or a thought I return to for several days. I've carried one from Tad's last letter longer than usual.

He wrote about bringing his family home from Gallup, NM to Dennehotso, AZ after Baby Paula (Marilyn Paula, but they're going with the middle-name tradition) was born in the Gallup hospital. It was raw, wet January weather. Fortunately they had a new car (for a very frugal person, Tad can't resist a new car or a new gadget), so the tires were very good and nothing was wrong yet with steering or brakes. As Tad described it, he was driving through pretty severe rain, with Larry and Patsy (now eight and five) in the back, and Lucille holding Paula next to him.

That's all Navajo reservation country: harsh, empty, miles and miles of not seeing another person if you're out in it. At Marsh Pass, Tad hit a very wet spot (which he realized in hindsight must have been dark ice, where it's thawed and refrozen to slickness but doesn't show) and the car began to slide slowly sideways. That was a terrible feeling, since the road there is next to a sheer drop hundreds of feet down. Tad said he didn't even know what he did except essentially nothing—no jerky or panicked or extreme reaction—just the tenderest, lightest application of the brake. And the car stopped, as far as he could tell, with the front wheel on Lucille's side already an inch or two out over the precipice (it makes my palms damp thinking about it again, but I have to record it anyway, to get it onto paper and out of my head).

I know the quiet conversational tone he must have used with Lucille, to tell her they were all going to move slowly out his and Larry's doors, onto the road. And then repeating that to Larry and Patsy, which, good children, they did. Tad is like Carl in his resourcefulness, and he knows anything can happen when you travel in empty country, so he's well prepared. Pretty soon he had a fire going in the large flat aluminum pan that's always in the trunk of his car. He also keeps a tarp that he was able to stretch from a big rock to an expandable set of poles he drove into the dirt over that fire, keeping his family warm and dry.

Tad then let himself look down the edge of the trunk and saw that indeed the car was placed pretty much as he had surmised: the passenger front tire was a little bit over the edge, and the back tire right on the edge. He wrote, "I still get a shudder as I write," which for Tad to put down on paper means something.

He walked out into the road, waiting and listening in the rain. He thought it wasn't more than half an hour until a wagon pulled by a team came upon them (which is its own miracle, considering how little travel that road sees). The driver was Navajo, and Tad reported with deserved pride that he'd picked up enough words to be able to explain their predicament in the man's tongue. Even if it's rudimentary, when you can speak to someone in his own language, the respect that indicates is significant.

So for a negotiated price, the man unhitched his wagon, used Tad's ropes (again, always waiting in the trunk) knotted to the front bumper of that new car, and those good horses pulled it slowly back into the center of the road. Tad said the Navajo didn't waste any facial expression, but did give him a look like, "You know how lucky you were here," and Tad nodded and thanked him again.

They got home safely.

What keeps coming back to me, picturing that car almost over the ledge, is how swiftly something changes from mundane to dangerous—more out here than back east, I guess. There are still more wild places here. And fewer people. And extreme weather, and rough roads. How long would it have been before someone might have seen the wreckage glinting down below, once the sun was back out? Would anyone have known where they had disappeared, to send a search? I'm guessing not. We would only have known at some point after not getting a letter next week that they didn't make it back from Gallup. My boy, my brave boy—of course now a man, father and provider, but always my boy. He didn't say if it stayed with him the way it has me, but knowing him I believe it must have.

Tad is some of both Carl and I, but he tends to carry dark things inside longer, as I do. Carl's seemingly able to whistle them right out of his head and move on to the next thing. Lucille seems practical, but I think she's just had to go through so much without sniveling that she doesn't talk about things that scare her. She simply goes about getting County Extension Service brochures and learning to mix cement, or nurse Larry through scarlet fever, or butcher and grind meat.

However, I'm guessing she had some girlish hopes and ideas of what her life might have been, that haven't been realized with Tad. He can be peremptory, and is not a gentle or courtly person. But Lucille certainly has a spirit of adventure, and he's given her that in great measure. Living in reservation communities with no or maybe one other white woman—she's needed every bit of that grit and pluck she has.

I remember after she brought Larry out of scarlet fever without permanent blindness, relying only on those pamphlets and her own instincts for nursing, she said, "That certainly made for an interesting couple of weeks." She didn't wail and shiver; she just remarked with equanimity. When my children were small, I used to pray for my children's spouses; the people they would grow up, meet, fall in love with, and marry. A church member in Gorin suggested that. With Lucille, my prayers were answered and then some.

Vultee

Jan. 31, 1938

Catherine is with us this year, because Genevieve, sweetest-natured of all our children, is ill. Cancer.

She knows it; I know it; she knows I know it. But no one says it out loud. Joshua is stretched to the limit with all the younger Coxes. Clara is teaching, but she keeps getting them through the paces of their days before and after school. Alice can be a big help with the younger ones; Betty is tiny, Helen and Jim in school and able to do a great deal for themselves. Dorothy, not old enough to be a real help, is still good with the baby and not ready to be away. Catherine has the most energy of all of them, and while she loves her mother dearly, she is strong enough to be elsewhere. So I know taking her—and having Larry come be a companion to her this school year—makes things easier on everyone. The two of them can be chums, being the same age, and my Genevieve won't have to see herself fade in Catherine's eyes.

Catherine is a straight-backed, brave little girl, and never says she needs anything. But at night after I brush my hair and braid it, I brush hers as well, singing softly the German lullabies I sang to all mine. Then I tuck her into her bed on our sofa in the living room with a soft oil lamp (Larry is on a pallet on that floor) and wait, 'til I see she's drifted off. Even the bravest of us need to be cosseted sometimes.

She and Larry got to have an adventure yesterday. It's been quiet since the Christmas holidays, for the most part. But the snowstorm that had kept them inside had lifted, and the two of them came running in before breakfast saying they wanted to go look at an airplane that was flying in circles. I told them it was all right as long as they had jackets, and then watched as they took off running toward the mesa, where I reckoned they'd realized they'd have a much better chance of seeing a low plane.

Pretty soon, it seemed the plane's pilot also saw them, skimming slowly over the mesa, banking and swooping back, repeating the pass three times. The fourth time it landed.

I was alert, but not actually frightened. Why would a pilot want to capture two fairly good-sized children? While I couldn't see what transpired between them, I could make out the three spots of color against the sandstone: Catherine's red coat, Larry's blue jacket, and the pilot with his white scarf. After a bit, the plane dipped a little as the pilot climbed back in. Then it made a wobbly taxi the full length of the mesa, seeming to drop at the end as if diving into air, before it went chugging steadily upward.

When they got back, Catherine and Larry were simmering with excitement. They'd been deemed worthy of attention from an actual pilot. Who landed, to talk to them! They explained that a different plane had disappeared in the snowstorm somewhere in this area, and this pilot thought they might be survivors of that crash. It was obvious once he landed that they were not the missing married couple. "And they're rich, Grandma," said Catherine. "That man who they were looking for was flying his very own plane!" For once they couldn't wait to get to school, to tell their classmates about being part of so dramatic an event.

Naturally, when Carl came home from the post office after the children were off to school, he had the whole story. A gentleman named Jerry Vultee and his wife, Sylvia, were flying home to California where they would see their six-month-old baby again. They'd left him for a whole month to do important things in Washington D.C. Part of my brain sniffed, "Oh, they're that kind," but then I realized there are many reasons to be away from your children. I pictured the loyal wife enduring receptions and small talk, just wanting to cradle that small soft body in her arms. In any case, it wasn't to be. They flew out of Winslow when they should have stayed on the ground to wait out a snowstorm. Did he go, even against good advice, to hurry back to their child? We will never know. Their plane crashed in the area out near Secret Mountain. It burned. They burned. Carl told me searchers found the charred frame of wreckage upside down, facing west.

I hope that baby will never find out what happened, when he gets older. That he'll never hear his parents were identified only by his watch and her jewelry. That Carl Mayhew said he'd heard "an awful unusual screech" and then "deafening silence" from the fogged-in area near Wilson's Mountain. Others reported seeing the flames, hearing a plane make several passes before a crash. Loss is hard to bear, even when it's not our own. I can drive myself half to distraction trying to decide if it's worse to lose a child, or for a child to lose its mother. "Neither," is the only answer, "neither is acceptable."

Some people said it was typical rich-folks behavior to fly into a snowstorm where any fool knew there'd be no visibility. I just think that six-month-old baby doesn't know anything about being rich or not. I hope his life turns out all right.

Couples

The last of our unmarried children is getting married!
I'd supposed by now that if it were to happen, it would have
already. Clara's been teaching in Denver for the past five years, writing
weekly letters that almost bring her spirit in them: brisk, bright, pur-
poseful from dawn to dark. She loves her students, loves her garden,
loves her life.

It occurs to me that Tad loves being a teacher because he takes
knowledge very seriously. He puts such value in Latin, literature,
grammar, geography. He values sharing it with young minds. Clara,
on the other hand, seems to come at it from the opposite direction: she
loves being with the students, so she teaches because that's the way she
spends time with them.

Her letters are full of this child's personality or that one; how she
helped two boys work out problems between them, how she was able
to get a couple of her dresses altered to surreptitiously pass to a student
who didn't have anything decent to wear. She celebrates each one of
them, it seems. They've been her life, and if she ever wished for a beau,
there was no whisper of it. But now she writes that Mac McBride asked
if he may make her his wife, and she accepted him.

We met Mac when we went to see her and the Coxes last Christmas.
He has a bit of a Scottish (Scotch? Scots? I should ask Clara) accent, and
seems a wonderful person. She's like a merry little sparrow, and he's
more like...hmm. A stork? Tall, mild, not flamboyant. But storks are

the legendary bringers of babies, and if it isn't carrying out the idea too far—so far it won't bear the weight and snaps off—he does bring happiness. Especially to her. I am overjoyed she will know that kind of companionship.

I understand that not everyone is cut out to be married. Some folks prefer more solitude, and others have restlessness, or a dedication to a profession, that make it a poor fit. Also, I remember when we had two women stay with us at the old house here in the early days, who said they were in a Boston marriage: living together, financially independent of either a father or husband. Both were teachers. I remember Carl wondering out loud to me that night how married they were: did they share their bed in the same way that we shared ours? Of course I didn't inquire, but they seemed to have the rhythms and patterns of a couple: one preparing the other's tea with a practiced hand, fond teasing touches as they passed. It isn't something you see often, but the world certainly does have a lot of different kinds of folks.

Some people collect little spoons. I've never understood why that's fun, but I see them a great many places, with the name of the town or whatever; I remember them at the Grand Canyon general store. It doesn't have to appeal to me for me to respect it.

Anyway, now I'm thinking about couples. Margaret and Stanton have been married these five years now, and he's certainly the quieter of the two. And unlike Mac and Clara, who seem to enjoy lots of lively discussion, mostly Margaret talks, with great certainty and emphasis, and Stanton is the listener. Which seems to work perfectly for them both.

That reminds me of one time when Carl was talking about the differences between his brothers, and how he and Ellsworth always interacted with no effort at all. Jacob, between the two in age, wasn't as easy. "We get along fine," he said, "but I have to do all the getting along." I think Margaret makes up her mind how they will do things, and Stanton does all the getting along.

Over the years it seems to me I've met a fair number of couples where the woman is frankly a bit hard to like: very opinionated, sometimes dismissive of her husband, or eager to tell everyone what we really must read, or do, or think. Often that husband is mild, amiable and goes along. I wonder "Why did he marry her?" Certainly it works the other way: kind women marry stern men. Quiet marries talkative—look at Carl and me. I've gotten used to the fact that, will me or nil me, he is going to bring people home to lunch. On one level he knows I don't care for it. But he loves both this town and me so much, that his desire to share his bounty with new-met friends outweighs the challenge it is to my shyness. Maybe he thinks if he does it long enough, I will one day slap my forehead in wonder and cry out, "For goodness sakes, I love meeting new people and only now realize it!"

Regardless, it's who he is, and who I am, so I always cook our noon dinner for four appetites. And rarely have leftovers. If three of us sit down, we send a boxed meal home with the single man who is visiting, and he walks away pleased.

Fourth of July

Actually today is the fifth; we got home so late last night we dropped into bed. But the Fourth is always the highlight of midsummer: conviviality and conscious excess from what Carl said the freed slave who raised him, Boyle, called can't-see to can't-see.

We're up early, getting our contributions ready for the party at Pine Flat. It's an event for the whole town, and some come down from Flagstaff or up from Cottonwood. The classics were there: Lady Baltimore cake, flag cakes with strawberries and blueberries and whipped cream, fresh corn on the cob, fried chicken (with that aroma you almost feel you could take a bite of). Tad and Lucille brought their brood down from Flagstaff, where he takes classes in the summertime. It's always wonderful to have those happy hugs from grandchildren, and see Carl's face light up when he hears their voices as they come up the walk. Larry was unusually lively, because he can't get over the free ice cream at the picnic; you bring your bowl and spoon, and can get in line as many times as you want. He kept asking Carl, "and you'll go with me again, Grampa, when I finish one? So after the chocolate, I can try the vanilla, and the strawberry, and then maybe the chocolate again?" He runs to being thin, so it did my heart good. Carl promised he'd get Larry as much as he wanted, "even if I have to roll you over there, you'll be so round," which made them both laugh.

Lucille still has to keep an eye on Paula because she's at that fearless toddler age, but somehow even so I've never seen a more competent mother, friend and helper.

T.C. (Carl) Schnebly with granddaughters
Paula, above, and Patsy Schnebly

Patsy was glad to see Annie Jordan, and the two ran off together as soon as we got to the picnic ground. I get a little embarrassed when people walk up with strangers in tow, "who just couldn't believe they got to meet the Sedona the town is named after," but Carl usually jumps in and starts asking them all manner of questions about where they're from, and why they came, and he's right—everyone has something interesting to say if you keep at it long enough.

And he does keep at it long enough.

After the firecrackers and rockets and all, we generally head home, but Helen and George Jordan invited us to their house. So we went with Tad's bunch; Paula curled up like a rosy little cherub in my arms who went right back off in a nest of pillows on Helen's bed. The rest of us had a last cookie with good milk, and George played his musical saw. It sounds so rustic, but he has a delicate touch, and by holding it between his knees at the handle and resting the other end on the floor, he bends it and then draws the bow across to produce different notes. The children were spellbound, and we all enjoyed the impromptu concert mightily.

George and Helen have been so generous to Carl and me; I see Ruth more because she's the one who needs the most help with those children, who are dear but spirited. She's so grateful, and I can always find a dozen things that need doing at her house. When I'm with Helen, we talk about art and music and things that nourish the soul. But both Mr. and Mrs. Jordans, Walter and Ruth, George and Helen, are a pure privilege to know. The town of Sedona got some true friends when they first came up from their dad's place in Clarkdale.

Visiting

March 1, 1940

We knew we were taking a risk, going up to Flagstaff. Carl had heard there could be more snow. But the Harts were driving up, and invited us along; we knew the Wallaces would be at home Sunday, and would welcome us. It was lovely weather when we set out; snow decorated both sides of the road up the switchbacks into Flagstaff. It gleamed even more brightly, contrasted against the vivid blue sky you get after snow clouds have moved out, as if the air has been rinsed extra clean.

It was lovely to see Billy and Ethel. Carl had teased me into wearing my new knickers. He missed seeing me in his overalls when we came back to Oak Creek, but the place has grown too much to risk being seen in those. So he went and bought me knickers! Actually, I love them. It reminds me of when we were here last time, and I could move so easily. So I decided at my age, I should do a bit more of what I want to do, and wore them into town.

Ethel also loved them, and was after Billy to get her some. "Never mind. In fact," she said. "I'll get them myself."

Visiting the Millers: four unknown guests on the right with Lucille
Schnebly sitting center, Sedona Schnebly to her right, another
unidentified guest, Ethel Miller Wallace, T.C. Schnebly holding a child

We had a feast at their table, three generations. Carl's at his best in
these times, telling stories that make everyone laugh. And it didn't stop.

Tad's family had come in from Parks, and Margaret and Stanton have Sunday dinner with his family if they aren't with us. There were plenty of people rocketing about. The Wallaces' house sits at the top of a hill, with the street going straight down toward the center of town, which draws neighbor children to go sledding after a storm. Today was bright and sunny, so there wasn't much to sled on, but once our group was excused from the table, the children went out front and began playing catch—actually the tiny ones rolled balls down that street, ran to get them and came back up to repeat the process. I'm amused, and touched, that small children can find such joy in activities that quickly wear out for adults. Children came pouring out of other houses. It's fun, in a world where so much has changed, that children outside still sound the same: calling, laughing, running. The sounds of children playing, and rain falling, are my favorite sounds.

Ethel and I love watching our mutual grandchild; Margaret and Stanton's Margaret Louise is the baby of the brood, with Paula already a big girl of four, Patsy eight, and Larry eleven. Because Parks is not even an hour's drive, they often come down to visit us on Sundays, and sometimes visit Margaret and Stanton or the Wallaces. Our other in-laws were lovely people at the respective weddings, but we really haven't seen them since. It's fun to hear all the grandchildren call us Aunt Dona and Uncle Carl, Uncle Billy and Aunt Ethel. It's a fine thing when one's family member is also friend, but it's a great unexpected blessing to have a friend become family.

Genevieve

G enevieve didn't get any better. Carl and I ended up going back to Colorado at the end of May for her last weeks. Alice is fourteen, Catherine twelve, Dorothy nine, Jimmy seven, Helen only five and poor Betty Lou, two. We have now buried another daughter. It's like losing an arm; wake up and for a moment think everything is fine, before remembering that empty space and having to adjust to it all over again. We're back in Sedona now, settling in. This is the first time I've had the energy to write at all.

At night those brave children all seemed younger. I gathered the youngest three on my lap in the big rocker, and could still stroke the hair of the others sitting next to me on the floor. For some reason, they like lullabies in German best. The one I sang most was Beethoven's "Ich Liebe Dich," which I also like in English.

"I love but thee as thou dost me,
at eve as on the morrow;
and no day dawns for you and me,
but that we share its sorrow."

But I think German kind of flows over, without having to hear actual words. So, "Ich liebe dich, so wie du mich, am abend und am morgen, noch war kein tag, wo du und ich, nicht teilten unsre sorgen."

My heart breaks for those dear children. As it did for Genevieve, with all the untold stories in her eyes, before she passed—eyes that looked at them so deep and so long, as if trying to see all the things she wouldn't be there for later on: graduations, weddings, babies. Seeing her have to let them go hurt me in a brand new way. Joshua was brave and wonderful. He never broke in front of the children. They were good together as husband and wife, and she'd been a good mother. The widower and family will be all right. But never the same.

It is strange, having two daughters gone ahead. So is Pearl older than Genevieve? To me she is still five, even though technically she is the big sister to the one who was only a toddler last time they were together. Place that under the mysteries of Heaven. I only know there aren't many funny jokes being told this year, and there are a lot of stories with no point to them. Or maybe it's me.

Bridges

Sept. 2, 1940

C arl just brought in a letter from Tad, who writes weekly from Parks. He has taken Larry to a boarding school in Utah. It's called Wasatch, Carl told me, named after a mountain range. Tad's been worried that Larry can't get as good an education as he deserves in Northern Arizona. I know it breaks Lucille's heart. Because Larry is so bright, Tad put him two years ahead of the boys his age in school, so now he will soon be twelve with a lot of fourteen-year-old boys. I worry for him as Lucille does.

But their trip up included this, which Carl read out loud to me:

"We stopped at the bridge by Cameron that crosses the Little Colorado, and I had Larry help me find large flat rocks. I didn't explain why, and I think he enjoyed the mystery. Then, when we got to the Navajo Bridge crossing the Colorado River, we parked and carried a rock back over the river. I told him to drop it. He saw for the first time what I always enjoy: the sandstone rock disappears against the same color of the red river water, so it's hard to be certain it landed. Then you hear the crack, the shot, the sound of the smack of stone on water, which is echoed five, six, seven or eight times, depending on its size. Larry's eyes lit up, and he ran back for the next rock.

"I think my son and I could have stayed all day if the supply of sandstone had let us. It's a good moment, and a good memory.

"Oh, and the reason we stop at the Cameron Bridge is that all the good rocks from around the Navajo Bridge went to the bottom of the river years ago."

This made us both happy. Tad can be stern with Larry. His expectations are high. But Larry is allowed to read at the table when none of the other children can, as Tad was allowed to with us. Tad wants Larry's good mind to be great. I hope his methods work, without breaking that boy's spirit.

Each child is different. We as parents do what we believe is best, or maybe what we just hope is best.

I do think this: if we love them with all our hearts, and ask God's help, we won't ruin them. As a child of parents who I believe made some mistakes, it's a great thing to grow old enough to forgive them, and see how we grew stronger from any pain they caused us.

My parents, like any parents, weren't born all-knowing; they were simply people who decided to have children. It can still hurt to remember how it felt when they acted the way they did about Carl. But it can feel good to believe we didn't have to make those same mistakes. If one of ours had married a Hottentot, we would have welcomed them in. We are fortunate that all our children-in-law: Lucille, Joshua, Hank's wife Annabelle, Mac and Stanton, are such fine individuals. I'd like to think it shows we were good parents, since our children made such wise marriages, but I've seen a great many couples where either husband or wife simply changed, later, and things came unraveled. So I think it's just good fortune.

From listening over the years to many women talking about their husbands, what I believe is this: any marriage is successful if both parties want it to be. They could be a tightrope walker and a Congressman, but if they want to love that spouse, more than they want anything else, it will work. Rich, poor, educated, humble—how much they both want it to work is the single determining factor of a marriage that succeeds. At first I was going to write "that lasts," but many of the poor loveless marriages drag on in perpetuity when sometimes they might have been better put out of their misery. I'm glad Carl and I wanted it to work so very much. Just now he walked in, saw me writing and left again. He didn't want to bother me. I'll stop and let him put out the lights.

War Again

N ow we're in it.

Pearl Harbor has been bombed by the Japanese.

When we came out of church after Bible study, everyone was talking about it. Planes dropped bombs that blew up the USS Arizona, and other ships there in the Hawaiian Islands also caught fire. I remember when the USS Arizona was first launched or dedicated or whatever, Carl read to me about the silver service made especially for it, engraved with images of the Grand Canyon and cactus.

Now it's been reduced to charred iron and death, far away.

Does it feel worse because that greatest ship lost bore our state's name? I feel guilty for admitting it, but probably so. Names have power; they matter. They link us to things. That's why Tad is Ellsworth Miller for his Uncle Dorsey Ellsworth and Miller for my family; Clara is Clara Amanda for Mutter and Carl's sister; Genevieve is Goldie Genevieve for my sister. Hank is Daniel Henry. Carl's great-great-grandfather Henry came from Switzerland to Maryland even before the Revolution, and built a plantation called the Garden of Eden. Carl's father and grandfather were Daniel Henry and Daniel Henry, Jr. Margaret Elizabeth is for Carl's sister Cora Elizabeth. Why am I talking about that now? Maybe to distract myself for even a moment, from those young sailors now burned and entombed in a watery grave by an island far from home.

My heart breaks for those mothers.

And we are at war.

Uncertainty and fear hang over everything, like our own cloud of spiritual ash, and we must give it time—as we would literal ash—to settle. Haven't we done this enough? Do we have to go through a Great War again?

Apparently we do.

Our boys are too old to enlist, but so many are not. God save us. I don't know what to do with myself. I want to do something constructive, but can't settle to anything. It all seems so frivolous. Except darning, which is the opposite of frivolous, but I just can't pick up the darning egg right now. I keep going from one room to another. I looked at the smoothly made bed, and ran the pine board I keep handy all the way across to make sure the covers are smooth. As if that needed doing. I want to forget about what happened. I want to have a good long talk about it. I can do neither.

Carl just came in to say Tad's car is pulling up! I guess the news spurred them to drive down.

I will play Flinch with our grandchildren.

Christmas Again

Dec. 22, 1941

I vow, it can't be this time of year already. It seems we just had Christmas. I recall each month since last Christmas, but time accelerates at such a rate. I clear the breakfast dishes and it seems like half an hour passes before I'm getting the plates back out for the noon dinner.

Last Christmas, Tad came and drove the two of us all the way to Parks to take the holiday dinner with his family. For him that's into Flagstaff and then down the switchbacks, so he had to be up before dawn to come get us, then drive all the way back past Flagstaff...and then do the entire trip in reverse starting before dusk to bring us home. We urged him to stay the night, but being Tad, he said he would sleep better back with the family. The teacherage there in Parks is tiny; Patsy (and Larry when he's home from school) will take hot bricks to a shed out back each night, where Lucille has made as comfortable a nest as possible, with a bed and quilts. There's no heat out there, but neither is there room in the house for them; Paula is tiny and sleeps in their very small bedroom.

That was a lovely day, I remember; Larry so excited to show us the slide as tall as a city building that he can slide down in warmer weather; it was all piled over with snow. He described how the children would use the waxed paper their sandwiches were wrapped in to make sliding even faster. I'm impressed no one's ever fallen off the side. Parks is in some seeming storm pocket, like Mund's Park between Oak Creek Canyon and Flagstaff; a geographic feature unknown to me makes storms bigger there. But it was warm inside, and delightful to see the children. Patsy's grown so much; I always see Lillie's thirst for life and love of excitement in her. Lucille somehow finds time, even with a toddler, to make fondant and fudge and all manner of treats. It's a good memory.

But this year they are down here, staying with us. Yesterday Tad and Lucille drove up towards Flagstaff a ways—they said they stopped in the forest near Fry Canyon—and she shot the Christmas turkey! Tad was so proud, bragging on how calmly she sighted down the barrel and pulled the trigger, and matter-of-factly went to fetch it. She could have been a pioneer anywhere, at any time, and made it work. She likes to build planters and terraces, mixing the cement and laying layers of brick or rock as competent as any man. But she is also an excellent seamstress, smocking exquisite designs on the girls' little dresses, and she loves to fix up old dolls. She did one for the wife of a teacher back in Chambers when they lived there.

So besides Lucille's turkey, we have the wonderful pies from the fruit here, and the usual side dishes. I'm so glad to be back in Oak Creek, where harvest yields such bounty. Joshua and the children will be visiting Clara in Denver. Margaret and Stanton will drive down from Flagstaff tomorrow! The best part of holiday is family.

Quilting

S ometimes over the years, I've thought the best thing to put on my headstone would be, "She carried a great many things from place to place." Steady and endless, I carried. First, the boards that would be Carl's overalls from the clothesline to our bed, where I could shake them and break the stiff clean fabric back into their wearable state again. Then, the grandchildren's overshoes from the porch outside to the mudroom, where I got the dried clods off and carried them yet again into the kitchen. Carried the dishes from the drain board to the cupboards, carried the crusts and bits to the chickens. Carried the watering can to the hose, to the plants, to the hose, to more plants. Carried Patsy's bonnet from the tree seat to the mudroom. Carried the mail to Carl's desk (something must have come up for him to not have looked through it yet).

But I knew that after the carrying would be quilting, and that always makes me smile inside. Quilting is as much about what I am not doing as what I am: it means I am not weeding or washing or ironing or canning, it means I can sit and listen and laugh a little. I've carried hot water for tea, and the powdered sugar cookies Paula calls rock cakes, and an applesauce loaf. But then I get to sit and sew with good friends for a few hours.

Little Paula loves quilting days as much as I do. (I can't believe our baby is five!) She likes to call the quilting frame her house. First she's on my lap, shy when the women who come in fuss over her pretty hair.

Then after we've been sitting for a bit, she slides off my lap and curls up on the floor. If I peek under the frame with the quilt hanging down around it, I see her surveying her tiny house like the kingdom she feels it is. Most times she ends up napping under there, curled like a puppy left under a Christmas tree, rosy and warm. I imagine she feels safe and loved, listening to the voices back and forth over her head.

I don't worry about what she might hear; women know how to say things so that children don't get confused, or too interested. There can be a whole paragraph in, "You know how he gets," or "She's a little too pretty for her own good." We've seen a lot of lives lived, and at this age we can generally tell when someone is taking the hard road to wisdom. But we also know you can't warn a young person away from the edge. Some stumble, some fall. Most get back up without too much harm. I don't know why some of us can take the world's word for things and not have to try them, while others believe themselves above consequences. Just one more way we're all different, I expect.

Marine

July 6, 1942

Tad! Truly? Did you have to?

Our firstborn just left. He's enlisted in the Marines. He's 44 years old! He was in the Army during the first war. He does not have to do this. And the Marines? They have the reputation for being the fiercest of all our armed services. How can Lucille let him? I know…there's no "let" when it comes to Tad. He is emperor of his own life. I'm sure she's furious, but would never say so, at least to him. They are moving out to Mountain View, California. He will go first, for his basic training. She and the children will follow with their possessions. I'm angry, even though I know it's because I'm so scared. I can't lose another child. Besides, his three children shouldn't have to worry about their father. How selfish. (Some would say noble, but I don't.)

The only good part is that this will bring Larry back from Wasatch. I don't think he's been happy there. We don't correspond a great deal, but what little I know makes me glad he can leave that place. He's just too young.

It's hard for me not to fret about the war. The headlines are grim. I try to remember Travois' old words about worry being prayer to the devil.

The only thing that seems to calm me down—because even prayer can become insistent and fearful—is to look at whatever is right in front of me, and concentrate on it.

Carl is happy and busy; despite long days working with the Jordans, his health holds.

Our children (those that are left to us) are thriving and enjoying their lives.

Our grandchildren are too young to fight.

Lucille wrote after they got to California that Tad was in the condition of a man twenty years his junior. It appears he will not be going overseas – we are so relieved -- and he works in the mail office sorting letters from, and for, the Pacific Fleet.

Ellsworth (Tad) and Lucille Schnebly, Moffett Field, CA

She works also, as a riveter, like the woman o the poster that urges mothers to help our country by learning a skill. The children are old enough to not be harmed by her being gone during the day. I'm grateful for all that.

This room where I sit is warm despite the weather, and the polished wood of the lap desk Carl made is familiar and smooth under my hand.

The apple pie dessert I made up in desperation once years ago when I didn't have time to make pie, and that Carl loves, cools for our noon dinner.

We are both able to walk on two good legs, have plenty of food to see us through, and don't wonder where we will sleep tonight. We are blessed.

I'm not writing so much. There are such gaps, when I flip back through these pages.

I simply don't feel impelled as I used to.

The other day Carl was reading me a letter from Alf Boltz, and I remembered my internal hue and cry when he first came to call on me. That figured in my young life as a crisis of epic proportion.

Now, it takes a lot for anything to figure as more than just a nuisance, or something to be puzzled out. I suppose once you've lived a while, you realize most things will pass, until one thing kills you and then the troubles are over. That's the compensation for the creaking joints that make the first few steps after standing up a little slow, the lines and creases that make me not recognize my knees as my own when I look at them.

Sometimes if Carl and I get involved in separate conversations at church and then my eye finds him again, for a moment I see the man the rest of the world sees: slightly gnarled and bent, with lips that have thinned over time, and a sharp chin, skin stretched over bone with no softening roundness. Then his eyes find me in return, and he is again my Carl, the man I first fell in love with.

I wonder if that happens the other way: does he see Aunt Dona or Mother Schnebly, the old woman who welcomes children and hands them cookies, as a faded, nondescript figure, before I again become his bride with Nature's own permanent wave?

It's all right if it's so, as long as he then sees the bride.

Dec. 12, 1944

This war drags on. Carl is gone much of the time, helping Walter and George Jordan get produce out. The troops need every apple they can get, and the orchards are working overtime.

Wouldn't it be pretty if they could. The orchards are doing what they do: provide a nourishing environment for nature to grow her apples.

But it's been cold, and the men have been out at night keeping the smudge pots filled with oil. It burns with thick black smoke to keep the trees warm, so the tender growing apples don't succumb to frost.

The other day Carl told me, as he was cleaning up after a long night, that Walter told him George is driving so much, he comes home from taking produce up to Flagstaff late at night, takes off his pants, shakes them out, and puts them back on to start a new day with a drive to Cottonwood. They are certainly doing their part for the war effort!

Carl bundles up to spend the better part of each night walking through the rows, making sure those burners are putting out that strongly scented smoke keeping the trees warm. Even our house reeks of it, despite his clothes waiting on the porch to be washed. It's a hard vigil for a man of any age, but in his way, Carl thrives on it. He's of use, in the company of good men, doing something important not just to us, but also to our soldiers far away. I would be gabbling and insensible if I had so little sleep, but he comes home at dawn, goes to bed for perhaps four hours, and springs up bright and ready to face another day.

He humbles me with his ability to simply keep going, cheerfully and without apparent stewing and fretting.

Aug. 15, 1945

The war is over.

It took bombs on Japan to finally end the thing once and for all; this after far too many men died over in Normandy on a beach under heavy fire to end the European side of the war. I had no idea we could do something which causes so much death and damage. But at least now we don't have to worry about California being invaded. It's done. We've listened to the radio as treaties were signed on a battleship named for our other state, the USS Missouri. Funny—my birth state was the name of the ship where the war ended, and my adopted state the name of the one where it began, at least for this country.

Again, as after what has gone from being called the Great War to World War I, we look around the world at the carnage, the destruction, and pray, "never again."

I hope Tad and his family will be coming home.

I am proud of Tad. I told Carl, "He's got both your strength and your determination."

We still don't know what secret things Lucille's position was involved in. After her riveting job, she changed to an important position in a big building called a wind tunnel, helping with some type of experiment with new kinds of airplanes. Tad said no one can know, but he intimated they might be able to fly somehow without propellers! Tad is very proud of her and the secrecy surrounding her position.

I guess the children have flourished. Larry has been working on base since finishing high school, and the girls enjoy base living. One horrible thing Tad wrote: a friend of Larry's was supposed to meet him for a movie, and never did. The next day they found his body! The San Francisco papers called it the Dollar Bill Murder, because the boy had been given one dollar to go out. I felt sorry for Larry being a pallbearer at his age. But this is the world in which we live.

Lucille doesn't write often—she's too busy—but did say that a woman named Inez, who has become a very good friend, keeps an eye on the girls when they get home from school. Patsy doesn't need much looking after, but Paula has a surrogate grandma. It's funny that when I was younger, the idea would have made me sad, but now I am grateful knowing someone cares about those girls and will guard them. Love makes us generous.

Before the next school year, they will be moving to Mayer, which is down near Prescott. We will see them often enough, I expect. Tad says Larry wants to enlist, but has to work for a bit before he will be allowed (he's almost 16, and can join with parental permission when he's 17). Right now he has a job on base—for a while he was on a garbage collection crew, but now he's surveying. So Tad thinks he can get him a job with Claude Etter's survey crew here in Oak Creek when they come back. Larry will be old enough to live in the house down by the creek, where they spent summers the past few years. I look forward to him being close by.

We all (and I think that's the biggest "we" I have ever included myself in, because it's the entire country) are so relieved the war is over. The small things have been bad enough: no meat (unless you have friends with cattle), no sugar, no gas for cars. But the biggest thing is trying not to let that corner of one's mind fear take hold, imagining foreign troops swarming across our soil. Tad wrote that sometimes he and Larry would see their big dirigibles that are docked at Moffett Field going out over the Pacific Ocean with depth charges loaded, and later coming back without them. What did those pilots see? Were there submarines full of Japanese soldiers in the San Francisco Bay?

We will never know for certain how close the enemy came, or how great the risk. I am simply grateful it's over.

And yet, I'm so sorry that everyone wasn't as blessed. Poor France, poor England, losing so many brave men, as well as mothers and children in the shelling. Furthermore, cathedrals and priceless paintings burned, that now no one will ever get to see. (Not to mention whatever those Germans stole and are keeping.)

Carl doesn't often get too upset, but when he reads some of those things to me out of the papers, I can tell he's angry. His feet jiggle on the floor so furiously, and sometimes he just shakes his head and folds his arms and actually shivers a little. He's seeing the same things in his head I am in mine. But we don't give voice to them. He goes to his desk, and I come here to my rocker with the wonderful lap desk he made, and write. We all handle things our own way.

Because we're in Oak Creek, we don't see as many gold stars in windows as they do in big cities, but every time I see one in Flagstaff it brings tears to my eyes. For a parent to outlive a child is the hardest thing that can happen, and I know it. Twice.

I wouldn't say this at church, because no one can know the mind of God, but I think that's why Jesus was sent. This is probably simplistic, but it's as if God thought, "How can I make people understand how much I love them?" And He knew that if He not only let His Own Son die, but in a cruel way, suffering in front of Him, that's the greatest sacrifice a parent could give. That's how much I love you, He said.

Now on both sides of the ocean (or all three sides, or whatever I mean, if you include Japan), so many mothers are torn and will never be whole again. It doesn't matter what the fight was for, or which side they were on. We are joined, in knowing those steps will never be heard outside our doors, that voice will never call for us. Anyone who loses a child suffers in a similar way, no matter what language we speak.

But at least for now, we have peace again. People can come home. Not all of them will come home the same. Some will be damaged by what they saw and what they had to do. But many will get to see children who were born while they were away, many will run into the arms of wives they married right before they left. And we will get to see Tad and his family! Those voices will fill this house again. Those children will be in my arms. My heart is full.

Sedona & Sedona

May 20, 1946

Most of the time I don't think about the fact that our post office and I share a name, although when I see it on letters it's no longer a surprise (I got over the strange combination of embarrassment and pride I felt in the early days). However, once in a while, I contemplate the fact that I'm both a person and a place—and, Carl told me today, at least for now, I am also a thing.

Schnebly home near Jordan Road, 1940s

We've moved from our little house at the base of Schnebly Hill Road up to a home close to the Walter and Ruth Jordans, in part so I can help Ruth out. After the CCC camps closed, there was no need to be down there anymore.

Anyway, one of the benefits is being much closer to the post office. Carl likes to go twice a day to get mail from both deliveries.

He came in from his daily rounds of the post office, Hitching Post Restaurant and Jordans' wearing a broad smile.

"Well, guess what, Dona," he said, clearly not wanting to give me time to guess. I could tell he was pleased. "When I went into the Hitching Post, Mr. Brolley had a special going. He called it The Sedona. Seems he's gotten ahold of some butter pecan ice cream, and he's doing this fancy thing with whipped cream and caramel sauce, and it's the Sedona. How does that sound to you?"

If a voice could be skipping like a child, that was how Carl sounded; just pleased as punch. I don't know if he likes seeing the town's name is actually going to stick, or what, but he was clearly delighted. It was all I could do to convince him that the lunch I have planned will do nicely, and we needn't drop everything to spend hard coin on this fancy dessert instead. Ham and apple slush and corn are sufficient, and already made. But I did realize, with a little start: I am a person, place and (for as long as a restaurant special lasts) a thing.

I am in Sedona the place...and I guess it could be posited that after all this time, Sedona the place is in me. (Sedona the dish is in Sedona the place but will never be in Sedona the person at Hitching Post prices. The Brolleys came from money, in Chicago, and I swear they still inhabit a different world than the one where I live. Money is nothing to them.) So the two Sedonas, place and person, overlap, or cohabitate—we share parts of ourselves with the other. Then there's Sedona the soul, the spirit, the essence of what fills this body I walk around in; that Sedona is eternal.

I doubt Sedona the town will be, what with it being so hard to get to, even with the new road going in. But I suppose some few will always live here, and more will visit as they always have, because of the looks of the place.

Anyway, it occurs to me I should enjoy this state of living in a place where I'm also the name of the town, because probably very few folk ever get to do that. Lincoln didn't live in Lincoln, Nebraska; Washington wasn't still alive when he got a state named for him. There is no person named Ash Fork (a good thing, I guess).

I have wondered a time or two: would Ellsworth have suggested they name the town Lillie if Carl had married her? What about Minnie? Edna? My name is more musical. I never thought to ask either brother that question. And I don't suppose it matters much. We aren't that big a place.

Golden Anniversary

Feb. 24, 1947

"Fifty years, Dona."

That's how Carl woke me today, saying that softly. He never wakes me; generally when I wake up and look over, he's looking back at me; maybe I moved, which woke him, before I knew I was awake. But today I guess he just was too excited to wait for me, and figured if any occasion is worthy of waking up one's wife it would be this.

We've been married fifty years.

I can't believe I've been alive for fifty years, let alone married that long. But I also don't recall a time we weren't together.

It seems everything that has happened was to the two of us, although clearly we grew up before meeting. Carl is as much a part of me as my own hands; in a way, his face is more familiar to me than my own, because I look at him more than I look in a mirror. Over time, we've been boiled down. It seems that babies are born pillowy and soft, somewhat formless in their plump little selves. As we get older, that extra moisture steeps away, leaving visible sinew and bone. The same thing happens to our character: children are all much alike, whereas the older we get and the more certain we become about how we see the world, it's as if we get more concentrated.

Carl had a softer, rounder face as a young man. Now what stands out is that very determined jaw. I guess I'm glad there will be pictures taken later, even though I am uncomfortable being in them. We are not the somewhat formless young people we were when we married, or when we came here the first time. We've been carved into different statues…statues that stand close to one another.

All the children have come. Today there will be a reception at the church, and then the Jordans are planning an outdoor gathering. That's when we will pose for photographs; as much as I hate seeing an old woman who is clearly how I look but nothing whatsoever like how I feel, I love seeing our family forever together on this day. The one when we marked fifty years wedded and our children come home to celebrate with us.

Golden anniversary gathering of Schnebly family, left to right: Clara, Tad, Sedona, Hank, T.C., Margaret

It's wonderful to contemplate. A half-century of Carl and I being the most important people in the world to each other.

"Golden" is a good word for that.

Mayor

Carl came home looking so pleased.

"I went to the post office, and there's a letter to me. Look at this! The address reads: 'To T. C. Schnebly, Mayor, Sultan, Pioneer, Homesteader, Trailblazer, Road Builder, Chieftain, Chamber of Commerce (one man), authentic tourist information, furnished free by the man who named it: SEDONA, ARIZONA.'"

He chuckled. He is all that! The letter came from a man who took his honeymoon here. Carl had given his bride one of his pincushions, and this gentleman simply wanted to thank Carl for his suggestions on what to see while in Oak Creek, and tell him that the town he'd help create is an unforgettable place.

Carl has everyone he brings home sign our guest book, and recently he called me in to say he had counted 900 signatures from 39 states since the current one was begun, about three years ago. (That's what comes of being Very Busy at his Desk all the time.)

I sometimes wonder if people are interested in all the things Carl tells them. Does anyone really care that Grasshopper Flat used to be called Copple Flat for one of the first white men who lived west of the town of Sedona, running his cattle there? Although even I think it's slightly amusing that Sterling Pass was named for a man whose first name I don't know, but he turned out to be a counterfeiter, when he was tracked back to his house for stealing beef cattle. I guess there's no telling what anyone finds interesting or not. But Carl's enthusiasm for the place, and his interest in other people, probably makes the interactions very positive. I guess if tourists didn't like him, all the people who come to lunch here would have politely refused instead.

It's quite a town now! The Hitching Post Restaurant, the post office, Hart Store, more commerce up in Indian Gardens. Of course Oak Creek Tavern, and Rainbow's End out toward Grasshopper Flat have been doing brisk business for a long time. Midgely Bridge, which keeps you from having to drive all the way around that long loop going up out of the canyon on the switchbacks, is wonderful. I know some wealthy people have visited and come back to build big houses, some with fancy names. Carl says an airlines man named Frye has built "The House of Apache Fire" down close to Red Rock Crossing. Mercy.

Our former land surely is quite valuable today, and I told Carl the other night that I'm so sorry he had to sell it and move. He'd quite likely be a millionaire if we'd stayed.

"I doubt there's a millionaire alive who is as happy as I am," he said. (Which makes me think there isn't a millionaire's wife as blessed as I am.)

There have also been a lot of movie people through Sedona; it seems like every time you turn around, you hear about another film being done here. I remember when Tad took Carl to Cottonwood to see one of them. It was called "Leave Her To Heaven." Carl came home and talked and talked about what it was like. He was tickled to see his beloved country up on that large screen, and people talking and moving around there. I remember how he was both rather honored and also annoyed when people were making a film called "California," and went through an act of using big ropes to lower covered wagons off Merry-Go-Round Rock on Schnebly Hill Road. He did get a chuckle out of watching them do all that, though. He wrote a letter to Larry, who was in Korea at the time, saying he wondered if he should point out no one ever did that, but he figured they probably knew that and just didn't care. It's a moving picture, not the truth.

I think most people who decide to live here are just folks. Although I know some are wealthy—Mr. Brolley was an important advertising executive in Chicago before, and came here because he no longer needed to work. Carl found out that he designed the Reddi-Wip can; that cream people use when they don't want to whip their own. Carl even bought one after he knew that, and the children had the time of their lives, laughing as he shook it vigorously and then filled their mouths with that white cream, while they turned up their faces like baby birds.

I guess Sedona the place is good for starting over, and always has been. After all, that's how we got here. Gorin wasn't going to be kind to Carl, so we came here. It's funny to hear people talk about pioneers, and realize they mean us. It makes me feel like a relic. To which Hank would say slyly, "And that's not true?"

March 8, 1948

I'm a fool.

I thought I could do it; thought I could keep putting those shingles up while Carl ran down to the post office. But I couldn't and I slipped, and the dratted ladder went down without me, and I had to wait 'til he got back to put it back up.

And he thought it was funny.

It wasn't funny.

It was ridiculous, and I'm so embarrassed, and he can't understand why I can't see the humor in it.

I just can't. It's who I am. Most of the time Carl and I are like two gears in a clock, turning smoothly together, but once in a while something gets jammed in the works, and right now if we had a barn I would go live in it.

It wouldn't do to go live in someone else's barn, and we don't have one of our own. This is between us, no one else.

But he can get on my nerves sometimes.

Larry

Nov. 22, 1948

Today Tad took Carl and me up to Flagstaff. He wanted us to see the new market, Food Town, I think, that had opened in town. We had held off going the first day because everyone was talking about the free ice cream samples, and we knew the wagons and trucks would stretch for blocks. But a month has passed, and the fuss has died down. It was quite a place: more canned goods than I imagined were made in the world—why would anyone need that many different kinds of beans?

And sure enough, there's a freezer that has ice cream in it all the time, which you can buy and take home. Well, I had put all the cup money in my pocketbook. And even though I saw Carl's puzzlement, because he's heard me go on often enough about paying for things we can make, I bought a container of some fancy kind with almond and fudge (we also bought a bit of ice to get it home safely). I've never done that before! Carl and Tad and Larry all love ice cream. And I love seeing happy eyes.

Tad had been curiously insistent that we be done shopping by three. We were, but after he turned the key to start the engine, we didn't drive somewhere else. We just sat in the car for almost five minutes, letting the radio play. Twice I started to ask the why of it, but Tad just shook his head as if waiting for instructions only he would recognize. And then, a song ended, and I heard, "Brown Credit Jewelers time, three o'clock." Which wouldn't have been so remarkable in itself, but it was Larry speaking. As if he were right there with us! Our Larry!

Larry Schnebly in radio publicity photo, Flagstaff

Of course, we knew people talked on the radio; to the degree that I could get past the magic of a voice being waves of sound, I understood that there were announcers. But this wasn't any announcer; this was our grandson. On the radio, exactly where you hear Edward R. Murrow, or President Roosevelt. Carl's eyes got so wide, and then he smiled as if he'd never stop, and shook his head. "That boy," he said softly. "That boy." Tad nodded briefly, and started the car. I don't think anyone could understand how proud you can be of a child or grandchild until you have them. It's a filling feeling.

Larry is special to Carl. I know he felt Tad was rough on him, oldest son or not. I felt so myself, but I understood: Tad knew life could be hard on a man, and he wanted to make sure Larry was hard enough in return. But Larry wasn't like Tad. Maybe he was like Tad would have been if Pearl hadn't died. He was easy, like Carl.

Anyway, Larry always adored Carl, and it went both ways. I remember once when Larry was about eight, he begged "Grampa" to take him swimming during the noontime break at the Camp. Carl walked over with him across the road to the steep slope that got them to the creek. I didn't follow, but I could hear Larry calling joyously, "Come in, Grampa! It's not cold! Come in!" Then Carl saying, "I know you think it can't be any fun just to watch, but I love watching you. No matter what you do. Show me you remember what I taught you about lying down on the water." And then splashes, and his praise. Larry told me years later he could always feel Carl's love, even if his words were about winding a watch. There was the love in his voice. And I understand that well. "Mother, shouldn't we stop wasting lamp oil?" is one of the sweetest lines outside a sonnet.

Fame

When we lived here the first time, Oak Creek Canyon was already known for its beauty, but not by very many people. Some came from the east, having heard about it, perhaps from a restless relative, like Ellsworth writing Carl. And people around Arizona Territory were familiar with it. But not at a level anything close to what it is now. People come from Chicago and Boston and San Francisco, already familiar with Courthouse Crossing and Steamboat Rock from pictures, movies and articles. A few have even heard of Schnebly Hill Road.

Doubtless, it is not like anyplace else on earth, from what I've seen in encyclopedias and geographic magazines. Several reasons: the contrast of the deep sienna land and such blue sky; the odd shapes and outlines, changing as you move between those rock formations, make being here feel like being part of a stereoscopic view.

People are so struck they can't stop telling us how amazing it is. They are excited; they want to share that excitement. I understand. What sometimes gets tiresome is feeling like we disappoint them if we don't match them gush for gush, rave for rave.

Once in a while, I meet one of these visitors at church. It's amusing how often they say, "This is God's country!" looking very proud, as if they've figured something out no one else has. Often, they add, "It must be amazing to have it named after you."

Well, just the town is, I say, not the whole canyon. And yes, it is amazing. But I told Carl that uneasy lies the head that wears a crown, if I could play a bit fast and loose with Henry IV. People seem to think I should be some mystical wraith, talking about the music of the spheres, and inspiration pouring from the rocks. Or that I should float about, a muse, merely being Sedona. Or pose on the Battleship Rock at sunset—shiver! We have had more than our share of artists. I don't know if people come and then get inspired, or if those who can copy scenery come because they want to be the ones to get something on canvas no one else has. But often these enthusiastic visitors looked a little disappointed when they meet me. They hoped for a sandstone sprite, and instead, they get this very reserved normal person quite probably scented faintly of potatoes or jam or something equally mundane.

Actually, that's fine with me. If they found me fascinating they'd scrutinize me more closely. And a brief meeting is more than sufficient for me. Sometimes they can get a little caught up in the poetry of the place and it spills over and makes a verbal mess. I've met a few who say the rocks have powers—not like turning flowers into birds, but powers to stir the blood or something.

"Don't you feel it?" they ask. I smile and shake my head. I don't want to feed rumors like that. Rocks don't have powers. God has powers.

While I don't hold with powerful rocks, I do know there is something different about being here than being anyplace else I've ever gone. It isn't good or bad. Just intensified.

Somehow Oak Creek Canyon takes everything you feel and magnifies it: if you are energetic, you become galvanized; if you are wistful, you become maudlin. Happy turns to giddy, lonely is desolate. Oak Creek Canyon is a more-so place, and it takes a strong person to be able to live here.

Or maybe that isn't true. Maybe anyone who wants to can learn to live here. Perhaps if you were weak when you get here, you and the canyon working together make you strong.

Now I sound like those folks. I'm going to go lay out the apricots to dry. That will be much more productive.

Jan. 3, 1950

We've been here almost 20 years now...this time. That makes it officially the place I have lived longest. I was 24 when we left Gorin the first time, so that was my longest residence. Then we were here a little over four years. And after that, in Boyero for 20. So now living in Oak Creek Canyon from both times just edges out Gorin as the most permanent home.

That's as it should be. Actually, it seems looking back that more happened in the first four years—1901 to 1905—than this past twenty here. Which have flown. When we arrived Margaret was only fifteen. Now every member of our flock has grown and married. And Genevieve's been gone these past ten years. God bless Clara. She doesn't say it, but I believe she avoided having children of her own to be able to mother the Cox bunch. She is such a constant presence to them, and no one could be better for children. She has a deft touch with her students as well as her nieces and nephews. They always feel at home with her.

Tad's three are grown and gone. Larry is working in Chicago right now, which makes me sad. He had a brief relationship with the Brolley girl from the Chicago family that owned the Hitching Post. It didn't go well. So he's in Barrington, which I gather is a very elegant and refined area of Chicago, living with her Uncle Ollie. I don't know much about his life, but from what Carl's read me out of letters, Uncle Ollie Hollister is a non-judgmental and steadying presence during a hard time. Also, apparently an excellent cook. I hope Larry goes back to college, but it's not my place to say so. Carl says he's working as a night watchman, and reading a great deal. I'm old enough to know God works on each of us in a different way, and He's not done with Larry yet.

Patsy is at ASC in Flagstaff. We don't see her a great deal, but she must be happy. That girl has spirit. I don't think of myself as spirited...

marrying Carl and getting disowned was my one rebellious act. And actually there was no rebellion involved; I didn't see marrying him as going against anyone. It was all I wanted, and I still think it was the smartest thing I could ever have done. But Patsy causes her family some concern. She takes life in great gulps. Which can be very exciting, but there are risks that make her parents worry.

Paula is with me often. With Tad and Lucille back here, I get to spend a great deal of time with that sweet girl. She reminds me of me, to Patsy's Lillie. The other sister is dashing, glamorous, unafraid, while Paula tends to hang back, as I did, feeling less remarkable, less interesting. She and I love time at the piano; she seems to crave music the way some people do company, or sugar. We garden, we sing, we talk about things in the Bible. She has Clara's equanimity, and Genevieve's quiet humor. She's better about wearing her sunbonnet outside than Patsy ever was.

The older I get the more I think there's something to the ancient idea that "kings are born to be kings and thieves are born to be thieves." Not that a cruel parent can't break a good child, or a damaged one be healed. But so much seems born in us. Paula never heard Genevieve's little narratives while she played, but sometimes when she's over, if I close my eyes I'm back in Boyero with my other girl on that wide clean parlor floor, lining up her dolls. Larry not only got Carl's odd crooked thumbs (and Tad's), but also the way Carl meets the world with an open face, and takes lively interest in every person. Like Kipling's, "...walk with kings, nor lose the common touch." Patsy has her mother's bearing, the bright hair, and her exact voice. But when she talks about a boy she knows, I can just see Lillie, who was physically darker but had the exact fizzing quality of being a little more alive than most people.

I'm sure all the grandchildren have bits of my children, their parents, which come out in them. But Tad's are the three I've always seen the most. Tad, for all he can be a bit harsh, a bit distant, has been a constant comfort and presence to me his entire life.

Manzanita

March 21, 1950

Speaking of Tad being a comfort and presence: I don't know what I'd do without him. Larry has come home! Actually, he's back at school in Flagstaff, but he was down for the weekend.

Anyway, Carl needed a new cane, and Tad told me after they got back this afternoon that the three of them, father, son, and grandson, had driven up Schnebly Hill Road to get one.

That makes it sound as if there's a men's store in Schnebly Hill Road. Of course not. But there is manzanita. Carl loves manzanita for a cane because it's such a hard wood. He can find a length and use it for a year or more before it wears down. The trick is finding a section that's long enough and fairly straight. Manzanita grows like it's confused about which way to go: twists and whorls and waves. So it takes some looking to get a good, long, fairly straight piece.

They drove up the road a piece and parked, and were looking around some stands of manzanita for a likely prospect. Tad told me that at one point he couldn't see Carl, so he walked over to the edge of the road and his father had scrambled down a very steep slope. "For crying out loud, Dad, what are you doing?" he called. Carl just waved him off. He'd seen the piece he wanted and by gosh, he was going to get it. Tad told me he dreaded having to come home and tell me that he had failed to take care of his father. (In that sentence I realized he still blames himself for "failing" to take care of Pearl the day she died, and I understand a bit better why he can seem bossy and sharp with his family, both older and younger members. Fear makes us sharp.)

Fortunately, there was no misadventure. Carl stubbornly refused help, and hacked and cut until he liberated his new cane from its peers and then had to make his way back up. I think he let Larry give him a hand up the final step...probably more to give Tad a bit of his dignity back than because he needed the help.

T.C. (Carl) Schnebly in his 80s, sitting outside in Sedona

Carl may be older, but he is determined to do everything he ever did, even if it takes longer. That stubborn set to his jaw shows me when his mind is made up, and I don't waste a breath trying to talk him out of whatever he's fixed on doing. Now he's out on the back porch, sanding and smoothing. He will stain this new cane and rely on it for months to come.

Church

Hank and Annabelle are visiting us with the grandchildren we see the least, Hal and Dixie. I savored getting to take them with us to our usual church service at Wayside Chapel. I remember so well the first time we lived here, and worship services were comprised of perhaps twenty people gathered in our front room, with me playing the piano, then listening to whoever was the most comfortable Bible reader go through some verses. But now the Jordans pick us up, although we could easily walk the few blocks. I still play the piano for services.

This morning everything was as usual, with Hank's family in the front row on my side. While I was playing "What A Friend We Have In Jesus," for our opening hymn, I heard little Hal hiss, "Gramma! Gramma!" and I looked over. He was staring in horror at the floor between his feet, and mine on the piano pedals. There was a centipede that I firmly believe was 18 inches long. I stopped playing and grabbed the broom I keep on the other side of the piano—for the look of things, it should be put away, but this happens from time to time. Thanking God for the years of dealing with unexpected rattlesnakes, I aimed swiftly enough to strike it directly. The key to killing vermin is never hesitate, never allow scuttle time. It took half a dozen good whacks, but I then joined the singers on the next verse.

Hal looked at me differently the rest of the day. He could barely wait till we'd left the church to tell everyone else in our party about it, although since they were sitting alongside him they had the event fairly well fixed in their heads. But what did privately please me was Hal's astonishment at my demeanor.

"Gramma looked like she'd just picked a piece of lint up off the floor, not killed a gigantic poison creepy creature!" he said. Bless him; he got extra biscuits for lunch.

Wayside Chapel has been such a blessing; I was treasurer and secretary so I know how long it took us to collect the funds to get the building. I wish we could afford a bell. Carl and I put away what money we can from his pension, for that purpose. We get $72 a month, "just for being old," as he puts it.

I'm so fortunate we have both piano and organ at church. I never mastered the organ; to me it seems a cross between a piano and bagpipes, although some get a lovely sound from it. But I love playing the piano. Someone said years ago, "Singing is praying twice," and I do think music is its own prayer. It adds a dimension. So if there is height and width, and then depth, there is also thinking a prayer, adding audible words to it, and adding music. It's full prayer. So "Old Gray Mare" probably doesn't catch God's attention, but maybe some of the world's most beautiful symphonies are parts of a prayer.

And anyone can make music! George Jordan's saw, a child's voice, or a professional orchestra. Nature makes music all the time, and some of us are fortunate enough to hear it often. Most every evening Carl and I sit outside, and last night were joined by Hank and Annabelle, while the children ran about, shouting with that excitement that seems to take hold of children around dusk.

They'd not seen the bench Carl put around the base of our juniper. My irises are growing everywhere, and the garden looks pretty. The talk is rarely spirited; part of the point of sitting outside is to let the day wind down around us. But Hank is always irrepressible, and had us all laughing, telling stories about when Clara's Mac took him to visit where he works, at the Atomic Energy Commission. Hank described how seriously everyone took their jobs, and how he joked about stealing secrets and suchlike, which did not go over well with anyone except Mac. Fortunately, he said, they all like Mac a great deal, so they didn't arrest Hank for cutting up. He is almost 43, but I still see that little boyish face when I watch him talk.

Hank also teased me because Carl had apparently mentioned that I'd gone to visit Oma Byrd. She's been going through a bit of a rough patch lately, Carl had told me, so I took her some preserves and such. She runs the Oak Creek Tavern and the Upper Store, so she wouldn't have time to get her garden into jars on top of that. Hank was tickled at the idea of me walking through the doors of the tavern, because of my WCTU work. I put up with a bit of joking, but I reminded him strongly that when Our Lord was on earth, He made it a point to be seen with the women judged unfairly by society. Oma is a very good person, regardless of her profession. I know she's fed at no charge a lot of men who couldn't afford the meals. Hank looked a little abashed, and then began talking about how the name "Oma" sounds like a noise an odd instrument might make, and began a tune using Omas until we were holding our sides again.

Diagnosis

July 26, 1950

We're back from Flagstaff, and the news isn't good. I've had a suspicion that whatever was causing me indigestion and feeling swollen, then unaccountably tired, might be something serious. Today was the second of two doctor's appointments; Tad drove Carl and I both times. I have cancer.

What a strange thing to write. Like writing, "Stop in the name of the queen!" or "I cannot tell a lie." Words that have meaning, and that people say. But always other people.

Carl looks terrible. Older. He went to lie down, which he never does. I think he doesn't want me to see his face. The doctor asked to talk to him alone, and I'm as sure as if I had been sitting in there with them that the doctor told him there's nothing they can do. It's often so with cancer, from what we've seen. While this certainly isn't good news, and perhaps I'm not fully realizing it yet, it's also not the worst thing that's ever happened. Any parent who outlives a child can tell you that. I've already outlived a logical life span.

July 27, 1950

It's always been easier for me than for Carl to say the hard thing. So I told him I knew. He looked relieved. "The doctor said I shouldn't tell you, but I knew you'd want to know. Of course, being you, you already do," he said.

We held hands, sitting side by side, not having to see one another's faces. That's how we've always talked about difficult matters. Several months, could be pain at the end. But there will also be good. We won't tell the children for a while; no point in long faces when nothing can be changed.

In the meantime, we will enjoy our days. I'm interested that the idea of travel doesn't appeal to me at all (Carl asked). I want what we have for as long as I can have it: getting up early, bringing him his morning cup, sitting quietly together, going over the day. Reading him letters from the children, hearing the news when he comes back from town. Right now I even want rolling my eyes when I see him coming back with strangers, then smiling because I can make him happy this way. He's bragged on my cooking to them already, and there's always a cobbler or pie or something for dessert from our (well, the Jordans') orchards.

I want to watch the flowers come up, and pull the dead blooms off to make more blossom. I want to hear the ravens. I love ravens. Saucy, unrepentant about making noise, seeming joyous and even cocky as they soar over, cawing, "You can't see what I can!" And they take such obvious pleasure in their view that I never begrudge it. I want to walk out to meet children who come running up to the door, and query them on Bible verses; see their faces light up when I bring over the cookie jar. (Where will they get cookies when I'm gone? Funny how that makes me significantly sad.)

Most people don't know anything's wrong yet, and that's a good thing. We can go to church together—Carl insisted on buying me a coat that's much too elegant, but when I made him get his suit, he said that I had to have something new as well. He's a dashing figure on Sundays in his snappy fedora...although I like him best in his khaki work clothes.

T.C. (Carl) and Sedona Schnebly before church

Mostly, I want to spend my time hearing Carl's voice. That's when everything is fine. How he loves to talk. I think his favorite times are setting out for downtown, eager to tell people about the area, often with one of his pincushions in his pocket for some wife or daughter he will surely meet.

He slices century plant into sections. It's just spongy enough to be perfect for pins. He's made me a dozen over the years, and now he signs his name on the underside. Sometimes we put cloth over the top, fastening it with pins around the edges, just to be fancy. I think his other favorite times are settling down at his desk in the afternoon to accomplish Important Things, and being with me. That isn't boastful; it's just true. We are happiest as two. I suspect the children find our lives rather quiet, but we are deeply content. We've done a great deal, travelled more miles than I ever thought possible when I was coming up. We helped start a town (thanks to brother Ellsworth) and raised a group of fine caring people. I've put up probably thousands of quarts of good fruits and vegetables over time. Carl can't run out unless he lives a dozen more years after me. That feels good.

I'm sure it will be hard for the children to get this news. From where I am, time accelerates at such a pace that I feel I will be welcoming them to Heaven in about twenty minutes. It won't be any time at all to me, but to them and the grandchildren it will feel a long, long while. Bless them. I am sorry to cause them any sorrow. But I also find myself thinking calmly and kindly, "This is how we all grow and learn." They will find out they get through it pretty well. Or, are very upset, and then realize later, with some faint surprise, "Oh, I guess I'm all right after all." Some pains last longer than others, but all of them fade over time. And there are so many delightful distractions during all seasons and all hours.

Enough. I get to put on the beans that have been soaking to cook, roll out a piecrust, and fold the pillowcases that have been out in the sun. I love that smell. It's like the whole outdoors in one naturally perfumed intake of air. I probably still have a lot of deep breaths of that scent ahead of me.

Understanding

I've not written much. I confess it's because I've been struggling with my previous words about acceptance. After the initial shock wore off, I found myself unsettled, and afraid—not of death, but of what might come between here and there. The worst part was not trusting my own body. How could it turn on me? I have fed and cared for and nourished it as best I could all these years…how could it turn traitor?

I haven't said this to Carl, but I can tell from how he looks that I'm not making much of a job of hiding it. I've prayed for help. I've always prayed for help. Once, a minister told Ethel Wallace that even ministers are only beggars telling other beggars where to find bread. Most of the important things I've done, I never could have done on my own.

But deliverence from these feelings didn't come from church, or not formally. Rescue, and respite, came from the garden.

I was out this morning while it was still cool, watering and pulling off old blooms. I looked out across this view we always enjoy, and at nature. And suddenly I saw this cancer in a very different light.

When a tall ponderosa gets struck by lightning, it loses its needles and dries to a snag. There are an unusual number of these at the top of Schnebly Hill Road, where it turns to go past the Munds' property into Flagstaff. Snags are stark, twisted, dramatic things. I find them beautiful, like sculpture. Eventually they topple and become deadfall, hosting small creatures and insects. We don't shake our heads and say, "That ponderosa turned on itself." It fulfilled its exact purpose in nature.

If a snowstorm drops two feet of white powder that covers everything with a magical hush, and then melts, we don't sadly say, "Well,

I guess that snow just couldn't survive." It watered the earth. Flowers have to die back in season. None of those are betrayal, or failure. They are in step with the symphony of the world.

As is this body I inhabit. Part of nature, for my time on earth. It's not letting me down, turning on me. Its season has come to exit.

I don't love leaving all this. But I feel a deep peace now, understanding that it's not that I've failed, or gone wrong. I'm as much a part of nature as any raindrop, any tree, any rock formation.

Oct. 28, 1950

I just sent Carl to mail a letter to Alf Boltz.

It's so funny to remember now, how aggrieved I was that he was my first gentleman caller. He's been a correspondent and friend, all these years. Several times he's come west and stayed with us. I've written to ask that he will make it a point to do that once a year after I'm gone.

Carl has always liked him—better than I did, in the beginning. He probably wouldn't have judged him even in our early school days

However...sometimes men and women do see members of their own gender differently from one another. There might be a woman none of the others approve of, while all the men follow her with their eyes and tell their wives she doesn't mean any harm, just likes to be looked at. Then, there's the man who men shake their heads about, not really trusting him, while women feel sorry for him, thinking he's hiding a broken heart under his swagger. Maybe both are right.

Alf turned out better than fine; got distinguished looking, married happily, and has several grown children. His wife passed away probably ten years ago, and now he's even been to Europe! So I know coming west won't prove a hardship. It will be good to have someone visiting regularly. Carl needs to talk; can't abide silence, never could, for very long. He and I can sit quietly because we don't need words to feel in communication. But he will get lonely. I'm sure his brother Mel will come sometimes as well. I'll write him next. And of course, the children will be around as much as they can, with their busy lives.

I also wrote Lillie; that was a hard one to do. We have been together, even when apart, since we can remember anything at all. She is still brisk and active. I hated to tell her that I don't get to write many more letters, if any.

But, I said, whenever you get to Heaven, it won't be more than a few days before you're showing me things I'd never thought to look for. That's what you do. You bring riches to my life because of the things you see, and the way you see them. You'll tease St. Peter when I merely stand in awe; you'll find Michelangelo and boldly tell him what you think he should have painted. You'll let them know you're there. And I will look forward to that, more than I can say.

I'm glad the Black family is happy to let us go down to the old place and visit the creek. I have so many memories there. I can just see the children playing, laughing and whooping when it was warm enough for them to wade and low enough to be safe. They learned to skip stones there, identify skeeter bugs, tell the sound of a beaver's tail slapping the surface, and other botany. I love that crisp sweet spicy scent it's always had, and the sound of cicadas that flourish once it's damp enough.

Perhaps it's like when you're around people you met when you were younger, part of you feels like you're that age again. Being at the creek reminds me of when I was there in my early 20s, and I feel younger. I remember how my back would hurt doing laundry in that cold water—so much better to do it on the back porch now! Back then I'd have to lay it out to dry everywhere (sheets for the guests filled our lines), and sometimes a raccoon or fox would track neat little red prints across when I wasn't paying enough attention. I swear, it would make me want to spit nails.

So now is better, even though there's no denying it takes me longer to get back up off the quilt I spread when I'm ready to leave. If Carl comes with me, he wanders across to check on "his" road. He likes to walk up to Bear Wallow, get the larger stones out of the roadway, generally pick up a little. He's always industrious. Hank and Clara are the only ones who never lived here, (although Genevieve left when she was only two). But they've visited as adults. When Clara and Mac were down, Carl had taken them both downtown to meet people. Later she said to me, "It's got your name, but it's Dad's place, isn't it?" She's so right.

Rainstorm

Nov. 12, 1950

Poor Carl—I just sent him to Jordan's to drop off a get-well card for Ruth's father-in-law because Carl heard at the Hitching Post today that he's ailing. And there's a wild Old Testament rainstorm raging out there; the house vibrates and shudders with thunder—bright lightning that's hard to get out of your eyes after it strikes. I've heard one crack so loud I know a tree went down somewhere nearby. Normally, I wouldn't ask Carl to go out in anything like this; while a card is always a nice thing, I did it mostly because I wanted to have him out of the house so I could get this package of papers finished and sealed, and leave a letter for him.

I believe it won't be long. Things just feel different inside, body and soul, like a restless shifting, similar to when a baby is getting ready to come. And that same need to get the house all in order that you feel—that nesting urge—before you deliver is back, only this time it's these papers. So that when I go, there's nothing left to be done.

Because I don't want to risk hurting anyone's feelings with my memories, I'm going to ask that this be kept sealed for 65 years. It's very possible no one will ever bother to open it. The whole thing could get thrown out. But I'll have tried to do something with these sheets: all this paper I've covered with words over a life; and this doesn't even count letters I've sent.

I let myself think it's possible some of it might be interesting to someone, although I wince as I write that. They are far more likely to wonder what that batty old woman thought she had to say. Fair enough. I just hold such reverence for the written word that I couldn't bring myself to burn these or consign them to the trash. So this can be closed, and stay closed for as long as a lifetime. By the time 65 years pass, that's long enough for everyone I love to have come to Heaven— or at least be old enough that anything I said won't matter. By the time they're in their 80s, they'll understand how this life is a preview. Like a baby before it's born can make out some light and sound, but muffled and faint, I think our sense of Heaven is completely unknowable. How could that baby in the womb picture the world and the wonders in it? That's how I am now, straining to guess at the unguessable.

But any parent understands the tremendous excitement of being close to laying eyes on a child. Both Pearl and Genevieve are waiting! I've not seen their dear faces for too long, and am eager to see what they look like and hear their voices. Probably Daisy will run out of the Heavenly gates first, followed by other doggies. Mutter and Papa, sisters and brothers, friends. What joy quivers in me, thinking of all this.

I do feel bad about leaving Carl. He looks so grave when he doesn't know I am watching him. He's dreading being alone, and if I could choose, I would let him leave first. It will be different for him, no doubt.

In part, he'll miss having someone to take care of. A while back, he was regretting that I didn't end up in a big house like we had in Boyero, or the one here that burned after we left. He regretted we didn't have a grand inheritance for our children, and that I help watch the Jordan children. Carl doesn't often get mournful, or think about things any way other than the way they are, but he was melancholy about it this one evening.

I told him he'd given me everything I ever wanted. He's given me love, and children, and adventure. It was only because of him that I got my big question answered: am I strong enough? I am—not always at the time, but overall. And, I said, he's given me things I didn't even dream I deserved to want: being the most important person in the world to someone, feeling precious and treasured. He could not, I told him, have taken better care of me, even with all the money in the world. And no matter what else we ever had, we always had a piano for me to play. He's given me music, everywhere we lived. And I've gotten to teach our children and grandchildren the famous first words of a musical life: "This is middle C." Whether or not any of them continue to play, they all seem to have an appreciation for music. That's a rich gift to have given them.

We've talked—some, because Carl looks so downcast I can't bear to do it very often—about the end and after; I've told him I don't want any flowers. Flowers are of the earth, and I will no longer be. Better there be more music, something the heavens can hear. Or a bell!

He'll throw himself into that project—the bell for Wayside Chapel—with the same energy and resolve he brings to everything, whether it's getting the mail, or straightening a nail, or helping heal a broken man's sense of himself. I know he'll keep busy, and I know he'll do fine. If there is a bell to be rung, I know I'll hear it in Heaven. It will be Carl giving me more music. And no matter how sweet the angels' harps, that will be my favorite sound; Carl sending his love from Earth to Heaven by the clear peal of a bell: calling a morning Alleluia if it's early in the day, or sending a final Amen in the evening. I suspect Carl will put considerable energy into getting a bell somehow. That will give him something to do, and a way to continue to take care of me. Which I won't need…but I suspect he will.

It just occurred to me: the last time I made a journey that felt this big was coming to Oak Creek in the first place. Everything I'd ever known would no longer be home, and something I couldn't imagine would be mine from then on. That's exactly how I feel right now.

Carl was the one who came to Oak Creek first: found our place here, and welcomed the children and me on that train platform in Jerome. This time I am going first. I'll be the one to welcome him when he comes Home. And with no disrespect intended, because I know "eye hath not seen, nor ear heard, the things which God hath prepared for them that love Him," it seems to me that whenever Carl does come, and I get to be the one to meet him at the end of his long journey, be in his arms again, and hear the familiar, "Well, Dona, it's good to be home…" that for me, will well and truly be Heaven.

Afterword

T.C. Schnebly lived four more years after his wife, and he did manage to get the money raised for a bell, which Hank found and shipped from Denver, that rang out from Wayside Chapel. Carl continued to walk downtown every day, meeting strangers, asking about their lives, pointing out landmarks and giving the women pincushions.

He died of a sudden heart attack; Alf Boltz was visiting, and came in to see Carl just returned with the mail, slumped over the washer on the back porch. That date and others are in the Family Bible & Census Data at the end.

Tad (Ellsworth) continued to teach his entire life, preferring to be principal and teacher in one-room schools in Northern Arizona, rather than applying for the district or state superintendent positions offered. He and Lucille always maintained a permanent home address in Sedona, and lived there full time from the mid-1950s until their deaths; hers in 1970 and his in 1975.

Larry worked in radio (with a brief stint back at NAU), then television in Tucson, where he also did football color work, voiceover and emceeing. He married Lee and they raised Laurie, Lisa, Lindsay and Lyle.

Patsy taught her entire professional life, first in California, then Northern Arizona. She married Lou and raised Michael and Stephanie in Winslow, after which she travelled tirelessly and widely.

Paula taught in Winslow, then moved to Tucson, where her husband Jack was a band director and she nurtured young children in day care. They raised Mel, Celeste and Lyric.

All those grandchildren grew up hearing stories of their great-grandparents, and went on to have families of their own, to whom they passed on the legacy of the great-grandparents who named Sedona.

Acknowledgements

While there is an "I" in writer, there's surely a "we" in every worthwhile book. This one would not have had a chance to exist without the generous sharing of family stories, most notably from Sedona's grandchildren. To my father, Larry, and his sisters, Patricia Schnebly Ceballos and Paula Schnebly Hokanson, great gratitude for all you told. Paula let us copy photographs years ago, and several I'd never seen from Pat's collection include T.C.'s signature on their wedding day, and their family on their golden anniversary. Larry was my Shipmate on a hundred journeys (including a few memorable ones along Schnebly Hill Road), during which I absorbed countless details that helped me with this project. We must have both received from T.C. what I call the red-setter gene: the one that which makes you joyously jump into any open car door without asking the destination.

Profound thanks to the extraordinary Nathan Shelton, who combined concept and content editing in a Herculean task that made what you read much better. I have learned much from his work; and on some days it was equally important that his comments—"a word-based, self-sustaining, catenating, mutually propagating chain reaction of verbal innovation"—made me guffaw.

Laurie Schnebly Campbell, as my older sister, has been my expert and leader since I was born. She also falls into the category of "if you want something done, ask a busy person." She somehow added one more plate to the twelve she was already spinning to proofread the entire manuscript. Then she pointed out dates, contradictions, absurdities—things which only an alert family member and editor would see—with great diplomacy and care.

Brooke Bessesen took time from her own writing to read, and then make gentle, carefully crafted and extremely valuable suggestions that vastly improved what you hold now.

Chuck Richards compiled a masterful and meticulous (and quite heavy) Schnebly history that I kept returning to for accurate dates and names; he literally wrote the book on the family.

I am grateful to the Sedona Historical Society, for sharing archives of the early years of the town.

Also I owe a huge debt to Northern Arizona University's Special Collections and Archives, where I have gazed in wonder at family papers I didn't know existed.

And lastly, thanks to my mother, Leona Koenig Schnebly, who endured years of my fascination with the other side of the family, while giving me the good values and unabashed encouragement the Koenigs taught her.

About This Book

During the writing process, people asked, "Will this be a biography? Historical fiction?" and I answered "yes."

Unless it's an autobiography—and maybe not even then—no one can truly know anyone's thoughts, or record every spoken word. Even our own memories alter and soften over time, so any memoir would be subject to inadvertent editing. A biographer needs to think carefully and long about how to share the known details, and then add what else may have happened. This is Sedona Arabella Miller Schnebly's life, as well as I can tell it.

I understand the desire to know: what really happened?

I used to claim the word "research" gave me hives, back before the ease of internet searches. Blessedly, that changed everything, so research has been long, wide and deep.

First, I talked to Sedona's children, grandchildren, and friends, to get various impressions of who she was. I read old newspaper stories, genealogical documents, census reports, magazine articles, and every letter written to or from a family member I could get my hands on.

Then I read about the times, looking up the popular songs of each year of her life to provide part of a cultural framework. I researched childbirth delivery methods for those years, read about styles, mechanical advances. These helped paint me a picture of the world when she walked it.

Finally, I read all I could about who else inhabited Sedona's world, as political leaders, fellow Arizonans, and neighbors. (In short, I made certain I wasn't in danger of saying Napoleon walked through the door.)

After all that, I would sit down, say a prayer that I be given the best possible words, think about what aspect of her life caught my interest that day, and begin writing. Generally, about 1,000 words would flow at a time, as if I were journalling about things that had happened to me. (It was unlike anything I've experienced, and I've written ten books.)

Tempting as it was to stir in my friends' names, names I needed but couldn't find, I would utter a quick prayer about, and write whatever came into my head. And having promised relatives from the beginning that I would never use "corset" and "creekside" in the same sentence, I have stayed rigorously true to who I believe the people here to have actually been. Everything written may have happened; we don't know enough to be certain. Were she and Pauline O'Neill friends? Maybe. Did an actual Dorothea take her to Flagstaff? Could have. Many things are from primary sources. For instance, the stories about their first Thanksgiving menu, Loring, moving Pearl's casket, the tutti frutti, the Boyero House, anthrax, CCC camp, the rattlesnakes and centipede, Marsh Pass, fixing the roof, and her last night come from immediate relatives.

Also, the people we call T.C. and Sedona called one another Carl and Dona, and called their son, my grandfather, Tad instead of Ellsworth.

There're facts, and there's truth, I've read. This has a heaping helping of the former, as well as a lot of the latter. And I hope, in combining them both, that this book answers the ancient, universal, human request, "Tell me a story."

Family Bible & Census Data

Sedona's family of origin:

Phillip Miller	b. 3/13/1843 Bonaparte, KS m. 1/16/1865		d. 7/01/06
Amanda Shaefer Miller	b. 1/27/1845 Chester, PA		d. 1/27/31

John Henry	b. 12/23/1866		d.10/4/72
Edward Frederick	b. 11/17/1868	m.1887	d. 1929
Minnie Lydia	b. 10/05/1870	m. George Egbert 1890	
Noah Phillip William	b. 1/24/1873	m. Ella Clement 1899	d. 1946
Amiel Otto	b. 3/13/1875	m. Daisy White 1906	d. 3/18/20
Sedona Arabella	b. 2/27/1877	m. T.C. 2/24/1897	d. 11/12/50
Lillie Veronica	b. 2/27/1879	m. Loring Johnson 8/8/1897	d.after 1971
Goldie Amelia	b. 8/19/1881	m. Rob't Otto Leftwich 8/20/1905	d.1949
Pearl Hannah	b. 10/19/1884		d. 3/20/02
Johnny	b. 1887		d. infant
Edna Amanda	b. 11/17/1888	m. Seth Trotter 1910	d.5/6/45
Lola	b. 12/23/1892		d. 12/2/95

T.C.'s family of origin:
(Father Daniel Henry Schnebly, Jr. moved family from Hagerstown, MD to Clark County, MO.)

Daniel Davis	b. 12/20/1864		d. 5/30/88
Cora Elizabeth	b. 3/12/1866		d. 7/30/49
Clara Ann	b. 5/2718/1867		d. 8/31/68
Theodore Carlton	b. 12/29/1868	m.2/24/1897	d. 3/13/54
Jacob Melvin	b. 5/3/1870		d. 11/15/59
Dorsey Ellsworth	b. 11/13/1872	m. Mary Higbee	d. 9/7/26
Maria Elizabeth	b. 4/241/1874		d. 1925
William Francis	b. 4/27/1876		d. 11/40

(Three younger children -- Nannie Myrtle, John Henry, Roy -- died as infants.)

T.C. & Sedona Schnebly:

Ellsworth Miller "Tad"	b. 3/9/1898	m. Lucille Finney 5/15/25	d. 3/26/75
Pearl Azalea	b. 11/18/1899		d. 6/05/05
Goldie Genevieve	b. 10/22/1903	m. Joshua Cox 1/02/25	d. 6/17/40
Daniel Henry "Hank"	b. 8/22/1907	m. Annabelle Wright 8/2/30	d. 12/25/79
Clara Amanda	b. 1/31/1912	m. H.E. McBride 05/22/39	d. 2/7/92
Margaret Elizabeth	b. 6/20/1915	m. Stanton Wallace 11/30/34	d. 9/15/98

Ellsworth (Tad) & Lucille Schnebly:

Lawrence Wilbur	b. 9/18/1928	m. Leona Koenig 6/20/53	
Evelyn Patricia	b. 12/26/1932	m. Lucio Ceballos 3/27/54	
Marilyn Paula	b. 1/4/1937	m. John Hokanson 12/22/56	d.12/13/2013

Genevieve & Joshua Cox:

Alice L.	b. 2/20/1926
Catherine B.	b. 2/3/1928
Dorothy Jean	b. 8/18/1930
James C.	b. 12/19/1932
Helen A.	b. 12/16/1934
Betty Lou	b. 7/18/1937

Hank & Annabelle Schnebly:

Harold (Hal)	b. 1/24/1935
Dixie Jean	b.11/10/1941

Margaret & Stanton Wallace:

Margaret Louise	b. 1/25/1940
Joanne	b. New Mexico

Census data:

1900: Scotland Co, MO, TC 31, Dona 23, Ellsworth 2, Pearl 6 mos. TC merchant hardware store, owned home.

1910: Scotland Co, MO. TC 41, Dona, 33, Ellsworth 12, Genevieve 6, Daniel Henry 2. TC merchant clothing store, Ellsworth worked in laundry, also in school. TC owned home.

1920: Lincoln Co, CO: TC, Sedona, Ellsworth, Genevieve, Henry, Clara 8, Margaret 4. TC general farmer.

1930: Lincoln Co, CO: TC 61, Sedona 53, Clara 18, Margaret 14. TC lists self as stock farmer, owns his land, valued at $2500. They have a radio.

T.C. & Sedona moved:

To Oak Creek Canyon 10/21/1901 (Post office est. 6.26/1902)

To Gorin 10/1905

To Boyero 1910 (homesteaded, town pop. 100)

To Phoenix 1931

Back to Sedona 1931

Made in the USA
Columbia, SC
04 September 2017